Women in
Modern America

A Brief History

Women in Modern America

A Brief History

Fourth Edition

LOIS W. BANNER

WADSWORTH
CENGAGE Learning·

Australia • Brazil • Japan • Korea • Mexico • Singapore • Spain • United Kingdom • United States

WADSWORTH
CENGAGE Learning™

**Women in Modern America:
A Brief History, Fourth Edition**
Lois W. Banner

Publisher: Clark Baxter

Development Editor: Richard Yoder

Technology Project Manager: Melinda Newfarmer

Marketing Manager: Lori Grebe Cook

Marketing Assistant: Mary Ho

Advertising Project Manager: Stacey Purviance

Project Manager, Editorial Production: Kimberly Adams

Print/Media Buyer: Emma Claydon

Permissions Editor: Stephanie Lee

Production Service and Compositor: G&S Book Services

Photo Researcher: Linda Sykes Picture Research, Inc.

Copy Editor: Karen Boyd

Cover Designer: Lisa Buckley

Cover Image: *Top row, left to right:* Eleanor Roosevelt and Zora Neale Hurston; *bottom row* Margaret Mead

For product information and technology assistance, contact us at **Cengage Learning Customer & Sales Support, 1-800-354-9706**

For permission to use material from this text or product, submit all requests online at **www.cengage.com/permissions**
Further permissions questions can be emailed to **permissionrequest@cengage.com**

Library of Congress Control Number: 2004104481

ISBN-13: 978-0-15-506350-1

ISBN-10: 0-15-506350-2

Wadsworth
20 Davis Drive
Belmont, CA 94002
USA

Cengage Learning is a leading provider of customized learning solutions with office locations around the globe, including Singapore, the United Kingdom, Australia, Mexico, Brazil, and Japan. Locate your local office at **www.cengage.com/global**

Cengage Learning products are represented in Canada by Nelson Education, Ltd.

To learn more about Wadsworth, visit **www.cengage.com/wadsworth**

Purchase any of our products at your local college store or at our preferred online store **www.CengageBrain.com**

Printed in the United States of America
2 3 4 5 6   15 14 13 12 11

FD167

Contents

PREFACE   xi

ABOUT THE AUTHOR   xv

1   THE EMERGENCE OF THE MODERN AMERICAN WOMAN, 1890   1

Women's Status in 1890   1

Legal Codes   2

Educational Opportunities   3

Medicine and Sexuality   6

A "Strange New Note"   8

Aging Women and Menopause   9

Women's Romantic Friendships   9

The Middle-Class Family   10

Employment   12

Inventors and Entrepreneurs   13

Discrimination Against Working Women   15

   Discrimination in the Professions: Feminization   16

   The Male Response: Masculinization   17

Rural and Urban Women   18

   Rural Women of the Midwest, South, and Southwest   18

   Urban Working Conditions   20

Immigration and Ethnicity Across the Nation   21

   European Immigration and Women's Work   21

   Asian Immigration   25

      Chinese Immigration   25

      Japanese Immigration   27

      Korean and Filipino Immigration   27

Race and Representation   28

   African American Women   29

   Native American Women   33

   Women and the Columbian Centennial of 1893   35

2   ORGANIZERS AND INNOVATORS: REFORMERS, FEMINISTS, UNION LEADERS, AND SUFFRAGISTS, 1890–1920   39

Women's Rights and Progressivism: A Case of Give and Take   40

   The Organizations: Growth and Changing Goals   41

   A Broad Spectrum   43

   Progressive Reform and Settlement Houses   45

   The "Female Dominion" of Reform   47

Women's Frailty, Special Legislation, and Maternal Feminism   47

Racism and Elitism in Anglo-American Women's Organizations   49

Diversity in Ethnic and Black Women's Organizations   49

The Artists   51

The Radicals   52

The New Scholars   53

Feminist Action Groups: A Faint Voice   56

Two Generations   57

Strikes and Unionists   58

The Consumers' League and the Women's Trade Union League   62

The New Sensuality   63

The Suffragists   64

Suffrage Deceived   64

Suffrage Achieved   65

Women and World War I   67

The Final Victory   68

**3   FREEDOM OR DISILLUSIONMENT?
THE 1920S   71**

Antifeminist Undercurrents and Feminist Conservatism   72

Sexuality   75

"Flaming Youth"—New Liberties, New Repressions, and Old Attitudes   75

Conservatism and Eugenics   78

Women at Work: Progress and Setbacks   80

Married Women at Work   81

Professional Women   82

Artists and Writers of Achievement   83

Mexican Immigration: Women, Work, and Acculturation   87

Working Women   88

Labor Unions in a Conservative Era   89

Women's Organizations in the 1920s   90

Women's Organizations in Transition   91

The Sheppard-Towner Act: Successes and Failures   94

The New Heroines   95

**4   WOMEN IN THE DEPRESSION AND WAR ERA,
1930–1945   101**

Feminism and Women's Organizations   102

Southern Women and the Antilynching Movement   103

Eleanor Roosevelt   104

The Women's Network and New Deal Programs   107

The NRA and New Deal Discrimination Against Women   109

Changes for the Working Woman   110

African American and Hispanic Women   112

Unions in an Age of Depression   113

The Importance of the Communist Party   114

Sexuality and Security   116

Marriage and Family in an Insecure Age   117

Lesbians and Gays: Oppressed Minorities   119

Popular Culture   120

Fashionable Appearances and Contradictions   120

Strong Women: Soaps, Sleuths, and Scarlett   121

Imagining Movies: West, Westerns, and Censorship   122

Race and Popular Culture   123

Women as Part of the War Effort During World War II   126

Women Take on Male Roles   127

Film Noir and Anxious Roles   127

Limitations During the War   129

Work After the War   132

Rebel Youth   133

5   A CONSERVATIVE ERA, 1945–1960   137

Anticommunism   138

Women Under Attack   140

Domesticity and the Family   141

The Back-to-the-Home Movement   142

The Evidence from Popular Culture   143

Styles in Dress   143

Movies   146

Television   147

Sex and Childrearing   148

A Sexual Underside   149

Playboy *and* Barbie   150

Feminism in the 1950s   153

New Economic, Demographic, and Medical Factors   155

The New Trends and the Persistence of Discrimination   156

Conformity and Male Discontent   157

The Youth Rebellion   157

The Civil Rights Movement   159

6   **PROGRESS AND BACKLASH,
     THE 1960S AND 1970S   163**

New Faces and New Music   164

Hippies and "Swinging Singles"   165

The Formation of NOW   168

The Feminist Movement After NOW   169

Discrimination Against Women   171

Sexuality and Power: Women's Bodies   172

Feminism: Cultural Impacts   173

Feminist Spirituality   175

Movies and Television: A Wasteland for Women   176

Minority Protest   177

   Native Americans   177

   Mexican Americans, Hispanics, Latinos   178

   African Americans   180

   Lesbians, Gays, and the Stonewall Riot   180

Legislative and Legal Successes   181

The Feminist Movement: United and Divided   181

   *Marriage and the Family; "Equality" Versus
   "Difference" Feminists*   182

   The Sex Wars   182

   Lesbians   183

   Women of Color   184

Feminist Achievements and the Houston National Women's
Conference   185

Backlash   186

   The New Right   186

   Pro-Life and Pro-Choice   187

   Backlash in the Media, in Appearances, and in Advertising   187

Disco and Punk   190

Recent Immigration   191

7   THE THIRD WAVE, 1980–2004   195

Politics Become Conservative   196

Backlash Continues   197

The Emergence of New Styles   199

   Fashions, Advertising, and Disco   199

   Rap and Hip-hop   200

   Madonna   201

The Anita Hill and Clarence Thomas Scandal   203

Feminism Takes New Forms   205

   "Unobtrusive Mobilization" and the Military   209

   Postmodernism   210

The Clinton Presidency   212

Generational Conflict   213

Third-Wave Feminism   214

The Recent Situation   218

The George W. Bush Presidency   218

Women and Aging in Contemporary Times   220

The Present: Revolutionary or Not?   221

BIBLIOGRAPHY   225

PHOTO CREDITS   251

INDEX   253

Preface

Until the middle years of the twentieth century, historians overlooked the history of women, as they focused their attention on governmental politics, war, and male power. Then in the 1960s a vigorous feminist movement appeared on the scene. It produced new female scholars and emboldened them to undertake studies on women in what became a vast and successful enterprise to reclaim women's lost past.

As part of this endeavor, *Women in Modern America* examines the history of women in the United States from 1890 to the present. This was an era of modernization, in which the nation experienced rapid technological, industrial, and commercial growth. Four periods stand out in this history. The first, from 1890 to 1920, was one of activism and innovation on the part of women. Many of the traditional discriminations against women were ended, and an impressive number of feminist and reform groups were organized. During the second period, from 1920 to 1960, feminist groups lost momentum, as the nation struggled with the sexual revolution of the 1920s, the severe economic downtown of the 1930s, and the waging of World War II and the reconstruction of peace at its end during the decades of the 1940s and 1950s. The third period, from 1960 to 1980, witnessed the emergence of a feminism more militant than any of its predecessors, as the Civil

Rights movement surfaced in response to racial segregation, and the student movement emerged in reaction to the Vietnam War. In the fourth period, from 1890 to the present, postfeminism and postmodernism have arisen and challenged the emphasis of the feminists of the 1960s and 1970s on male patriarchy, female objectification, and change through electoral politics. As capitalism and consumerism have become triumphant with the fall of communism and the end of the "Cold War," postfeminists and postmodernists look to advancing the cause of women through subverting cultural styles, especially in the media, and to encouraging women to reshape themselves according to a model of male power and sexual manipulation. Meanwhile, a powerful conservative coalition, rooted in Christian fundamentalism, is challenging both the feminists and the postfeminists.

In *Women in Modern America* I examine the history of various groups in the years from 1890 to the present, including female reformers, working-class women, immigrant and ethnic women, farm women, women of color, and lesbians, as these histories interact with my four-part periodization. I focus on the dramatic and continuing struggle waged by determined women of all social classes and ethnicities to achieve rights for women. Realizing that the history of women is deeply intertwined with that of men, I include brief discussions of the history of men, drawing from the work of scholars in the new field of men's history. Following current usage, I employ the term "first wave" for the feminist movement between 1890 and 1920; "second wave" for the reborn feminist movement of the 1960s and 1970s; and "third wave" for the postfeminists who have formed their own movement for women's rights in recent years.

Moreover, I attend to central themes that have dominated my four periods. These themes have included the progress of industrialization and the move to the cities on the part of the American population. They encompass changing attitudes and behaviors in sexual expression and marriage. They extend to the growing power of the mass media and of consumer culture, represented by advertising and the enormous success of brand names, as well as the expansion of the economy and of certain occupations within it that were identified with women (such as secretarial work) and technological advances that offered women more leisure time. Finally, discrimination toward racial, ethnic, and sexual minorities has been endemic during the course of the history that I cover, as well as movements to end such incursions on individual liberties and social democracy.

This is the third time that I have revised this book. In this new edition, I have continued the emphasis of previous editions on the politics of women's organizations and on the difference between generations as a force for change. I have expanded the material on birth control, abortion, eugenics, and sterilization abuse, following the direction of recent scholarship in the field. Responding to the interests of the students I teach and to the growth in studies on gender in the fields of communications and media studies, I have expanded my coverage of the movies, television, and popular music. Thus this edition includes discussions of individuals like Madonna and Queen Latifah and movements in music like rock and hip-hop.

I wrote the first edition of *Women in Modern America* in the early 1970s. At that point women's history was a new topic, and I was an assistant professor as well as a young wife and mother. I taught at Douglass College of Rutgers University, the state university of New Jersey. Then a women's college, Douglass was among the first institutions of higher learning in the nation to generate courses on women across the curriculum as well as a women's studies program. Inspired by the feminist movement of the 1960s, I, like many other women, expressed my solidarity with women by joining the movement for women's rights and, as an academic, taking up the new field of women's history as my specialty. It was as though, to use the popular metaphor, an ocean wave had washed over me, carrying me along in its wake. In my case, it inspired me toward—and permitted me to have—a career as a university professor. Without "second-wave" feminism I would never have written this book nor have been able to enter the professorial ranks.

My children are now grown, and I have been a professor at the University of Southern California for several decades. I have participated in the growth to maturity of the field of women's history as well as that of women's studies. I have witnessed the development of the fields of men's history and men's studies, and of gender history and gender studies. I have watched the appearance and growth of gay and lesbian studies and, most recently, of queer theory, and I have drawn on their insights in this book. During the years that I have worked on *Women in Modern America,* I have written a biography of Elizabeth Cady Stanton, the major women's rights leader of the nineteenth century. I have also written histories of physical appearance and fashion in the United States, of the high school culture of the 1950s and the cultural radicalism and spiritualism of the 1960s, and of aging women in Western culture from the Greeks to the present. Most recently, I have examined the lives of anthropologists and intimate friends, Margaret Mead and Ruth Benedict, the greatest female intellectuals of the twentieth century. I have incorporated insights and material from all these books in *Women in Modern America.*

At the beginning of the twentieth century, feminist author Charlotte Perkins Gilman, in her utopian novel *Herland* (1915), called for men and women to honor one another and to work together for a world in which aggression and violence would be outlawed and the sensitive caring of motherhood would become a model of behavior for both men and women.

At the middle of the century, in *Male and Female* (1949), Margaret Mead called for a society in which men and women would be divided by individual characteristics, not by anatomy, and both would participate in creating homes and raising the next generation. At the end of the century, in her utopian novel *The Left Hand of Darkness,* Ursula Le Guin proposed a model of androgyny, in which humans would shift between being male and female and both would gestate and bear children.

Whether the powerful force of technology can produce the situation that Le Guin describes—or whether it is desirable—remains to be seen. Yet taken together, the three statements by Gilman, Mead, and Le Guin point to the history of women in modern America as a force for change. The statement of purpose for the National Organization for Women at its founding convention in 1967 declared that women must speak out "in behalf of their own equality, freedom, and human dignity—not in pleas for special privilege, nor in enmity toward men—but in an active self-respecting partnership with men." And that partnership, as the course of the women's movement would make clear over the next forty years, would include women and men of all ethnicities, sexualities, ages, and social classes, as the United States struggled—and continues to struggle—to fulfill its promise. That promise was stated profoundly by Thomas Jefferson in the Declaration of Independence as the goal of providing "life, liberty, and the pursuit of happiness" to all.

To help the reader who wishes to pursue any particular aspect of this history more fully, I have provided a critical bibliography at the end of the book.

Lois W. Banner

About the Author

Lois W. Banner was born and raised in Los Angeles, California. A graduate of the University of California at Los Angeles, she holds M.A. and Ph.D. degrees from Columbia University in New York City. She is the author of *Elizabeth Cady Stanton* (1979), *American Beauty* (1983), *In Full Flower: Aging Women, Power, and Sexuality* (1992), *Finding Fran: History and Memory in the Lives of Two Women* (1998), and *Intertwined Lives: Margaret Mead, Ruth Benedict and Their Circle* (2003). She has taught at Rutgers University, Princeton University, the University of Scranton, the University of Maryland–Baltimore County, George Washington University, Hamilton College, Stanford University, and UCLA. She is a past president of the American Studies Association and the American Historical Association–Pacific Coast Branch. She lives in Los Angeles, California, where she teaches history and gender studies at the University of Southern California.

The Emergence of the Modern American Woman

1890

At the opening of the twentieth century, women's status had been completely transformed in most respects.

SUFFRAGIST, IDA HUSTED HARPER

WOMEN'S STATUS IN 1890

Over the course of the nineteenth century, women entered high schools and colleges, took up careers and sports, entered the workforce, and formed organizations for self-improvement and reform. By the 1890s legal codes restricting women's rights were modified in state after state; Victorian restrictions on sexuality were eroding, and women were profiting from medical advances in fields like obstetrics and gynecology. The United States was undergoing vast and rapid industrial growth. A national system of railroads had been completed. Heavy industries such as oil and steel had emerged, and mass-produced consumption goods such as packaged cereals and food

Opposite: Suffragists Elizabeth Cady Stanton and Susan B. Anthony

in tin cans had been developed. Business consolidation and a managerial expansion were occurring; they would lead the way to the modern corporate and consumption economy. These developments would have a major impact on American women of all ethnicities, social classes, and ages.

The modern woman of the 1890s, called "The New Woman," was a prominent figure in literature and art, as well as in real life. Her model was the tall and athletic Gibson Girl, drawn by artist Charles Dana Gibson in *Life* magazine—then a humor magazine containing critical commentary, jokes, and drawings of beautiful women. Instead of the trailing, flounced gowns of the nineteenth-century Victorian woman, the Gibson Girl often wore a dark skirt and a simple shirtwaist blouse. She loosened her tight-laced corset—the torture instrument of nineteenth-century dress—that produced the fashionable eighteen-inch waistline while it damaged internal organs. Gibson's pictures centered on the traditional themes of courtship and marriage, and he rarely depicted his figure as a working woman in a factory or office. Yet he drew her playing tennis and golf, bicycling, and even driving an automobile. The Victorian "True Woman," a model for the nineteenth century, was "pious, pure, obedient, and domestic." She submitted to her husband and remained at home. The New Woman was replacing her.[1]

Yet discrimination against women still existed, especially against working-class women, ethnic women, and women of color. A huge new immigration of Jews and Slavs from Eastern Europe and Italians and Greeks from the Mediterranean entered the United States between 1890 and 1920. Chinese and Japanese from Asia and Mexicans from across the southern border came to California and the West. These immigrants often had darker skin than Anglo-Americans and were generally without funds. They arrived from Jewish, Catholic, and Buddhist cultures that differed from the culture of earlier migrants from England, Germany, and Scandinavia, who were predominately Protestant and light-skinned. Such differences fueled mainstream and Anglo-American acceptance of Social Darwinism. It was adapted from the theory of evolution proposed by Charles Darwin in his *Origin of Species* (1859), and it had first become popular in the 1870s. Social Darwinism contended that nuclear families, heterosexual males, corporate capitalism, and the white race occupied the high point of evolutionary development. Drawing from Darwin's biological model of human evolution, it justified unregulated capitalism by asserting that society was like a jungle, where competition among animals predominated and the "fittest" survived.

Legal Codes

By 1890, individual states had come a long way in amending statutes that, based on the English common law, defined wives as chattels of their husbands, with no control over their earnings, children, or property. Such laws had been in place since the colonial era, but these laws did not apply to single women. But since most women married, unmarried women beyond their mid-twenties were not a large group. Most states passed laws during the nineteenth century that gave wives control over their inherited property and their earnings, although some states continued to prohibit women from entering business partnerships or signing contracts without the consent of their husbands. In many states married women were still denied rights over their children. In the case of divorce, however, children were increasingly awarded to mothers in the latter years of the century, in line with the belief that women were biologically intended to raise children.

Only a few states gave women the right to vote. In some, women could vote in local school-board and municipal elections, but only four states allowed women to vote in state and federal elections: Wyoming, Utah, Colorado, and Idaho. The Fifteenth Amendment, passed in 1870, gave the right to vote to African Americans, but it did not include women in its provisions. In 1874 the Supreme Court ruled in *Minor v. Happersett* that voting was not guaranteed by citizenship (as women's rights advocates argued). Thus voting rights could be withheld from women.

It took over a century of feminist agitation to abolish discriminatory laws against women. As late as 1930, one-fourth of the states did not allow wives to make contracts, while in seventeen states married women's property rights over real estate were not equal to those of their husbands. Moreover, there was no legal recognition of marital rape until the 1970s.

Educational Opportunities

Women had made major gains in education by 1890. In 1800 it was difficult for them to secure any education. No colleges accepted them. In many areas of the country, grammar schools restricted their pupils to boys or allowed girls to attend only in the summer, when sons worked on family farms and classrooms were vacant. It was considered sufficient that girls learn to read and write. Either their mothers taught them these skills or they learned them at local "dame" schools established by unmarried, older women for this purpose. A woman with advanced education was regarded with suspicion for usurping a male prerogative and threatening the separate spheres of domesticity for women and public activity for men. Mockingly, women who were well educated were called "bluestockings." This term derived from the blue stockings worn by members of women's intellectual groups in England in the 1750s.

By the end of the century, however, elementary and secondary education was open to girls. In the antebellum era, private academies (high schools) for girls were founded, and as local public school systems expanded in size and numbers, girls were included as students. In fact, because boys

© Culver Pictures

The International Council of Women. The Suffragist Executive Committee (including foreign delegates) that arranged the first International Council of Women in 1888. In the front row are Susan B. Anthony (second from left) and Elizabeth Cady Stanton (fourth from left). Anthony and Stanton led the women's rights and women's suffrage movements from the early nineteenth century until they both died in the 1900s. Anna Howard Shaw and Carrie Chapman Catt then took over leadership of the National American Suffrage Association.

dropped out of school more often than girls to seek paid employment, by 1890 more girls than boys were graduating from high school. Higher education, too, was open to women by then. A few colleges opened their doors to women in the antebellum period—notably Oberlin in 1837 and Antioch in 1853. As states were established, their legislatures founded both universities, which generally admitted women, and teacher-training schools, which attracted many women students. (The teacher-training schools evolved into today's "state" universities.) After the Civil War, a number of prominent colleges for women were founded, particularly in the Northeast. They included Vassar (1865), Wellesley (1875), Smith (1875), and Bryn Mawr (1885). New coeducational private colleges also appeared, such as Cornell University (1877) and the University of Chicago (1893). By 1900, 80 percent of the colleges and universities in the nation admitted women.

African Americans in the South had been forbidden to learn to read and write under slavery. After the Civil War they flocked to schools to become

Immigrant Women at Ellis Island. Five immigrant women sit outside at Ellis Island, the immigrant receiving station in New York Bay that processed millions of immigrants to the United States at the turn of the century. Men usually emigrated first, to find employment and housing. Once established, they would send for their wives, children, and parents as part of the largest diasporic movement of people in global history.

literate, although racist white governments often hampered their efforts with inadequate funding for their schools. In response, private African American academies and colleges were founded. In 1884 two Northern white women from the Baptist Women's Home Mission founded Spelman College in Atlanta. They named the school after Laura Spelman Rockefeller, a member of the wealthy Rockefeller family, who provided them with financial backing. In 1886 Lucy C. Laney, a member of the first graduating class at all-black Atlanta University in Atlanta, Georgia, founded Haines Normal and Industrial Institute in Augusta, Georgia. At that point Georgia had no public high schools for blacks, and both Spelman and Haines established preparatory departments to bring their students up to the college level. By 1912, there were fourteen black women's colleges across the United States, mostly in the South. Most of these schools prepared their students to become teachers. Progressive Northern colleges like Antioch and Oberlin admitted a few black women each year.

Mexican women in the United States lived primarily in Texas, California, and the Southwest during this period, and assertive women among them (mostly unmarried) organized *escuelitas,* or small schools, in places where public education was not provided for Mexican children. These schools taught English and reading. Given the devotion of Mexicans to the Catholic Church, they also provided religious education. Catholic nunneries also existed, and their members often took on education and child welfare as part of their mission. They established schools, as well as orphan asylums, for children whose parents had abandoned them or couldn't afford to raise them.

MEDICINE AND SEXUALITY

The 1890s was a time of advance in the medical treatment of women. From 1850 to 1900, life expectancy for women rose from forty to fifty-one years. Better sanitation and new vaccines for diseases like yellow fever were partly responsible for the improvement. In addition, the introduction of antiseptic techniques in delivering babies greatly reduced the incidence of puerperal fever, an infection of childbirth that had killed women for centuries and that was especially prevalent in eras before the 1890s, when doctors didn't wash their hands before performing medical procedures. Developments in gynecological surgery made curable such chronic and debilitating female disorders as a prolapsed uterus, usually resulting from childbearing. However, the "hysterical" or neurotic woman, who suffered from severe depression or emotional outbursts and who was unmarried, might still be advised to marry to cure her difficulty. Or doctors might remove her uterus, a procedure first attempted in 1881 and called a "hysterectomy." This procedure and the term created to name it came from the ancient belief that the uterus controlled female emotions, a belief that was still current in the nineteenth century. (The operation is used today to eliminate physical problems like uterine tumors.)

By the 1890s doctors were viewing women less as fragile creatures who were prone to illness. For decades educators and doctors had debated whether or not a woman's physiology could withstand the rigors of a college education. In 1873 Dr. Edward H. Clarke, in his influential *Sex in Education*, had contended that intensive studying could ruin a woman's health and make her infertile. By 1890, however, studies showed that college women had excellent health.

Many individuals still remained reticent about sex, regarding it as an act that should be confined to marriage and intended for procreation. Masturbation, often called "the solitary vice," was generally viewed as immoral and bound to result in illness and even insanity or homosexuality. Sex was often a taboo subject between parents and children, especially in the middle class. For many girls, the onset of menstruation was a shock because, given Victorian prudery, no one had told them about it. It was not uncommon for a bride to marry knowing nothing about sexual intercourse. Novelist Frances Parkinson Keyes stated that in her affluent circle, the mother of the bride was supposed to have "a little talk" with her daughter shortly before the wedding ceremony, but mothers were often so embarrassed about discussing the subject that they said nothing enlightening.[2] The traditional view that sex was primarily for procreation was still widespread. Even married middle-class women often remained secluded during pregnancy. The "double standard," under which men had sex outside marriage with impunity while women were expected to remain virgins, was in force, at least among the middle class. Especially in urban areas, prostitution flourished.

In the 1870s legal restrictions on sex had increased as the federal government and most states outlawed abortion and even birth control. "Social purity" was a goal of many late-nineteenth-century Victorians, and even of some liberal reformers, who feared that access to birth control freed men to pursue satisfaction of their sex drive, which was supposedly greater than that of women, outside marriage. In 1873 Congress passed the Comstock Law, named after its chief proponent—the New York City antivice crusader, Anthony Comstock. As a young man Comstock had moved from Vermont to New York and had become a clerk in a store there. Appalled by the amount of pornography the other young male clerks were reading, he secured the backing of the New York City Young Men's Christian Association (YMCA) to launch a crusade against immorality in American life.

The Comstock Law banned the dissemination in interstate commerce of pornography, abortion devices, and "any drug, medicine, article, or thing designed, adapted, or intended for preventing conception." Soon after, twenty-four states enacted versions of the federal Comstock Law to restrict such trade on the state level.

Under the common law, birth control was legal. Abortion was permitted until the "quickening" stage, when the pregnant woman first feels the fetus moving in the womb, which occurs around the fifth month of pregnancy. In the early nineteenth century, however, scientists discovered that the egg was fertilized soon after intercourse, and some doctors became uneasy about defining life as beginning at five months of pregnancy. They were also critical of poorly trained abortionists. The motives of other doctors against abortion, however, were not so disinterested. Many were trying to turn medicine into a modern profession, with standards of training and practice that would give them greater control. Abortion prohibitions would drive out many physicians outside the medical establishment who employed homeopathic, natural techniques. These alternative doctors included women who were willing to perform abortions. Moreover, anti-abortionists were concerned about rising rates of abortion among Anglo-American middle-class women. By 1870 as many as one in five pregnancies to such women ended in abortion.

Despite the prohibition on all forms of abortion included in the federal and state Comstock Acts, often as a result of campaigns led by male doctors, women of all classes and communities continued to undergo the procedure, and some doctors and midwives continued to perform it. For the most part, abortionists were prosecuted only when patients died, although some had to pay off the police to stay in business. Moreover, contraceptive devices such as condoms and vaginal sponges were available, though how reliable these early devices were is debatable. They were designed and sold by small entrepreneurs—often immigrants and women—who marketed them through handbills they passed out and advertisements they placed in newspapers. To avoid prosecution, these entrepreneurs used euphemisms to describe their products, claiming that they would promote women's health or end "women's complaints." The latter phrase was commonly used to refer to the physical problems connected to menstruation and menopause.

A "Strange New Note"

Family size decreased in the late nineteenth century, as it had since 1800. In 1804 the birth rate was about seven children per family. By 1880 it had decreased to 4.24, and by 1900 it had decreased to 3.56. This "demographic transition," as historians call it, was a key development in the history of modern women, for it freed them from constant childbirth and allowed flexibility in life choices. Whether women employed continence, vaginal sponges, or douching as their form of birth control, or whether they requested their partners to practice coitus interruptus or use condoms (historians disagree over the use of each method), women were asserting control over their lives.

Writing about the frontier Illinois of her youth, novelist Mary Austin dated women's adoption of birth control, then called "voluntary motherhood," from about 1870. "The pioneer stress was over," she wrote, and with it had ended "the day of large families, families of from a dozen to fifteen." According to Austin, "a strange new note had come into the thinking of the granddaughters of the women who had borne their dozen or so cheerfully and with the conviction of the will of God strong in them." And this "strange new note," according to Austin, grew out of women's desire to participate in the public world outside the home.[3]

Aging Women and Menopause

New opportunities for women, in addition to their increased life expectancy and improved health, brought more positive attitudes toward their aging. Eminent women, such as actress Lillian Russell and suffragist Susan B. Anthony, remained vigorous well into their fifties and sixties. Older women dominated women's reform organizations, and commentators in newspapers and magazines referred to a "renaissance of the middle aged."[4] Grandmothers were still viewed mostly as sexless and domestic—white-haired creatures who doted on grandchildren. However, an alternative image portrayed them, with children grown, as free to take on new roles as activists in a variety of organizations or as consumers of the new consumption and beauty products being marketed in this era of commercial expansion. Some doctors even suggested that menopause was a positive experience and that only a minority of women suffered from such symptoms as insomnia and severe heat flashes. In ethnic and black cultures, in particular, aging women were honored for their wisdom, and they often served as folk healers and midwives.

Yet ageism and poverty remained issues for older Americans, especially in an era without pension plans, Social Security payments, or "old age" homes. State poorhouses and workhouses, established early in the nineteenth century to deal with poverty through institutionalization, were on the way out by the 1890s. However, they still contained old people without families willing to support them and who had no place else to go.

Women's Romantic Friendships

A culture of romantic friendships among women came into being in the mid-nineteenth century, and it still existed in 1890. It was produced by the Victorian separation between the genders and by its prohibitions on sexuality before marriage at a time when the age of first marriage was rising, producing numbers of unmarried young people in their late teens and early twenties. Moreover, a demographic imbalance (more women than men) occurred in areas of the Northeast and the South after the deaths of millions of men during the Civil War. Allowing bonds of affection between young women to develop would aid them in not giving in to the strong sexual drive of young men until they married. Women wrote passionate letters to one another, and sometimes they lived together on a long-term basis in what were called "Boston marriages." (The term was derived from Henry James's 1886 novel, *The Bostonians*, which focuses on the romantic friendship between two women.) Frances Willard, head of the Women's Christian Temperance Union (WCTU) between 1879 and 1898, wrote "The loves of women for each other grow more numerous every day. . . . That so little should be said about them surprises me, for they are everywhere."[5]

Some of these partnerships between women may have been sexual. However, the term lesbian, coined in France in the late nineteenth century, was not yet in use in the United States. ("Lesbian" was derived from the island of Lesbos, where Sappho, the ancient poet who wrote woman-centered verse, had lived in the seventh century BC.) Homosexuality was primarily a discreet and hidden behavior. Most people considered it an inherited genetic perversion connected to mental illness. In every state, "sodomy" laws, on the books since the colonial era, forbade most forms of sex outside of heterosexual intercourse, including oral sex, bestiality, and sometimes even masturbation. Homosexuality as an identity wasn't criminalized; in fact, the word wasn't coined until 1869. A German-Hungarian writer, Karoly Maria Benkert (whose pseudonym was Karl Kertbeny) invented the word; it was first used in English in 1895. Before then, individuals today called "homosexual" were called "perverts" or "inverts." The term "invert" referred to the belief that individuals who were attracted only to their own gender would become the other gender, with men taking on feminine characteristics and women taking on masculine characteristics. The terms "gay" and "lesbian" were not in widespread use until the 1930s.

By the 1890s, many medical specialists, such as Sigmund Freud, were attempting to catalogue sexual behavior and identity as a way of understanding them. They devised terms such as sadomasochism, transvestitism, and sexual fetish still in use today. They were loosely grouped together under the rubric of a new specialty called "sexology." They questioned the belief that homosexuals were "perverts," viewing them as simply different from the norm, as, for example, left-handed people are. Homophobia was so strong in American society, however, that organizations of homosexuals agitating for homosexual rights would not appear in the United States until the 1950s. Before then it would have been too dangerous to attempt to form such organizations.

THE MIDDLE-CLASS FAMILY

During these years of early modernization, the middle class was undergoing a vast expansion and regrouping across the nation. The managerial needs of a complex industrial society created not only new business magnates but also scores of new middle-level plant managers, insurance underwriters, and salesmen. Between 1870 and 1910, their total multiplied eight times. In 1910, they numbered almost five million individuals. Often upwardly mobile, they wore a "white collar" on their shirts as the symbol of emancipation from "blue collar" manual labor. Their wives formed a new leisure group, who participated in reform activities, did a lot of shopping, or still took pleasure in managing a home and family.

A decline in family functions accompanied the modernizing process. Schools took over education, and doctors took over health care; production of goods and services shifted from a rural economy to urban factories and offices over the course of the nineteenth century. A consumption-oriented economy began to appear, and by the 1890s it produced brand-name products, widespread advertising, and large urban department stores, many of which were lavishly designed as Moorish palaces or with Japanese or Parisian motifs. The department stores had large plate-glass windows facing the street, in which wax mannequins dressed in the latest fashions were displayed.

Women were responsible for 85 percent of the nation's consumption, surveys showed. New consumption activities developed for them: "window shopping," for example, and "bargain hunting." Shoplifting, called "kleptomania" by the day's psychologists, became a problem, even among middle-class women. Some seemed dazzled by the displays in the department stores and obsessed by the consumption ethic while rebelling against it.

New laborsaving devices such as sewing machines and carpet sweepers were a boon to housewives, but public health reformers called for increased cleanliness, and some of the new devices actually increased work. The new coal furnaces, for example, emitted dust and ashes. All studies showed that, even with new laborsaving devices, the requirements of housekeeping increased to fill the hours of the day. Moreover, servants were increasingly less available. Between 1890 and 1920, the ratio of domestic servants to the general population fell by half, as young working-class and immigrant women moved into factory and clerical work, which they preferred. Such jobs in factories and offices were demanding, but housework could require even more labor, and housewives could be even more dictatorial than factory foremen and bosses, especially since female servants usually lived in their employers' homes. Moreover, domestic work in individual homes was isolating, while factories often employed large numbers of young women and men, who socialized in the workplace and went out together after hours. By the 1920s the majority of domestics were older black women who came during the day and returned to their own homes in the evenings.

As middle-class families grew smaller, childrearing became more complex. The new domestic science movement produced many books advising wives on home management, thus reinforcing the housekeeping and childrearing role for women. New magazines like the *Ladies' Home Journal* and *Good Housekeeping* spread that message, while women joined organizations for the study of childrearing. In 1912 these groups joined together into the Federation for Child Study, which expanded its focus over time to become a participant in the movement for women's rights.

New rights for women increased their expectations of marital happiness. At the same time, increased life expectancy brought an increase in the length of many marriages; death less often provided a release from marital discontent. In the colonial era the wife had been primarily an economic "helpmeet" to her husband, while the Victorian wife provided spiritual uplift and domestic management in the home. The modern family, however, was supposed to fulfill the emotional needs of its members. What commentators in the 1920s called the "companionate marriage" had appeared by the 1890s. Divorce was on the rise; in 1905 one out of twelve marriages ended in divorce.

Historian Margaret Marsh, however, contends that this era witnessed a rise in family cohesion among the middle class. Suburban living increased, she asserts, as trolley lines and railroads connected suburbs to cities. Outdoor family games became popular: badminton, Ping-Pong, bicycling. In middle-class homes, the living room for the whole family replaced the wife's parlor and the husband's study of the Victorian home.

EMPLOYMENT

In 1870 about 15 percent of all women over sixteen years of age were regularly employed away from home for wages; by 1900 the figure had risen to 20 percent. In 1840 Harriet Martineau, prominent English feminist and author, contended that only seven occupations in the United States were open to women: teaching, needlework, keeping boarders, setting type, working as servants, or laboring in bookbinding and cotton factories. (She failed to mention prostitution.) By 1890, however, women were represented in all but nine of the 369 occupations listed in the federal census. Most of the women working outside the home for wages were young and unmarried. In 1900 only 5 percent of the nation's married women were so employed; by 1910 the figure stood at 11 percent.

With expanding technology and the rise of the corporate economy, women became typists and stenographers. They began to dominate such professions as nursing and teaching. Over the course of the nineteenth century, they entered the ministry, law, and medicine. Elizabeth Blackwell was the nation's first licensed Anglo-American female doctor in 1850; Rebecca Lee Crumpler became the first African American female doctor in 1867. Arabella Mansfield was the first licensed Anglo-American lawyer in 1869; Charlotte Ray the first African American lawyer in 1872.

In the theater, leading ladies like Lillian Russell commanded huge salaries and avid newspaper publicity, while women performers did the "hootchy-kootchy" in vaudeville, displayed their bodies in burlesque, and took to the high wire as trapeze artists in the circus. Helen Mary Butler toured the country with an all-female band, and semiprofessional women's baseball teams were formed. Schoolteacher Annie Taylor in 1901 was the first person to go over Niagara Falls in a barrel. Journalist Elizabeth Seaman, who called herself Nellie Bly, specialized in exposés of the exploitation of working women. To obtain her information, she worked in a paper box factory, spent time in prison, and posed as a high-class prostitute. In 1889 she traveled around the world in seventy-two days to prove that a woman could complete the trip in less than the eighty days it had taken the fictional Phileas Fogg in Jules Verne's *Around the World in Eighty Days*.

Inventors and Entrepreneurs

Between 1890 and 1930 women received over five thousand patents for inventions ranging from dressmaking supplies to scientific instruments. They also became entrepreneurs, mostly in family businesses catering to women's interests. Lydia Pinkham dominated the patent medicine market with an herbal compound she brewed in her kitchen, to be taken orally and containing 19 percent alcohol as a preservative. She advertised it extensively as a cure-all for women's gynecological complaints. Mary Ann Magnin created I. Magnin's in San Francisco in 1877. (Respecting Victorian conventions about women remaining at home, she avoided attaching her own name to the name of her department store and took the initial "I" from her husband's name, Isaac.) Carrie Marcus Neiman was the force behind the department store Neiman Marcus in Dallas, founded in 1907.

In 1895 Lena Himmelstein emigrated from Lithuania to New York. By 1910, as the dress designer Lane Bryant she challenged the taboo that pregnant women must stay at home by designing maternity clothes to be worn outdoors. She also broke new ground by designing clothing for "stout" women; her stores for "full-figured" women remain popular today. In 1911 Helen Lansdowne Resor, one of the first women advertising writers, created the famed Woodbury Soap slogan, "The skin you love to touch."

Women took on entrepreneurial roles associated with men. Stock market tycoon Hetty Green (called the "witch of Wall Street") amassed a fortune of over $100 million by her death in 1916. African American Maggie Lena Walker of Richmond, Virginia, expanded the failing Independent Order of St. Luke's, which provided life and burial insurance, into a major bank for African Americans. She was the first woman in the United States to become the president of a bank. African American Sarah Breedlove

© Harcourt Brace Library

Vassar College Advertisement. Vassar College advertises for students in the *American Agriculturalist,* April 1877. Vassar was the first college for women in the nation, and its administration wanted to soothe parents' concerns about sending their daughters away from home. Thus in this advertisement the college is described as a family, under the supervision of a Lady Principle, with daily prayers in the chapel, and a resident female physician. To counter fears that higher education was detrimental to young womens' health, the advertisement mentions the existence of a gymnasium, with opportunity for "beautiful recreation."

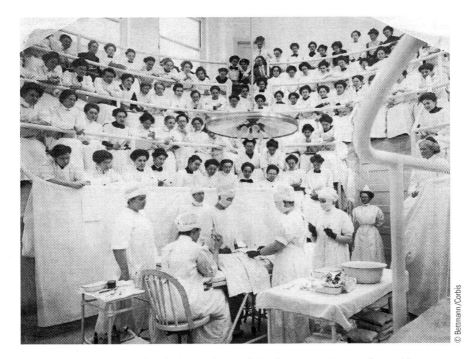

Female Surgeons. An undated photo of one of the first operations performed by female surgeons. Elizabeth Blackwell was the first female medical graduate in 1849. By the turn of the century, 5 percent of physicians were women, a rate that did not increase until the 1970s.

Walker was a pioneer in the beauty business. She invented lotions and hair products that she marketed through a sales staff of hundreds of black women who went door to door. Intent on furthering racial pride, she didn't especially advertise her hair straightening lotion, although it was a best seller among her clients. She called herself Madame C. J. Walker to convey dignity to her name at a time when most whites called blacks by their first name only.

Discrimination Against Working Women

The "New Woman" and the "Gibson Girl" symbolized the new era of opportunities for women, but they also masked discriminations against working women and ethnic women. Indeed, most women were usually employed at the bottom of the occupational hierarchy. The census of 1910 reveals that over 50 percent of working women worked as farm laborers or as domestic servants: 18 percent in the former occupation and 37 percent in the latter. Nearly 30 percent of working women were employed in manufacturing, mostly in textile, clothing, food, cigar, and shoemaking industries. They had previously done piecework for the latter two industries in their homes. Eight percent of women were employed in the professions (mostly as teachers and nurses) and 5 percent in clerical occupations. About 4 percent were employed in trade (mostly as saleswomen). A small percent were employed in transportation and in public service, primarily as telephone and telegraph operators.

In almost every category of work, skills were divided into men's and women's jobs, and women performed the less prestigious and lower-paid tasks. This situation resulted partly from the fact that most factory women were young and unmarried and therefore transient members of the workforce. In general, however, women in industry had little chance for advancement. They were the assemblers, not the skilled operatives. A long-term female employee might become a forewoman over a group of female workers. But even in this position, she would be paid less than male foremen, just as female workers across the board were paid less than male workers, even when their jobs were similar.

Discrimination in the Professions: Feminization This division between men's and women's work was also characteristic of the professions. Most female lawyers performed office work, collecting claims or preparing probate papers. Female doctors were most often in general practice and their clients were mostly women and children. They could expect less remuneration for their services than men, although women's rights advocates might seek them out for treatment.

The majority of women who entered the professions became teachers and nurses, in line with women's traditional family roles of educator and nurse. As women moved into these fields in large numbers, men either left them for other careers or moved up to managerial positions. Subsequently, pay and status decreased. "Feminization" is the term sociologists have coined for this pattern of lessened pay and status when women become the majority in a profession. By 1910, 77 percent of all teachers were women. Like female factory workers, they were mostly young and single. They clustered in grade schools and high schools, while men dominated administrative positions in such schools as well as university teaching. Sometimes women were denied promotion in education and clerical work because of the so-called marriage bar. This informal practice involved firing women if they married and refusing to promote unmarried women because it was presumed that they would marry and quit their jobs.

Such a pattern of "feminization" also existed in librarianship and in clerical work. Over the course of the twentieth century the latter occupation became the major employer of female workers. Clerical work first opened to women when typewriter manufacturers discovered that attractive female demonstrators sold more machines than men and that women could be paid less than men for the same work. Once women became typists and stenographers, men left the clerical field, which they had previously dominated. Office work was better paid and had more prestige than factory work for women, but it had its problems. For several decades, typists were called "typewriters," and the confusion between women and their machines was the subject of jokes in office conversation, in magazines, and on the variety stage. Moreover, when clerical work had been done mostly by men, the occupation was a stepping-stone to management. When women took it over, that was no longer the case.

The Male Response: Masculinization As women left the home for education and employment, a general fear arose that the entire culture might be "feminized." In response, what historians call "masculinization" occurred. This trend involved, as in office work, limiting women to subsidiary positions. In the case of the academic social sciences and public careers in the field, differing gender tracks appeared: men became sociologists and research scientists, while women became social workers and psychologists in schools and welfare agencies. The former professions, associated with men, had more status and were paid more than the latter.

Moreover, in the 1890s virility became the ideal in appearance and behavior for men, as the United States embarked on an imperial venture in the Spanish-American war, taking over Cuba, Puerto Rico, and the Philippines at its end. Engaging in bodybuilding and watching prizefighting matches and football games became popular activities for men. Macho cultural models for them appeared, such as the Western cowboy and Tarzan, the Anglo-American "ape man." Owen Wister created the cowboy in his 1906 novel *The Virginian*; his cowboy was from the South and had fought in the Civil War. The figure brought the cattle rustlers who were stealing privately owned cows grazing on a Western range to justice, prevailing over their leader in a duel with guns. The prim, pacifist schoolteacher from the East with whom the cowboy was romantically involved and who represented civilization learned that male justice often required violence. These characters and actions would become standard in the cowboy genre.

Tarzan was created by Californian Edgar Rice Burroughs and was featured in many novels by Burroughs and later in many films. The son of an English nobleman, Tarzan was left alone in Africa when his parents died. He was found by apes and was raised by them in the jungle. As the product of both civilization and savagery, he reflected the views of Social Darwinists about the superiority of the "savage" white male. He represented the new ideal for men. Even the Boy Scouts, an organization that began in England in the 1900s and was brought to the United States in 1910, reflected the newer, more aggressive masculine ideal. The goal of the organization, as stated in its handbook, was to teach boys the "manly virtues" associated with the outdoors and raw nature. They were to become like the tough, independent male hunters, trappers, and scouts of the frontier period of American history, who led the way for the Anglo-American conquest of the continent.

Juliet Low founded the first Girl Scout troop in the United States in 1912. She modeled it after troops existing in England. Like the Boy Scouts, the Girl Scouts included outdoor camping as part of their activities. Learning independence was one of their goals in this age of the "New Woman." Reflecting the era's belief that women were more emotional and spiritual than men, the Girl Scouts also focused on teaching members to form beter relations with each other and to contribute to the betterment of society.

RURAL AND URBAN WOMEN

By the 1890s the urban population was vastly increasing in size, due to immigration and the movement from farms to cities. Yet before the 1920s the majority of Americans lived on farms. Whether they lived in rural or urban areas, however, many women contributed to the family economy through remunerative employment outside the home or paid work within it. This was true of both married and unmarried women.

Rural Women of the Midwest, South, and Southwest

By 1890 the frontier era was ending in the West. Large cities such as Chicago and Denver had been founded, and small towns dotted the landscape. Given increasing mechanization and the productivity gains achieved by increased acreage, large farms, some owned by corporations, began to appear. Yet farming remained typically a family enterprise, and women were still involved in it. In addition to housekeeping chores, farmwives cared for the family's vegetable plot and for poultry and eggs for family use. During harvest time, they cooked for farmhands. Among nonwealthy farm families, daughters often worked as teachers or as domestic servants in other households to supplement the family income.

Farm life could be volatile. Farm income was dependent on variable crop production, which caused uncertainty, as did the movement of farmers to the cities. Divorce rates were higher in the West than in the East, although less stringent divorce laws in many western states partly produced this difference. Midwestern farmwives complained of hard work and isolation. But churches sponsored sewing circles and community dinners, and many women on farms and in small towns belonged to the WCTU.

Not all adult farmwomen were married. The sizable percentage of working women classified in the census of 1900 as farmworkers (18 percent) included single women who hired themselves out, like men, to pick crops and do farm chores. Most of them were African American women in the South. The census of 1900 also counted 300,000 women—mostly native-born whites—who were farmers, planters, and overseers. Most of these women were widows working land they had inherited. Some of them worked farmland they acquired under the 1865 Homestead Act, which provided that any individual who headed a family could qualify for a grant of 160 acres by living on that land for five years. In Colorado and Wyoming, women filed about 12 percent of such claims.

In the South, a prolonged post–Civil War agricultural depression forced white as well as black women on farms to join husbands and fathers in the fields, while daughters found employment in rural textile mills. The situation for black farmers and their families was particularly difficult, since the ending of slavery did not bring them real emancipation. Rather, an agricultural peonage developed that resembled their situation under slavery. Under this system, called "sharecropping," blacks farmed land owned by white planters who allotted them a yearly share of the crops. Because the white planters controlled the local government and economy, that share was often very small. And because the white merchants were often relatives or associates of the plantation owners, the sharecroppers were often considerably in debt to these merchants for seeds and supplies. Sharecropping families lived in small one- or two-room cabins, often lacking glass windows, screens, running water, or proper sanitation.

A variant situation developed in the Southwest, including Texas, New Mexico, Arizona, and California—areas that Mexico ceded to the United States in 1850 after the Mexican-American war. Throughout these regions Anglo-Americans used a combination of money and political influence to enclose common grazing land and to buy out Hispanic owners and combine their subsistence farms into cattle ranches and "factory" farms. In the process, the original owners were reduced to tenant farmers and field hands. The Anglo-American owners also recruited cheap laborers from Mexican families coming into the United States, especially after the Mexican Revolution of 1910 created havoc in Mexico and produced mass immigration to the North. Other immigrants from Mexico, especially single men, found employment as seasonal farm laborers and as workers in southwestern mines and on the railroads then being built. Their wives and families sometimes accompanied them, and the women cared for their families, worked as domestics and cooks, and took in boarders to contribute to the family economy. They exhibited a pattern of work often apparent among married immigrant women.

Urban Working Conditions

In all industrial and service occupations, conditions were difficult for female workers. Employers paid low wages and overlooked state safety laws with impunity. Waitresses often worked under unsanitary conditions and depended on tips for a living. Even department-store saleswomen—with positions of higher status—often had no vacations and no rest breaks. Many women did seasonal work and were laid off during slack periods. Male supervisors could be aggressive, and sexual harassment was not uncommon.

Similar exploitative conditions existed in factory labor for women. The women's garment industry, a major industrial employer of women, was representative. Centered in cities, it was organized around both production in factories and sewing done by women in their homes. Individual entrepreneurs and subcontractors also often set up small workshops in tenement apartments where rents were low and they could hire women who lived nearby for a pittance. This cheap method of production became a national scandal because of the unsafe and unsanitary conditions of the small workshops, which came to be called "sweatshops."

Even in the large garment factories female employees worked ten hours a day during the week and a half day on Saturday. They had to buy their own equipment. They worked at tasks less prestigious and lower-paid than those of men. Men were the cutters and pressers (positions of higher authority and pay) and women were the sewers and finishers. They suffered other indignities. In 1911, for example, the Triangle Shirtwaist Company in New York City became notorious as the scene of a major industrial fire. Many lives were lost in the fire because, to discourage pilferage, the only exit from the building was locked during working hours.

Many middle-class Americans at the time believed that working-class women worked to acquire "pin-money" for clothes and entertainment, not because they had to. Yet all investigative studies concluded that this belief was incorrect. Daughters of the working class worked because limited family incomes required that they contribute to the family economy. Most young, unmarried working women lived with their families not to save money to spend on themselves but because there was insufficient housing in American cities for them to live on their own, because many immigrant families considered it a disgrace for unmarried women to live alone, and because many working women were not paid sufficient wages to afford a single room, much less an apartment. A 1910 survey of Chicago department-store saleswomen showed that as many as 30 percent of these workers earned little more than a subsistence wage.

IMMIGRATION AND ETHNICITY ACROSS THE NATION

Large numbers of immigrants fleeing economic upheaval and political tyranny in Europe and drawn by economic opportunity to the United States began to appear in the 1880s. Chinese and Japanese individuals looking for economic opportunity also came to the United States. Koreans and Filipinos were recruited to work on the sugar and pineapple plantations in Hawaii, before many of them migrated to the mainland. Many immigrants during this period were single men who sent money home to families. But immigrant women also crossed the oceans to the United States. Once in the new country, wives and daughters went to work to contribute to the family economy, while they and their husbands and fathers endured the virulent nativism of the period.

European Immigration and Women's Work

Entering the United States through Ellis Island in New York City's harbor, European immigrants remained in Eastern cities and worked as poorly paid laborers in factories and mines. They jammed tenement flats in decaying city districts and crowded company towns in the New England mills and the Pennsylvania mining fields. Earlier German and Scandinavian immigrants had the funds to settle on midwestern farmlands, but the Italians, Slavs, Greeks, and Jews, who were the majority of turn-of-century immigrants, did not have such resources.

Moreover, much of this migration, except for the Jews, was composed of men who went back and forth to the United States to take advantage of work opportunities, leaving families behind. Some settled permanently in the United States with their families, but many didn't. As for the Jews, many immigrated to the United States because of the virulent anti-Semitism in Eastern Europe in the late nineteenth century. Facing severe religious and political reprisals, including threats against their lives and their jobs in their country of origin, they had no intention of going back.

Among working-class women in general, mostly unmarried young women worked for remuneration outside the home. For immigrant women, the percentages were high. In 1900, approximately 25 percent of

Nellie Bly. "Nellie Bly" was the pseudonym for journalist Elizabeth Cochrane Seaman, who adopted it from a popular Stephen Foster song. She entered journalism in 1885, when she was not yet twenty, quickly moving to the *New York World,* one of New York's major newspapers. Bly abandoned the genteel style of the few female journalists of the day to report on poor working conditions in factories, the problems of the working girl, and slums. She feigned insanity to spend time in a state asylum; she made paper boxes in a factory; she had herself arrested to report on conditions in jails; and she posed as a high-class prostitute to expose its clients. In 1889 she journeyed round the world in seventy-two days to prove that a woman could complete the trip in less than the eighty days it had taken the fictional Phileas Fogg in Jules Verne's novel, *Around the World in Eighty Days.*

COPYRIGHT 1890.
529. PUEBLO MAIDEN,
ISLETA, N.M.

© Corbis

Pueblo Woman. Pueblo societies were generally matrilineal in organization, with women serving as potters, taking responsibility for the household, and contributing as substantially to the family economy as the men. Some Pueblo societies lived in large "apartment-like" structures, made of adobe, with ladders used to gain access to the upper floors.

unmarried immigrant women worked, compared with 15 percent of native-born women. Immigrant women entering the workforce encountered a gender hierarchy that reflected their own culture's values as well as the nativism of the period. White native-born women monopolized clerical work, sales work, and semiskilled factory labor. Immigrant Slavic women found employment in unskilled factory labor and in domestic work. Many Jewish women entered the garment industry, in which they were sometimes employed in skilled positions because they had done such work in the shtetls, or the Eastern European towns from which they came. The work patterns of Italian women were influenced by their strongly patriarchal culture, in which male family members guarded the virtue of unmarried women. Young Italian women avoided working in sales or as domestics because in these positions they might find themselves alone with men to whom they were not related.

In addition to the impact of ethnic values and mainstream nativism, women's industrial employment was also determined by the type of work available in a particular area and the location of factories in relation to the location of ethnic neighborhoods. Women in cities like New York and Philadelphia with a variety of light industries were more likely to work in factories than women in heavy-industry towns, like Buffalo and Cincinnati. In general, women were not considered strong enough to perform the physical labor heavy industry required. In Pittsburgh, however, Italian women were employed in a variety of industries because the proximity of industrial sectors of the city to Italian neighborhoods allowed male family members to oversee them. In textile towns like Lawrence, Massachusetts, the mills employed entire families, including women and children.

Even though immigrant women bore primary responsibility for domestic tasks and childrearing, many contributed to the family economy, no matter how patriarchal their culture. Italian and Polish wives, for example, had often lived and worked independently in their countries of origin when their husbands and fathers went back and forth to the United States. In Buffalo, New York, Italian married women picked crops in the summers on nearby farms; they had done so in Italy. Married Jewish women in New York City pushed vending carts and tended family stores, as they had in the shtetls. In Los Angeles, Mexican American women were sometimes the first family members to take up new work. Like New York City Jewish women, they became street vendors, in their case selling homemade tamales and other Mexican food.

Married immigrant women who were not employed for wages outside the home often made money within it. Much of this work went unrecorded by census takers, since women often did not want to reveal work they did that might demean their husband's sense of masculinity. The "breadwinner ethic," which decreed that men should support their families unaided, was strong throughout American culture. Married immigrant women did laundry and ironing in their homes for middle-class women. These were substantial tasks in an age with neither electric washing machines nor wash-and-wear fabrics. Or they did piecework in their homes for garment factories. They housed boarders, accommodating the large numbers of single men who came to the United States on a short-term basis for work. In Homestead, Pennsylvania, a single industry town constructed for workers and their families who were employed by the Carnegie Steel Company, there was a large number of unmarried male workers and little opportunity for employment for women outside their homes. Thus more than 40 percent of families housed at least one paying boarder.

Asian Immigration

Chinese Immigration In the nineteenth century, most Chinese immigrants were single men who entered the country through San Francisco and who worked on building the transcontinental railroad and in the gold mines in California. Settling mostly on the West Coast, they often sent money to their families in the overpopulated and economically depressed Chinese province of Kwantung from which many of them came. Expecting to return to China, many married before they left their homeland, though they were often unable to save enough money from poorly paid work in the United States to return. Immigrant Chinese women in this period were mostly prostitutes, kidnapped or purchased from their families by the Tong associations that were powerful in many Chinatowns in the cities of the West. They smuggled these women into the United States as financial investments and to insure that Chinese men would not become involved with American women and would remain loyal to their families of origin. Other women, however, migrated as servants or as daughters of wealthy parents who had the funds to bring families and servants to the United States.

According to historian Peggy Pascoe, some women who came to the United States as prostitutes saw the occupation as a way of finding a husband, supporting a poverty-stricken family at home, or escaping the very confining daughter-in-law role that was standard in China and that resembled a de facto form of slavery. In order to escape their owners, some prostitutes in San Francisco brought prospective husbands (often former clients) to the Chinese Mission Home, established by Protestant women, for protection. Women abused by their husbands also sometimes came to the Mission Home for protection.

West Coast nativism against the Chinese was virulent, and in 1882 the federal Congress prohibited any further Chinese immigration, with the exception of professionals, merchants, and students—a small number of individuals in any case. The predominantly male character of Chinese communities was continued for many decades. At the same time, state miscegenation laws prohibited them from marrying white women. In 1900 there were 1,887 Chinese men in the United States for every one hundred Chinese women, or a ratio of almost nineteen to one. In China, family structure was decidedly patriarchal. Male sons, as carriers of the family lineage, were prized, and daughters were devalued. In China married couples lived with the husband's family, which was extended in composition, and young wives served their husbands and mothers-in-law. Once they were middle aged and their sons were grown, they might themselves take on the powerful mother-in-law role.

This structure broke down in the United States, where limited immigration often produced nuclear families without mothers-in-law present, while financial need often necessitated that wives work with husbands in stores, restaurants, and laundries. (Chinese laundries first appeared in the United States during the California gold rush of 1848, which was mostly male in composition. With few women available to do domestic work and with Anglo-Americans taking up most of the mining claims, Chinese men, at the bottom of the occupational and status hierarchy, took up washing and ironing as a means of employment.) Once in the United States, Chinese women rarely left their homes to work as domestics or factory employees. Moreover, traditionalism could control them in other ways. For centuries in China, beauty in women was associated with small feet. Thus in families of any affluence, girls' feet were tightly bound in bandages so that they would not grow. This painful process produced tiny, deformed feet in adult women. (The European Cinderella folktale, revolving around Cinderella's small feet, probably originated in China.) One Chinese woman in the early twentieth century, living in Butte, Montana, rarely left her home. On hearing of the Chinese Revolution in 1911, in which the nationalist, democratic forces decreed an end to foot binding, she unbound her feet. It was a "symbolic act of personal emancipation." She subsequently discarded her Chinese clothing for American dress.[6]

Some Chinese-American women did achieve commercial and professional success. Gue Gim Wah, for example, came to the United States with her merchant father in 1912. She married the manager of a boarding house in Nevada, and she helped him run the hostelry. In 1942 she opened her own restaurant, Wah's Café, featuring the Chinese food cooked in her family. The restaurant became famous throughout the region, and it remained in operation for many decades. Restaurants serving ethnic food were often established by immigrant families, and they often became popular among the general population.

Japanese Immigration Japanese immigrants first came to the United States in the 1870s as workers on Hawaiian sugar plantations. Subsequently, some came from Hawaii to California because Chinese exclusion opened up jobs on the mainland that Chinese immigrants had previously held. However, the Japanese soon encountered a strong nativist reaction from the Anglo-Americans. Given Japan's military strength, President Theodore Roosevelt was reluctant to offend the Japanese government through direct exclusion. Thus in 1907 he signed a "Gentlemen's Agreement" with the Japanese rulers, under which they agreed to restrict Japanese emigration to the United States. Because by the terms of this treaty wives in Japan were allowed to join their husbands in the United States, the Japanese did not have the same problem with family formation as the Chinese, for whom the policy was to exclude all women, even wives.

The notion of romantic love was not strong in these Asian cultures. Thus Japanese men in the United States solved the problem of finding Japanese wives through the "picture bride" exchange. Under this system, marriage brokers circulated pictures of young women living in Japan who wanted husbands among Japanese men in the United States who wanted wives. Once a marriage was agreed upon, the woman in Japan and the man in the United States were married in Japan by proxy, making the woman eligible to immigrate to the United States. Many Japanese women met their husbands for the first time at the San Francisco boat dock. In 1907 the small Japanese-American community in the United States was located primarily in California, and it numbered about fifty thousand individuals. Men outnumbered women four to one. By 1920, however, as a result of the "picture bride" exchange, the gender imbalance among Japanese Americans had ended.

In contrast to the Chinese, the Japanese tended to locate in farm areas rather than in cities. Many became specialists in fruits and vegetables being introduced into the United States: in California's Imperial Valley, for example, they pioneered in growing cantaloupes. They engaged in what came to be called "truck" farming because they often sold their produce from the backs of trucks or brought it by trucks to small specialty markets in the cities. Many grew prosperous as a result of these enterprises. Wives worked alongside husbands, sometimes in the fields. In addition, they maintained the traditional Japanese family, in which their role, like that of Chinese women, was one of service.

Korean and Filipino Immigration The experience of the tiny group of Korean immigrants to the United States in these years was similar to that of the Japanese. About seven thousand Koreans came to the United States between 1902 and 1905, immigrating primarily to Hawaii. They were hired in Korea to work in the fields on Hawaiian sugar plantations because the Japanese laborers there were engaging in strikes, and the plantation owners correctly presumed that the Koreans and the Japanese, speaking different languages and from different cultures, would not join together in labor protests. About one thousand of the original number of Koreans migrated to California, where they worked as migrant crop laborers. Like the Japanese, they also engaged in truck farming outside the cities. In 1905, as a result of the Russo-Japanese war, Korea became a possession of Japan and thus subject to the 1907 "Gentlemen's Agreement." Like Japanese men, Korean men imported "picture brides" as wives. These women found adjustment to life in the United States especially difficult. Traditionalism was so strong in Korea that families of any means confined their women to "inner rooms" and forbade them to go out during the day. In the United States, however, many had to work alongside their husbands in the fields and take in boarders to make ends meet.

In Korea, American missionaries had converted many Korean women and their families to Christianity from the Buddhism that was the religion of many Asian countries. The new religion, with female figures like the Virgin Mary and the female missionaries of the New Testament, offered women less-confining gender arrangements than the traditional culture. In the United States Korean women became known for their support of the movement for Korean independence from Japan. Picture brides, many of whom were educated, were especially involved in the work of public education and fundraising for this cause.

The Hawaiian sugar planters also imported young, unmarried Filipino men to work on their plantations. Filipino women hesitated to leave the Philippines because of the strength of the family structure and their close ties to blood relatives, which were retained after marriage. As a result, since Hawaii had no miscegenation laws and Filipinos had no "picture bride exchange," Filipino men married women of other ethnicities. The same result occurred among the Chinese and the Japanese in Hawaii, although many of them preferred to marry women from their homeland.

RACE AND REPRESENTATION

Given widespread interracial sexual intercourse, especially under slavery, large numbers of black people had light skin. Such individuals sometimes held an elite status among blacks, and some "passed" as white. Among the Anglo-American majority, definitions of "race" and of "black" and "white" have shifted over time. In the racist period of the 1890s and after, what are today called "ethnicities" were often defined as races, and dark-skinned Europeans from the Mediterranean and from Eastern Europe were often defined as inferior to light-skinned people. Italian immigrants in New Orleans, for example, were stigmatized because they took up occupations like tenant farming and farm labor that local custom decreed to be "black"-oriented labor. The Italians were called "dagos" and "white niggers." In Louisiana, Mississippi, and West Virginia, they were lynched for alleged crimes.

African Americans were at the bottom of these complex hierarchies of raced subjects, although the miscegenation laws that were often applied to Asians, stigmatizing them as a "yellow peril" or a "Mongolian" people inferior to "white" Caucasians, were very oppressive. Another new conception of race preached the superiority of Northern "Teutonic" peoples, who had blonde hair and fair skin, as superior to all other nationalities and ethnicities. By contrast, the Indians were "savages" and "redskins," and their conquest by the United States was justified in terms of the superiority of the new nation and its "white" citizens bringing "civilization" to the West.

An example of the complexities of definitions of race, interwoven with gender, is provided by the controversy over race that erupted in the copper-mining town of Clifton, Arizona, in 1904. Women in a number of Mexican American families in Clifton arranged to adopt a group of Irish children from the New York City Foundling Home, a Catholic orphan asylum run by Irish nuns. The Mexican American women believed that they were engaging in a humanitarian act in line with their Catholic faith. These women, from northern Mexico, were light skinned, and they considered themselves "white." At the same time the Anglo-Americans in New York City considered the Irish laboring class to be an inferior race, stigmatizing them as "near black." For their part, the nuns of the Foundling Home were mostly interested in placing the children in Catholic homes—and the Mexicans were Catholic. Once the children, mostly blonde-haired, arrived in Clifton, the Anglo-Americans there, who were Protestant, decided that the children were "white." Anglo women stirred up a hysteria that resulted in the Anglo men forming vigilante squads, which kidnapped the orphans from the Mexican American families who were caring for them and placed them with Anglo families. The courts decided for the Anglo families, who kept the Irish orphans and raised them.

African American Women

In the years before World War I, African Americans remained concentrated in the South, but many began the movement to northern cities that would be a major feature of their history until the 1980s. In the North, segregation

Black Women in the Workforce. An unusual example of African American women employed in a factory sawmill. In 1900 nearly 50 percent of black women worked outside the home, while only 15 percent of Anglo-American women did so. Most black women worked either as domestics or as farmworkers. Note that these women are wearing bifurcated skirts, a fashion that would have been considered unseemly before World War I.

could be subtle, since it often resulted from blacks living in areas separate from whites, rather than from overt and legalized segregation. In the South, all areas of life—from schools to cemeteries—were segregated by the 1890s. "Riots"—in which whites looted and pillaged black communities—were regularly unleashed as a means of social control. The lynchings of black men (and sometimes black women) were also employed for this purpose. Lynchings were community events, with thousands of whites present. Public officials attended them, and the spectators participated in torturing the victim. The most common charge against the victims of lynchings was the rape of a white woman—although the charge was often inaccurate or the sex was consensual. (Sometimes it involved a prostitute.) Yet the charge supported the mythology that black men were dangerously oversexed, while it concealed a truer reality in which white men more often sexually victimized black women, just as they had under slavery.

Mainstream Anglo-American culture also stereotyped black women, like black men, as oversexed and naturally promiscuous. Or they were regarded as "mammies," as docile, devoted servants of whites who had happily raised the plantation owners' children under slavery. In Southern black schools, female students were taught to dress and to behave as formally as possible when off campus to discourage the attentions of white men. Some

Aunt Jemima. A twentieth-century version of the iconic "mammy" of the romanticized antebellum South, Aunt Jemima was introduced at the Columbian Exposition of 1893. The booth at the Exposition where a large, smiling black woman made pancakes for sale was so popular that she became both the name and the image on the label of a pancake mix. Most scholars believe that the mammy figure rarely existed and that she was a fiction invented to justify slavery in the white mind.

states forbade black women to use the titles "Miss" or "Mrs." or to try on clothing before purchasing it. The penalty for committing rape against a black woman was less stringent than when a white woman was the victim. Separate washrooms were provided for white women and men in public places, but black women and men often had to share the same facilities.

Faced with such difficulties, black women were raised to be both independent and cautious. American blacks came from African societies that were matrilineal (descent traced through the mother), and female independence had been furthered under slavery, which undermined family ties. African American women expected to assume as much responsibility for family support as their husbands and fathers did. And they could often find work more easily as domestics than their husbands could as laborers.

In 1900, 43 percent of African American women were employed outside the home, compared with 15 percent of Anglo-American women and 25 percent of immigrant women. One-fourth of black married women were in the workforce, compared with less than 4 percent of white wives. Almost all African American women were employed as farmworkers or domestics. Sales and clerical work, in addition to factory labor, were almost completely denied them.

African American women did enter professions that served the black community. In medicine black women constituted a higher percentage of black doctors than white women did of white doctors. In 1910, 13 percent of all black doctors were women, while the figure among white doctors was 6 percent. Economic realities partly determined African American women's professional participation. For the most part upwardly mobile black women could not enter the expanding field of clerical work and thus had to secure professional training. Most educated black women became schoolteachers; many of them were more educated than their husbands.

Nursing, like school teaching, was a nonelite profession open to African American women. White training hospitals and schools, however, for the most part excluded them. As a result, African Americans established a national network of two hundred training hospitals and schools, which trained black women as nurses and served black communities. Funds raised by black women's clubs provided the initial support for most of them, although some white philanthropic foundations, like the Rockefeller Foundation, also provided support.

Discrimination and poverty, in addition to black migration from the South to the North, placed stress on the African American family structure, leaving many women as heads of households. Yet such a family pattern did not necessarily reflect social disorganization or result from male desertion. Death rates among black men were higher than among black women, and this trend produced many widows. And the Northern migration contained a disproportionate number of women, for whom there were not enough black men to marry. Yet most African Americans continued to live in nuclear families, as they had attempted to do under slavery, and as they have done ever since the emancipation of blacks from slavery after the Civil War.

Native American Women

By the 1890s the United States army had conquered the Native American tribes and forced most of them onto reservations, usually located on the least desirable portion of their original land. Concurrently, Anglo-Americans fenced in their former communal grazing lands for private cattle ranches and farms. Anglo-Americans regarded the land as something to be exploited for individual profit, but the Native Americans revered the earth and thought in terms of preserving it for the benefit of the entire community.

There were many Native American societies, with differing languages, social arrangements, and customs. Some, like the Pueblo tribes of New Mexico and Arizona, had been settled agriculturalists for several centuries before the Anglo-American conquest; others, like the many tribes of the Plains, had been nomadic hunters and gatherers, subsisting on the vast herds of buffalo that roamed the plains before the Anglo-Americans decimated them in the nineteenth century. In 1900 more than one hundred languages were still in use among Native American tribes. Some Indian societies practiced patrilineal descent (through the male line); others were matrilineal. Most Native Americans lived in extended families, linked together through clans; most societies had little concept of the individual ownership of property, the bedrock of American capitalism.

In many Native American tribes women held great authority. In many societies, they were centrally involved in the economy. In many of them, they grew or gathered most of the societies' food and controlled distribution of it, while the men hunted, fished, or tended the animals. These divisions of labor between women and men could be complex. Among the Chumash Indians of California, for example, in gathering acorns, a staple of their diet, men climbed the trees and struck the acorns to the ground while women collected them. In the Pueblo societies of the Southwest, women were the potters, who worked the clay from "Mother Earth." They made the impressive pots decorated with geometric patterns that are collectors' items today. Among the Navajo, weaving was a major activity, and men were the primary weavers. Among the Plains Indians, where beadwork was an important product, it was women who stitched the beads onto hides and other material. Cherokee women voted with the men in selecting the society's leaders; among the Iroquois of upstate New York, councils of women elected the tribal chieftains. Among the Hopis of eastern Arizona, the male village leader was assisted by a female relative called the "keeper of the fire," while clans were headed by older women in the communities who were considered clan mothers.

In this society women owned the houses, and inheritance passed through the youngest daughter, in a system known as ultimogeniture. Some Native American societies held a rite to honor girls at the onset of menstruation; all tribes respected aging people for their wisdom. In many Native American religions a female figure heads the pantheon. Among the Iroquois the revered figure is Sky Woman; among the Hopi, Hard Beings Woman. The Lakotas believe that woman was created first and that man was then fashioned out of a drop of her menstrual blood.

In many Native American societies men whom we would consider homosexuals, and whom early European explorers of the North American continent called "berdaches," took on the roles of tricksters and shamans. In many societies they were honored as spiritual beings who mediated between the genders. Sometimes they dressed in women's dress; sometimes they took wives; among California Native Americans they became wives to men in polygamous marriages that also included female wives. They often functioned as tribal "prostitutes," or in their terms, sacred sexual beings who in sexual intercourse brought union with the divine. They had a different name in each society; the Navajos called them "nadle"; the Assiniboine called them "winktan." In some societies "lesbian" women joined men in hunting expeditions, although scholars agree that Indian societies allowed women to change their gender role without having to become female "berdaches," while men's gender position was more rigidly defined. Some scholars contend, however, that most female "men-women" were postmenopausal, since menstruation was connected to a female identity, and only with the end of childbearing could women occupy a cross-gender role.

The United States had difficulty understanding Native American cultures, for their societies were mirror opposites of capitalism, while their religions and lifestyles seemed primitive to Anglo-Americans. Their skin color consigned them to the category of nonwhite. Under the Dawes Severalty Act (1887), individual land ownership was imposed on Native American tribes as a way of instilling them with Anglo-American values, seen as superior under the prevailing doctrine of Social Darwinism. Each individual family was given 160 acres, and the surplus acreage (often large in size) was sold to white families and speculators. Native American children were often removed from their families and placed in boarding schools, where they were taught Anglo-American values. Protestant missionaries also established schools and converted many Native Americans to Christianity.

The U.S. policy undermined the social and economic function of many tribes, as they both adopted American institutions and kept to their old ways. Among the Plains Indians tribes, the destruction of the wild buffalo herds destroyed their accustomed livelihood, the men's warlike ways, and the center of their ritual life. The American policy, which placed Native Americans on farms, proved devastating to many Native American men, who regarded farming as a woman's activity. According to historian Karen Anderson, Native Americans lost most of the lands that they had held in 1880 through a combination of fraud and coercion at the hands of the federal government and private interests. Whites were especially successful at securing valuable agricultural, mining, and timberlands. The Native Americans, however, managed to maintain many of their old rituals and structures and to create new ones. The Native American Church, for example, which flourished in the Southwest, was a pan-tribal religious organization that incorporated religious rituals from several tribes with Christian doctrines and with the taking of peyote, a natural hallucinogen, that was part of traditional religious practice. (In a reversal of the usual federal drug policy, members of the Native American Church in the U.S. military are permitted to take peyote in their services.) The Native Americans were susceptible to Anglo-European diseases and to alcoholism, which most scholars believe was a function of cultural breakdown, more than a genetic predisposition. Moreover, they often were relegated to arid, unproductive land, a factor that furthered poverty and alienation among them.

Some did achieve success in the Anglo-American educational system. Ella Deloria, the daughter of a Lakota mother and an Anglo missionary father, studied anthropology at Columbia University in the late 1920s and returned to her tribe to record social arrangements and folktales. Among the Cherokees, Anglo men and their Cherokee wives, together with full-blooded Cherokee parents, founded the Cherokee Female Seminary. Graduates of the seminary became educators, businesswomen, physicians, and social workers. Educated women sometimes returned to their communities of origin to teach at the boarding schools the U.S. government had established.

The government policy of turning Native American societies into a version of Anglo-American society remained in place until the 1930s, when John Collier, director of the Bureau of Indian Affairs, persuaded Congress in 1934 to pass the Indian Reorganization Act. Under this act traditional Native American cultures were to be encouraged, and tribal governments were created to promote self-determination. Economic development among the Native Americans was to be supported. This act and its implementation provided an impetus for a revitalization of Native American culture.

Women and the Columbian Centennial of 1893

In 1893 women captured public attention by participating in the Chicago Columbian Exposition, a "world's fair" celebrating Columbus's discovery of America four centuries earlier. The exposition was housed in a specially constructed beaux-arts "white city," and its buildings were mainly classical in style. It was intended as a symbol to transcend the dirt and grime of industrialization. Its buildings were built of a substance like plaster of paris and were not meant to last. Massive female figures stood everywhere, representing such values as "Faith," "Virtue," and "Freedom." A special women's building, planned by women, housed a display of arts, inventions, and handicrafts by women and provided a forum for speeches and conferences. It had a childcare center and a restaurant managed by women. Architect Sophia Hayden, the first woman to complete the program in architecture at MIT, designed the women's building. Adjacent to the main buildings of the Exposition was a midway, containing re-creations of native villages from throughout the world. In the Egyptian village Farida Mazhur, named "Little Egypt," did the "danse du ventre," or belly dance, in a 1,500-seat theater and became a sensation. In the following decades she and numerous imitators would appear on the vaudeville stage.

The participation of women in the fair was widely reported. Early in the nineteenth century, it had been considered a disgrace for a woman's name to appear in print. Now, as one observer noted, women were constantly "in the glare of publicity."[7]

Yet there was racism at this fair, even among the female leaders. The women's building featured a display of "women's work in savagery," which contained belts from Fiji, basketry from Samoa, and artifacts from Africa. Yet African American women were not allowed to participate in the building's programs. Black leaders Fannie Barrier Williams and Anna Julia Cooper gave speeches at the fair attacking the racism the white women displayed at the fair and elsewhere. Barrier Williams, born in upstate New York, was a talented musician who was active in social welfare work for blacks in Chicago. Anna Julia Cooper, raised in North Carolina, attended Oberlin College and taught at Dunbar High School in Washington, D.C., for most of her adult life. She devoted herself to the achievement of equal college education for women and for blacks. She attained a Ph.D. at the Sorbonne at the age of sixty-five, and she wrote her doctoral dissertation on the French attitude toward its slave colony Haiti during the French Revolution of the eighteenth century.

In contrast to these authoritative women of color at the Centennial, the Betty Crocker baking company hired a black woman of smiling demeanor and ample girth to make and serve pancakes from their new pancake mix at a booth on the fair's midway. She proved to be so popular that, dubbed "Aunt Jemima," she became the official Betty Crocker trademark. The racist "mammy" stereotype, which reduced African American women to domesticity and childrearing, bore little relationship to the actual situation under slavery, under which African American women were exploited and

brutalized. Most historians now agree that such a figure rarely existed in reality, but she nonetheless became a fixture of early twentieth-century popular culture.

Rooted in the past, celebrating "whiteness" and the "virtues" of civilization, the Columbian Exposition of 1893 still pointed to the future. The
trademark "Aunt Jemima" underscored the growing power of commercialism and consumerism, while "Little Egypt" indicated the growth of a freer,
yet more objectified, sexuality for women. As women became freer to express their sexuality over the course of the twentieth century, they increasingly became sexualized objects in advertising, pornography, and "pinups." Yet female leadership in the women's building at the Exposition also
highlighted another trend. That trend was their movement out of the home
into the public sphere, as they became both creators and supporters of a major revolution to reshape the relationships between the genders in American society.

NOTES

1. This classic description of the Victorian domestic woman was coined by
   Barbara Welter, "The Cult of True Womanhood, 1820–1860," in *Dimity
   Convictions: The American Woman in the Nineteenth Century* (Athens, Ohio:
   Ohio University Press, 1976), 21.

2. Frances Parkinson Keyes, *All Flags Flying: Reminiscences of Frances Parkinson
   Keyes* (New York: McGraw Hill, 1972), 5.

3. Mary Austin, *Earth Horizon: Autobiography* (New York: Literary Guild of
   America, 1932), 31.

4. Anne H. Wharton, "The Prolongation of Youthfulness in Modern
   Women," *Chataqua Collection*, Elizabeth Bancroft Schlesinger Library,
   Radcliffe College, p. 85.

5. Frances Willard, *Glimpses of Fifty Years: The Autobiography of an American
   Woman* (Chicago: Woman's Temperance Publication Association, 1889),
   641–42.

6. Rose Hum Lee, *The Chinese in the United States of America* (Hong Kong:
   Hong Kong University Press, 1960), 192–93.

7. Lydia Commander, *The American Idea* (1907; reprint ed., New York: Arno
   Press, 1972), 144.

2

Organizers
and Innovators:
Reformers, Feminists,
Union Leaders,
and Suffragists

1890–1920

Between 1890 and World War I, organized women were vigorous and active. Historians have sometimes interpreted the women's movement of these years as monopolized by the drive for women's suffrage. In fact, a range of innovative programs appeared, and women's organizations proliferated. Not since women joined the antebellum antislavery and temperance movements and Northern women formed the Sanitary Commission during the Civil War for charitable service had so many women belonged to so many organizations. Most organized women were involved in social reform activities, and Anglo-American women were the majority of their members. But women of color had their own organizations in their churches and their communities, and some women of all races joined radical movements, participating in socialist and anarchist groups. (Socialists wanted worker participation in the ownership of industries; anarchists wanted society and politics to be organized around small groups that cooperated with each other.) Both Anglo and ethnic working-class women joined labor unions, another form of organization involving women. By 1914, most

Opposite: The "New Woman" of the 1890s: The Gibson Girl

women's reform groups had joined together behind women's suffrage as a common goal.

By that year, many young urban women and men were rebelling against Victorianism by participating in the new sexualized culture of dance halls, movie houses, and amusement parks, like Coney Island near New York City, that appeared in this modernizing era. The revolt against the older morality began among working-class young people in the 1900s, and by the 1920s it spread to the middle class. It drew from the impulse of the age toward social change, while in reaction to it some conservative reformers were motivated to form organizations dedicated to preserving the Victorian ideals of sobriety, order, and sexual restraint. By 1920 the revolt against Victorianism would become a major social force, while the conservative reaction would also grow in size and enter the mainstream of politics.

WOMEN'S RIGHTS
AND PROGRESSIVISM: A CASE
OF GIVE AND TAKE

The women's movement of the pre–World War I era both drew from and furthered the general reform movement known as Progressivism that existed between 1890 and 1920. Both movements were partly inspired by the excesses of unregulated industrialization, which was especially evident during the depression of the 1890s. During that decade unemployment was high and workers in industry often protested low wages and poor working conditions by striking against their employers. In the past, historians viewed Progressivism as a movement of male reformers to reform the political process, or of alienated professionals attempting to re-create an older, simpler society, or of certain businesses lobbying for favorable legislation. A more recent interpretation stresses reform goals like child-welfare legislation and finds a main source of the reform impulse in women's desire to expand their role outside the home to provide better lives for their families. In addition, the growth in women's rights over the course of the nineteenth century and the advent of the "new woman" also inspired women to join reform organizations.

Throughout the nineteenth century, female reformers had justified their involvement in reform by invoking the Victorian belief in the moral superiority of women's "pious and pure" nature. Surely, the argument went, women should be allowed to extend that virtue outside the home, so that the general public might benefit from it. Drawing from the belief in women's moral superiority, some female reformers during the Progressive era contended that men were responsible for the high rates of prostitution and of venereal disease that existed and that men should be brought up to women's high moral standard. Excoriating the "double standard," they called for a "single standard" of morality. Under that standard men, like women, would remain celibate until marriage and then faithful to their wives. Often unmarried, female reformers sometimes used rhetoric extolling women's solidarity and their presumed moral superiority to men in their speeches and publications that could make them sound antimale.

Another justification for women's participation in reform was that managing a home, with its multifaceted tasks, was excellent training for managing government. Because of their domestic involvement, women could be superb "municipal housekeepers." Besides, mainstream writers often satirized male reformers as effeminate and ineffective. Only non-masculine men, it was alleged, would participate in such a "feminine" activity. Dr. Alice Hamilton, a pioneer in industrial medicine, which investigated chemicals and other pollutants as a cause of worker illness, found her gender an advantage in her work. Most Americans, she contended, believed that because of women's empathy and spirituality, they naturally put the health of workers over the profits of owners. Such an impulse in a man, she asserted, was regarded as unmanly or as radical.[1]

Religion also inspired women to participate in Progressive reform. According to historian Anne Firor Scott, the public life of every Southern woman in this period began in a church society. In addition, the evangelical impulse in the South to perfect society motivated religious organizations like the Methodist Board of Foreign Missions to support women's clubs and suffrage organizations, as well as to send religious missionaries to Africa and Asia. In the North, the "Social Gospel" movement of this era in Protestant churches, which urged Christians toward social benevolence by focusing on Christ's imperative to help the poor, drew many pious women into joining Progressive reform organizations. Social reformer Jane Addams, for example, was a devout Christian. For college she attended Presbyterian Rockford College in Illinois, which urged its graduates to become religious missionaries. Addams translated that religious imperative into secular terms by founding Hull House, a "settlement" house in the slums of Chicago that brought together a community of individuals working to improve life in the neighborhood.

The Organizations: Growth and Changing Goals

The largest women's organization in this era was the Women's Christian Temperance Union, which was strongest in the Midwest and the South and in rural areas and small towns. Its charismatic president Frances Willard proclaimed a campaign to "Do Everything." Under her leadership the organization worked not only to persuade city councils and state legislatures to prohibit the sale and consumption of alcohol but also for such reforms as kindergartens in public schools, police matrons for female prisoners in jails, and laws prohibiting child labor. Willard secured WCTU support for the peace movement, which was dedicated to ending war, and for the Knights of Labor, the major trade union of the late nineteenth century. In 1896, Willard's conservative opponents gained control of the WCTU and focused it on temperance. During Willard's leadership, however, the organization taught many women to have a sense of social responsibility. Women often joined the WCTU and then became involved in the female suffrage movement and in Progressive reform. As Willard put it, their "consciousness" of themselves and their society was raised.[2]

The women's clubs that flourished in this era also often took up reform. Popular journalist Jane Croly, who published her work under the pseudonym Jennie June, founded the first women's club, Sorosis (or sisterhood), in New York City in 1868. Many of the subsequent clubs that appeared in towns and cities throughout the nation were established as lecture and discussion groups with an emphasis on art and literature. Lectures on such subjects sometimes led to drives to beautify cities by planting flowers and trees. These activities in turn generated an interest in creating public parks and playgrounds and in expanding municipal services with a bearing on family welfare. One mother's concern about her children's schooling might lead to an investigation of the local school system or to the introduction of kindergartens, an educational innovation begun in Germany in this era. Women's campaigns for street cleaning came into existence, according to one observer, because: "It is their dresses which must sweep up the debris."[3] In 1890, Jane Croly, among others, organized the General Federation of Women's Clubs, and the national organization pressured the local clubs to undertake reform.

Women's clubs formed coalitions with other organizations. When a hurricane in Galveston, Texas, wiped out portions of the city in 1901, clubwomen and others organized a Women's Health Protective Association. This organization persuaded the city government to adopt health and sanitation measures, ranging from the inspection of milk for suspicious bacteria to the establishment of clinics to treat individuals suffering from tuberculosis, which was epidemic in that age. In Dallas, Texas, a coalition headed by the Dallas Federation of Women's Clubs, the Women's Forum, and the Council of Mothers successfully lobbied for city ordinances on health and sanitation and for changes in policies regarding education that would lead to better schools.

The Chicago Civic Club and the Boston Women's Municipal League led drives in their cities to raise the money to buy and improve overcrowded tenement apartment houses to show that landlords could improve such buildings and still make a profit. Federations of women's clubs in Iowa, Ohio, Pennsylvania, and Michigan were responsible for the creation of juvenile court systems in those states. A letter-writing campaign coordinated by women's organizations played an important role in the passage of the federal Pure Food and Drug Act of 1906. Historian Daphne Spain contends that Progressive female reformers succeeded in so many urban reform endeavors that they saved American cities from falling into chaos.

Women in colleges and universities sometimes organized sororities, following the example of the fraternities male students established in this era. The first such sorority was Alpha Delta Pi, founded at Wesleyan Female College in Macon, Georgia, in 1851. Black sororities also appeared at African American institutions. The most important black sorority was Delta Sigma Theta, formed at Howard University in Washington, D.C., in 1913. Both the black and white sororities were created to encourage a sense of sisterhood among their members, and both had secret rituals and a membership composed only of individuals selected by the existing members. Often elitist and focused on dating, they relegated activities on behalf of social welfare to a secondary position in their agendas. Delta Sigma Theta, however, focused on political and social issues. It encouraged its members to become agents of racial change. Its members became known for their contributions in later life to the arts, to community leadership, and to politics.

A Broad Spectrum

The broad spectrum of women's groups in the Progressive period included organizations with differing goals. The Young Women's Christian Association (YWCA) focused on recreation and housing for young working women in cities. The Association of Collegiate Alumnae (later the American Association of University Women) worked for municipal reform and raised money for college scholarships for women. In 1909 Ellen Richards, the first female graduate of MIT and later a professor there, established the American Home Economics Association to create a specialization for women in the sciences. Fields like chemistry and physics had generally either excluded them or relegated them to practical tracks. Responding to the crisis for homemakers caused by the lack of servants, the American Home Economics Association in the 1910s attempted to upgrade the status of domestic work and to provide better training in it for immigrant girls.

The Protective Agency for Women and Children, founded in 1885 in Chicago by delegates from fifteen women's associations in the city, sent women fleeing abusive husbands to a shelter operated by the Woman's Club of Chicago. The Protective Agency also provided counseling and legal assistance to rape victims. Even the nativist Daughters of the American Revolution—composed of women who had an ancestor who fought in the

American Revolution—participated in the reform impulse. The organization undertook letter-writing campaigns on behalf of conservation and child-labor reform.

Progressive women also participated in the "social purity" movement, a coalition of organizations that lobbied successfully for the creation of vice commissions in many cities to expose prostitution and to suggest ways to deal with it. They were also behind efforts to censor immoral behavior in the movies, to establish reformatories for "delinquent" girls, and to raise the age of consent—the age at which a girl is considered adult enough by law to consent voluntarily to sex. (Until she reaches that age, such an act is considered "statutory rape" on the part of the male involved.) In some states at the beginning of the twentieth century, the age of consent was as young as twelve years.

Women became leaders in Progressive organizations. Albion Fellows Bacon of Evansville, Indiana, was married and the mother of four children. She began her reform career as a volunteer member of the sanitation committee of Evansville's Civic Improvement Society, a group focused on securing improvements in the city's sewers and its water supply in order to decrease the incidence of disease. She then worked as a "friendly visitor" for Evansville's associated charities. ("Friendly visitors" were the predecessors of today's social workers.) Bacon decided that inadequate housing lay at the heart of poverty. She launched a statewide campaign in Indiana for laws regulating housing—a goal she achieved in 1913.

Katharine Bement Davis, a Vassar graduate with a doctorate in sociology, headed a Philadelphia settlement house before becoming superintendent of the new Women's Reformatory in Bedford Hills, New York, in 1901. Under her leadership, the Bedford Hills institution became "the most active penal experiment station in America."[4] She instituted an extensive educational program in basic reading and math skills and a training program in skills such as carpentry. She also had inmates renovate the grounds and run the physical plant as a way of teaching them landscaping and business management. In 1914 Davis became Commissioner of Corrections for New York City. Three years later she took the job of General Secretary of the Bureau of Social Hygiene of the Rockefeller Foundation. In this position, she supervised studies of prostitution, narcotics addiction, and the sexual behavior of women. Her study of this behavior, based on the responses to a detailed questionnaire of 2,200 women (mostly high school and college graduates), is considered a pioneering work.

Some women, like Albion Fellows Bacon of Indiana, moved from voluntary work to paid employment because of the expertise they had acquired as volunteers. In North Carolina, women spearheaded a movement to establish welfare departments in every county of the state. Subsequently, women who lobbied for the reform were appointed directors of the county departments. Women who worked as volunteers in settlement houses also sometimes moved into social welfare positions in local, state, and national bureaucracies.

Women also became leaders in male-dominated Progressive organizations. Lillian Wald, who founded the Henry Street Settlement in New York City in 1895, reported that in 1894 her name was dropped from the list of potential members of a New York commission on industrial safety because male members feared that if a woman were present, they could not take off their coats and roll up their shirtsleeves.[5] Yet men and women worked together in organizations such as the Consumers' League, the National Child Labor Committee, the National Association for the Advancement of Colored People (NAACP), and the Urban League. The NAACP was founded in 1909 by black and white men and women to serve as a spearhead to gain civil rights for blacks. The Urban League was founded in 1910 to work for improving the social conditions for blacks in the cities.

Progressive Reform and Settlement Houses

A major example of the ingenuity of women in the Progressive reform movement was the creation of settlement houses. The two most famous were Hull House in Chicago, founded by Jane Addams in 1889, and Lillian Wald's Henry Street in New York City. Settlement residents were mostly college graduates, fueled with a dedication to humanity and determined to prove to a skeptical public that educated women could be as forceful and innovative as men. Faced after college with the choices of marrying, training for professions that still discriminated against women, or taking low-status jobs as schoolteachers or nurses, they responded with typical American ingenuity. They invented their own profession by buying houses in urban slums where they lived and from which they provided social services to the poor and the new immigrants who lived in the neighborhood. Settlement-house work fit women's traditional role of service. Men as well as women took it up, but men did not control it. By 1900 there were one hundred settlements nationwide.

For some college graduates, settlement work was an interlude before marriage or a brief experience of idealism (like the Peace Corps of the 1960s). Some female settlement-house workers married male coworkers. Others became social workers or entered a profession. A few, like Jane Addams and Lillian Wald, remained at the settlement houses throughout their lives. Wald's Henry Street settlement, established as a visiting nurse service, became a center for social and educational work. Jane Addams's Hull House expanded to eleven buildings, and they included a gymnasium, an art gallery, a kindergarten, an apartment building for female workers, and numerous meeting rooms.

The residents of Hull House gained the authority to become leaders in other women's organizations and to influence mayors and state and national legislatures. Jane Addams wrote eleven books and hundreds of articles, and she lectured throughout the nation. She lived in a "Boston marriage" with Mary Rozet Smith, a major financial backer of Hull House. Some of her colleagues were appointed to government positions. Julia Lathrop became the first female member of the Illinois State Board of Charities and the first director of the Children's Bureau of the federal government, established in 1912. Sophonisba Breckinridge became dean of the pioneer School of Civics and Philanthropy of the University of Chicago. Florence Kelley became head of the National Consumers' League, which focused on attaining special legislation for working women.

Settlement houses were not the only community social welfare centers in this period. Some public schools, often inspired by the settlement houses, took up a similar mission. They offered courses in domestic science and skilled trades to adults in the evenings, provided free medical exams for families, and built public baths. School representatives visited students' homes to give instruction on child rearing and on middle-class Anglo-American values, such as cleanliness, thrift, and self-discipline.

According to historian Elizabeth Lasch-Quinn, most settlement houses ignored African Americans. Community centers for them were established by a coalition of black and white YWCAs, the Women's Home Mission Society of the Methodist Church, the black women's clubs, and the National Urban League. Individual black women also founded community centers. In 1911 Jane Hunter, a nursing graduate who had great difficulty in finding a job or adequate housing in Cleveland, set up a Working Girls' Home Association in the city to assist black women in a similar situation. In 1917 she opened a twenty-three-room residence for single, black, working women. By 1928, the residence, now called the Phillis Wheatley Association, after the renowned eighteenth-century black female poet, had 135 bedrooms and an employment agency to help residents find work. Other black women set up such residences and agencies in other cities, following Jane Hunter's example. Or, sometimes they derived their inspiration from women involved in such reforms who had belonged to the friendship networks they had established in college and continued after they graduated.

In her study of the backgrounds and careers of 145 social welfare leaders from the 1890s to the 1940s, historian Linda Gordon found that most of the black women in her sample were educators, while the white women were social workers. She also found that most of the black women were married, often to prominent black men, while the white women remained single. (Twenty-eight percent of them lived in "Boston marriages.") The black women saw themselves as part of the community they served, while the white women often saw their charges as "the other." This attitude led them to stress teaching their clients middle-class morality and its work ethic.

Whether their clients were lacking in such values—or whether poverty and a different language and mores were the problem—remains debatable. Still, learning English and the values and customs of the Anglo-American mainstream were important for immigrant success. In 1889 Baltimore Jewish leader Henrietta Szold established a night school in the city to teach "Americanization" to immigrants from Eastern Europe. Within a decade these schools had spread to the other Northeastern cities in which large numbers of Eastern European immigrants were settling. Many of these immigrants were Jews who did not want to lose their Jewish heritage. Responding to this impulse, Szold also established Hebrew schools and Jewish centers in Baltimore, as did other Jewish leaders in other cities.

The "Female Dominion" of Reform

According to historian Robyn Muncy, female reformers in the settlement houses and in social reform organizations were networked through the Children's Bureau in the federal Department of Labor. Women who staffed the bureau worked to establish similar bureaus at the state level. Schools like the University of Chicago's School of Civics and Philanthropy trained women to staff these agencies. The federal and state bureaus, in addition to women's local and national organizations, formed a "female dominion" in reform. As a result of their efforts, many states by 1920 had passed laws extending special legislation to women in the form of maximum hours and minimum wages, as well as laws providing "pensions" to needy mothers raising children alone.

WOMEN'S FRAILTY,
SPECIAL LEGISLATION,
AND MATERNAL FEMINISM

Seen in retrospect, there were weaknesses in the ideology and action of female reformers in the era from 1890 to World War I. These weaknesses were particularly evident in the conservative implications of the attitudes of some of them toward gender, under which they viewed women as both superior to men and as needing special protection from the state. Such attitudes contributed to the decline of the women's rights movement in the 1920s, for they seemed out of date to many feminists in that era.

The attachment of organized women of this age to the campaign for special legislation for working women and for mother's pensions reveals an underlying gender conservatism. The Women's Trade Union League organized women into unions, but it also lobbied for the passage by state legislatures of maximum hour and minimum wage laws that would apply only to female workers. The courts had overruled special legislation for workers on the grounds that it violated the common-law doctrine of "freedom of contract" between worker and employer, based on the principle that the individual worker and the owner of an industry were equal in negotiating hours and pay. They might, however, be willing to validate such legislation for women. The women's rights supporters of such legislation argued, however, that much factory labor was too difficult for women because they were physically weaker than men and were potential mothers whose reproductive capabilities might be hurt by such labor.

In 1908, the National Consumers' League prepared the brief on the basis of which the Supreme Court rendered its first decision upholding a minimum wage law for women (*Muller v. Oregon*). The decision made legal history because it was also the first time the Supreme Court based a ruling on sociological data, not just legal precedent. The brief, however, declared that "physicians are agreed that women are in general weaker than men in muscular strength and in nervous energy."[6] It cited contemporary studies contending that women who worked strained their bodies and bore unhealthy children, overlooking the differing conclusions of other scholars. The Court agreed with the Consumer's League brief.

The movement for mother's pensions was launched in 1909 at a White House Conference on the Care of Dependent Children. It was spearheaded by the National Congress of Mothers and the General Federation of Women's Clubs. The first state to pass such legislation was Illinois in 1911, and many other states soon followed. Yet the campaign for such legislation, like that for special legislation for working women, was also based on the premise that women were biologically different from men. "Maternal feminists" —as recent historians have designated them—based their arguments for these payments on women's presumed "natural" ability as mothers and on the need for children to be raised by mothers at home. These payments were viewed as a benefit, not a necessary provision that a government ought to provide its citizens.

Although soldiers receive pensions from the government, women raising children are not placed in the same category of "extraordinary service" to the state. Between 1880 and 1910 about 28 percent of American men 65 and older received Civil War pensions, as did three hundred thousand widows, orphans, and other dependents of soldiers killed in battle. The payments to mothers raising children alone were called "pensions," but they were not viewed as a basic right of "citizen-mothers." Maternal feminists, who were drawn from a broad coalition of groups, acceded to the argument that these pensions were a benefit, not a right. That decision set the stage for the vitriolic attacks against welfare in the recent era. Moreover, the women's organizations were not able to prevent most of the state legislatures from adding moral eligibility requirements to the welfare legislation they passed. Under those requirements divorced women, never-married women, and black women were excluded. In some cases, attendance at "Americanization" programs was required of immigrant welfare mothers.

RACISM AND ELITISM
IN ANGLO-AMERICAN
WOMEN'S ORGANIZATIONS

Some historians of women contend that the Anglo-American women's organizations in this era were racist, nativist, and elitist. Indeed, most barred women of color from membership. Suffrage leaders used racist and nativist arguments, asserting that white women should be granted suffrage to counter the votes of uneducated ethnic and black men. The YWCA, which had black members, had a better record on race than most Anglo-American organizations. Most of its black organizations at the local level, however, were separate from its white locals. Anglo-American middle-class women joined with working-class women in organizations to improve the conditions of work for women in service jobs and in industry, but the middle-class women often patronized their working-class allies. By the end of this era, however, female suffrage united reform women, and the suffrage organizations included working women in their ranks.

DIVERSITY IN ETHNIC AND BLACK
WOMEN'S ORGANIZATIONS

Women of racial and ethnic groups formed their own organizations, partly because their social networks were located in their own communities but more importantly because most of the Anglo-American women's organizations excluded them. Within the Jewish community, the National Council of Jewish Women, founded in 1893, encouraged American Jewish organizations to adopt social service as a goal. By the 1890s, Zionism, the movement to establish a separate Jewish state, was strong among American Jews. Hadassah, the women's Zionist organization, was formed in 1912 to provide funds for medical services for the Jewish community in Palestine. In 1913 a group of well-to-do Chinese women in San Francisco founded the nation's first Chinese women's club—the Chinese Women's Jeleab (Self-Reliance) Association.

After the Civil War, African American women founded local clubs, and in 1895 these clubs federated into the National Association of Colored Women (NACW). Its main purpose was social welfare; it was the nation's first social-service agency for African Americans. It was founded nearly fifteen years before the NAACP and the Urban League. Indeed, the black women's clubs eventually undertook much of the grassroots organizing for these two groups.

African American women often played key roles in black churches, which had long been central institutions of black communities. Thus it was natural that they would become leaders in social welfare in their communities. Local black women's clubs established day nurseries, playgrounds, old people's homes, and homes for female juvenile delinquents. They worked for better housing and schools and for more employment opportunities for African American women. The motto of the NACW was "Lifting as We Climb." It indicated its members' belief in black self-help, middle-class morality, social mobility, and racial solidarity and pride.

According to historian Glenda Gilmore, Southern black women achieved in their communities every progressive reform that Southern white women achieved in theirs, and they did it without extensive financial resources or the civic protection of their husbands, who had been excluded from voting despite the Fourteenth Amendment. These women had no illusions that they could overturn the strict system of segregation that Southern whites had imposed on them by the 1890s; under what were called the "Jim Crow" laws every public institution—from hospitals to restaurants to bathrooms—was segregated and voting rights were rescinded. Rather, Southern black women avoided confrontation with Anglo-Americans, adopted a façade of indifference, and persisted in getting what they wanted. "They set their shoulders," writes Gilmore, "fixed their facial expressions, [and] watched their language . . . because they knew that racial progress depended on it."[7]

Above all, they challenged Southern sexual mores, including the view that black women were naturally promiscuous. Journalist Ida B. Wells, an outspoken activist, fueled this campaign when in 1892 she wrote a series of articles in the newspaper she had founded in Memphis, Tennessee, denouncing the lynching of black men. Her office was bombed. She fled to Chicago, where she crusaded against lynching, took up social welfare work in the African American community, and married a prominent black lawyer, Ferdinand Barnett. She founded the first black female suffrage organization, served as probation officer for the Chicago municipal court, and worked with Jane Addams to prevent the creation of separate schools for black children in Chicago.

Mexican American women in the Southwest also participated in organizations to better their communities. Given their strong commitment to family and the Catholic Church, their involvement in social welfare characteristically took the form of providing food, lodging, and some education to those in need through family and church associations. They joined *cofradias* (lay organizations), sponsored by the Catholic Church, which helped church members in periods of crisis. They also served as *beatas,* unsanctified religious or community leaders or healers, who effected cures through the practice of folk medicine, using plants and herbs. Sometimes they became nuns, joining nunneries where they might establish schools or orphanages.

A number of Mexican women, however, radicalized by the Mexican War for Independence in 1910, worked in Mexico and the United States to organize workers, protest abuses against them, and establish mutual aid societies among them. Sara Estela Ramirez of El Paso was a poet, a political speaker, and an early supporter of the Mexican Revolution. Raised and educated by Catholic nuns in El Paso, she followed, according to historian Linda Gordon, their model of "female authority, activism, discipline, commitment to a cause, and skepticism about men's inevitable supremacy." Ramirez and others like her were forerunners of the Mexican American women who became labor organizers in the 1930s and after.

THE ARTISTS

Women were also leaders in the arts and crafts movement, which encouraged rural people to continue doing the native and folk crafts that were quickly disappearing in this modernizing era. A national network of women's exchanges marketed and also distributed these crafts. An Episcopal missionary on the White Earth Reservation in Minnesota, inhabited by Chippawa Indians, founded The Sibyl Center Indian Lace Association and sold the lace the Indian women made through Episcopal women on the East Coast. Settlement worker Susan Chester Lyman left Jane Addams's Hull House in 1894 to settle in the mountains near Asheville, North Carolina. She founded the Log Cabin Settlement there, where she revived the local craft of weaving bedspreads, which had almost died out. She marketed the work through the Women's Exchange in Asheville.

Men created and managed the major museums in the nation, many of which were founded in the late nineteenth century. Museums like the Metropolitan Museum of Art in New York City rarely bought the work of female artists. Louisine Havemeyer, heir to the Havemeyer sugar fortune, donated her huge collection to the Met, but it contained only works by men. An exception to the bias of art museums and collectors in favor of men was the Pennsylvania Museum, which collected decorative arts, regarded as women's work. That museum contained many paintings and artifacts produced by women.

There were some famous female artists in this era. Mary Cassatt was known as a painter of women and children. African American sculptor May Howard Jackson exhibited her work at the Pennsylvania Academy of Fine Art. Adelaide Johnson sculpted busts of Susan B. Anthony, Elizabeth Cady Stanton, and Lucretia Mott as part of her Memorial to the Pioneers of the Woman Suffrage Movement, which still stands in the U.S. Capitol building. By 1900, a majority of American art students were women, as were a large proportion of the artists who exhibited work in galleries.

Women's magazines employed many female artists, such as Nell Brinkley, whose "Brinkley Girl" became the successor in popularity to the Gibson Girl. In contrast to Gibson, Brinkley drew working women and women of color in addition to upper-class women. Her curly headed women, increasingly small and dynamic, led the way to the "flapper" model for women in the 1920s. Female artists who identified with the reform movements of the era created posters and designs for the women's suffrage movement. Norah Hamilton, a sister of Alice Hamilton, the pioneer in industrial medicine, illustrated books on the settlement houses and founded the Hull House Art School. Their sister Edith became a scholar of classical antiquity and the editor of a renowned collection of Greek mythology.

THE RADICALS

Radical Anglo-American and ethnic women created a ferment of new ideas in this era. Though they advocated many of the same causes as the moderates, they were more militant in their ideas and actions regarding social reform. Charlotte Perkins Gilman called for the building of apartment complexes with cleaning services, day nurseries, and general area kitchens where prepared food was available so that women would be freed from domestic tasks in order to actualize themselves through work. Other radical women (and men) called for the opening of every occupation to women, for unrestricted divorce, and for the adoption of simple, uniform clothing, without much decoration and without the uncomfortable corsets that were still in style. Some called for the communalization of the family and espoused free love. Men and women in the anarchist movement did not marry on principle; instead, they lived in monogamous unions in which both partners were free to have sex with other individuals. Many outspoken radicals lived in Greenwich Village, a bohemian center for New York City and the nation.

The fiery Emma Goldman, a Jewish immigrant from Eastern Europe, was a major radical leader. Responding to the exploitation she experienced as a garment worker, she rejected capitalism to espouse anarchism. A magnetic speaker, she crisscrossed the nation, drawing huge crowds and often encountering hostile police and private vigilantes. In reply, she vigorously defended her right to free speech. She was also the first individual to agitate publicly for the legalization of birth control. Stripped of her citizenship in 1908, she was deported, along with other radicals, after World War I.

The feminist movement, then as in the 1960s, was international in scope. Swedish feminist Ellen Key advocated that mothers raise their children alone and that the state pay them to do so. She was an influential voice in both Europe and the United States behind state pensions for mothers with underage children. English feminist Cicely Hamilton fulminated against marriage, which she viewed as an economic arrangement for women—a trade they entered for lack of any other. Olive Schreiner of South Africa, in her influential *Women and Labor* (1911), turned Darwinian beliefs about women's evolutionary inferiority upside down by arguing that only self-reliant women could bear healthy children and that humanity was destroying itself by giving middle-class women nothing to do. Schreiner coined the much-used term "sex parasitism" to describe the position of married women.

THE NEW SCHOLARS

A new kind of female scholar contributed to the crusade for women's emancipation. Like feminist scholars in the 1970s, they searched the past and the present for evidence of female oppression and women's activism. Although small in numbers, they were featured in feminist publications and cited in the general media. Female scholars in science argued that men as well as women underwent periodic emotional disturbance based on hormonal cycles. On the basis of new evidence that women were better able to

Henry Street Settlement. Henry Street Settlement House nurses on their way to the homes of the poor and needy in New York. Founded by Lillian Wald in 1895, Henry Street provided public health nursing in their homes to the poor who couldn't afford doctors. Quickly expanding beyond its initial medical orientation, Henry Street became a full-scale settlement house, a neighborhood center for civic, educational, social, and philanthropic work. Both Lillian Wald personally and Henry Street more generally took on leading roles in civic campaigns to eradicate tuberculosis, improve housing, and establish more parks and playgrounds.

© Sophia Smith Collection, Smith College

Birth Control Review. Volunteers selling copies of the "Birth Control Review." Margaret Sanger's pioneering publication first appeared in 1917. Sanger opened her first birth control clinic in 1915. In 1921 she organized the American Birth Control League, the national lobbying organization that later became the Planned Parenthood Federation of America (1942). By 1938 Sanger and her supporters had established over three hundred clinics nationwide.

resist pain than men and that they lived longer, some feminists theorized that women were, in fact, superior to men in the process of evolution. Using data from early societies, some female scholars speculated that the first human societies had been matriarchal, with women in control.

Female novelists and playwrights also explored the relationship of women to men and to society. In *Herland* (1915) Charlotte Perkins Gilman constructed a feminist utopia. Women live alone in it, in a society they have created in a remote South American forest. They reproduce by parthengenesis (the spontaneous generation of offspring without male participation), and they teach three men who wander into their society the female virtues of pacifism and humanitarianism, which Gilman regarded as natural female traits. In her short story "The Yellow Wallpaper," based on her own life, Gilman portrayed a woman who is driven mad by domesticity and her patronizing male physician. Gilman experienced a nervous breakdown several years after she married. To heal herself, she left her husband and their home in Providence, Rhode Island, to move to Pasadena, California, where she lived an independent life and supported herself through her writing.

Edith Wharton in a number of novels, including *House of Mirth* (1908) and *The Age of Innocence* (1920), explored the oppression of women in upper-class New York society. She had been raised in that society and rebelled against it, spending many years living in Europe.

Danish playwright Henrik Ibsen, in his renowned and still performed *A Doll's House* (1879), portrayed a woman slowly becoming aware of her oppression in a traditional marriage. Nora slams the door on her husband as she leaves him for good at the end of the play. That gesture became a famed symbol of women asserting independence from traditional marital arrangements. Susan Glaspell, a founder in 1914 of the Provinceton Players in Greenwich Village, went further. In plays like *The Verge* (1921), the story of a woman attempting to graft a new plant into being, she depicted male infidelity, female bonding, and women rejecting marriage and family to fight for personal independence—even when in *The Verge* that independence involved killing the husband who had oppressed the female protagonist in their marriage.

FEMINIST ACTION GROUPS: A FAINT VOICE

Despite their literary and scholarly endeavors, militant women for the most part did not form organizations for women's rights. An exception was the Feminist Alliance, formed by radicals in Greenwich Village. Its members worked for the repeal of the New York City prohibition against employing married women as schoolteachers and formed committees of doctors and lawyers who wrote law and medical schools protesting their quotas on admitting women. The Feminist Alliance discussed building one of Charlotte Perkins Gilman's professionally staffed apartment buildings, but they never did so. Its membership, however, was small. Many members were career women with limited time to dedicate to the Feminist Alliance, and many already worked for the Socialist Party, women's suffrage, or the birth control movement. Those activities took all the time they had to spare from their jobs.

A second Greenwich Village group was called Heterodoxy. Its members included Charlotte Perkins Gilman, Susan Glaspell, and other prominent female writers and reformers. They met every other week over lunch to discuss their personal issues as women, engaging in an activity similar to the "consciousness raising" of feminist groups of the 1960s. That activity was designed to raise women's self-confidence and their feminist commitment by sharing their experiences of oppression in a group setting with other women.

The radicals initiated the movement to legalize birth control. Emma Goldman pioneered in calling publicly for the reform, and Margaret Sanger followed her lead. A suburban matron raising several children in a New York City suburb, Sanger so detested her life that she came close to having a nervous breakdown. In 1910 she moved to New York City, and she became heavily involved in radical groups there. She organized strikes and rallies for the Socialist Party and for the International Workers' of the World (IWW), an anarchist union. She also worked as a visiting nurse in Manhattan's Lower East Side. The experience of watching an impoverished mother die from a botched abortion motivated her to focus on attaining the legalization of birth control, a term she coined.

Deciding that women needed a form of contraception over which they had complete control, she went to Europe to search for a diaphragm that was completely reliable, and she found one in Holland that is still in use today. She founded her first birth control clinic in 1916. The police immediately closed the clinic, but in the subsequent trial the judge ruled that an 1873 New York statute that allowed doctors to prescribe condoms for venereal disease could be extended to provide women with contraceptive advice for "the cure and prevention of disease." Thus Sanger was empowered to continue her clinic and to establish other ones, while the female doctors who staffed them kept careful records to refute the claims of male doctors that diaphragms were ineffective and that they caused cancer.

The support of the radicals added strength to the coalition of women that achieved female suffrage. The radicals also gave moral support to women and men who were trying to establish new roles in their lives. But the conservative opposition to fundamental reform was strong. Sanger, for example, spent twenty years working to achieve the complete legalization of birth control, which was slowly achieved through court decisions and the repealing by legislatures of state laws prohibiting birth control.

TWO GENERATIONS

By 1910 two groups—one older and one younger—had emerged in the women's movement. Women in the older group, centered in the suffrage movement and the settlement houses, held more traditional ideas about sex and sexuality, and were primarily interested in social reform and suffrage. Women in the younger generation—many of them professionals involved in careers—were sexually more liberal than their elders, and they were concerned about women's internal psychological liberation, their sense of themselves as independent beings. Such a personal change, they contended, was needed before political emancipation and social change could be achieved. The discussions at Heterodoxy centering around members telling their life stories reflected this goal.

The ideas of the younger women were both radical and conservative for their age. They adopted the new term "feminism" (which had been coined in France) to describe their position. Their feminism included both older ideas about the need for political emancipation for women and newer ideas about psychological liberation and about combining careers with motherhood. They were often socialists, and they criticized the older women's rights advocates for not marrying and for often being, they thought, anti-male. They didn't like the belief of the older women's rights leaders in women's moral superiority, and although they supported mothers' pensions, they split on the issue of special legislation for working women. They praised writings of Ellen Key that argued that men and women had different natures and that stressed the importance of motherhood, both for social progress and for individual fulfillment. Birth control was a major issue for them. Yet finding a way to combine marriage and motherhood with remunerative employment or a career was a central feature of their feminism. That issue would be of major concern to all women in the 1920s, as well as in the decades after.

STRIKES AND UNIONISTS

Working women joined labor unions during this era and became leaders in them. Mary "Mother" Jones, born in 1830, devoted her long life of one hundred years to organizing laborers in the most oppressive industries in the nation—coal, western mining, and southern textile mills. The fiery oratory of socialist Elizabeth Gurley Flynn brought her to public prominence in 1907 at the age of seventeen. In 1909 she led a successful free speech movement in Spokane when the city council prohibited IWW speakers from speaking on city streets, and after that she worked as an organizer among female garment workers. In 1920 she was a founding member of the American Civil Liberties Union (ACLU), devoted to the protection of the constitutional right to free speech guaranteed in the First Amendment. She continued to work as a union organizer in the 1920s and 1930s.

Women also participated in local strikes and labor organizations. Layoffs of workers or wage cuts could rouse the anger of female workers as well as of men. In 1898 female glove makers in Chicago went on strike when new assembly line techniques were introduced. They had tolerated piecework wages, tyrannical male foremen, and having to buy their own equipment. But the threat of a wage cut was too much. In 1905, in Troy, New York, eight thousand women working in commercial laundries went on strike because of the introduction of fines for talking and lateness, irregular work assignments, and a new machine—all of which had the effect of cutting wages.

Between 1909 and 1913 such episodes became common, particularly in the garment industry. In 1909, twenty thousand shirtwaist workers in New York City and Philadelphia took to the streets in the early century's most famous women's strike. In 1910 in New York City, sixty thousand workers in the cloak and suit business struck; 10 percent of these workers were women. Strike activity that year spread to garment workers in Chicago, Cleveland, and Milwaukee. In 1911, protesting the unsafe conditions that produced the terrible fire at the Triangle Shirtwaist Company in New York City that year, eighty thousand workers marched up Fifth Avenue for four hours.

In 1912 the determination of striking female textile workers in Lawrence, Massachusetts, was central to the success of one of the decade's most violent confrontations between industry and labor. The strike involved ten thousand woolen textile workers of almost forty different nationalities, and women and children were involved, since they were almost half the workers in the industry. Workers believed that they deserved a living wage—one that would allow them to support themselves without having to ask for governmental assistance. When a pay cut was announced, they struck. The strike began among female Polish workers. The owners hired strikebreakers and guards, and the local police, supporting the owners, clashed repeatedly with the strikers. These incidents aroused public sympathy for the strikers when even women and children were beaten. Contributions to the strike fund were sent from across the nation, and radicals like Margaret Sanger and Elizabeth Gurley Flynn came from elsewhere to join the workers on the picket lines. Soup kitchens and childcare centers were organized. Although the strikers won their demands, the owners were able to rescind them several years later.

These strikes in Lawrence and elsewhere demonstrated that working women in the early twentieth century had the capacity for labor militancy and large-scale organization. The International Ladies' Garment Workers Union (ILGWU), founded in 1900 as an American Federation of Labor (AFL) affiliate, greatly increased its membership as a result of these strikes. By 1913 it was the third largest AFL affiliate.

Yet for strikes to succeed locally and gain national momentum was

difficult. Employers had behind them the power of the courts, which readily issued injunctions to stop strikes, and the police, who often did not hes-
itate to use force against female strikers. The shirtwaist workers' strike of
1909 succeeded in part because a number of well-to-do philanthropists
joined the picket lines. Their participation brought public sympathy to the
strikers and forced the owners to settle. Even in this strike, however, not all
the workers were successful. Women at the Triangle Shirtwaist Company,
among the organizers of the strike, gained no concessions from their employer. Instead, a number of them were killed in the devastating Triangle
fire of 1911.

Moreover, unionizing female workers was difficult. In 1900 about 3 percent of factory women were unionized; in 1913 after the garment strikes,
only 6 percent were. Such low figures reflected the seasonal nature of the
workforce and the timidity of the women in the face of aggressive supervisors. Moreover, employers often hired women from different immigrant
backgrounds, with different languages and social customs, to limit their
interaction and their willingness to join a union. This was a tactic they also
employed in hiring men.

Women also failed to unionize because labor unions hesitated to organize them. The Knights of Labor had flourished in the 1880s. The Knights
was a general federation of workers, including both skilled and unskilled
workers, and it recruited women as members. But the Knights didn't survive the 1890s; they were destroyed by the economic downturn of the
1890s and the favoritism of the courts toward employers. Moreover, violence occasioned by battles between striking workers and the armed guards
that employers hired often turned public opinion against them. With the
disappearance of the Knights, the AFL, founded in 1886 and composed
mainly of skilled craftsmen, came to dominate organized labor. Given the
difficulties of unionizing workers in general, skilled workers, the elite
among laborers, often had little interest in taking on the problems of unskilled laborers. (The craft-based AFL also excluded African Americans
and most immigrant males from membership, in addition to women.) Nor
did AFL members want to encourage job competition from women, always a cheap source of labor. The AFL was devoted to the "breadwinner
ethic."

The national AFL constitution prohibited sex discrimination among
local unions, and most nominally complied. But because women and men
performed different tasks in most industries, union leaders eliminated
women from membership by simply excluding women's work when defining the crafts included in their union. One official of the International
Association of Machinists contended that "a machinist is born and not

made. One must have a feeling for machines, and women haven't got that."[8]
Such beliefs about women dominated many skilled crafts. Even in the few
AFL unions like the ILGWU, where female members predominated, the
officers were invariably men—with the exception of the secretary, who
was frequently a woman.

There were other reasons for the exclusion of women. For men, the
union was a refuge from the family, a place of male bonding, and an escape
from everyday life. Unions generally met in saloons, which were places of
male camaraderie. Many wives of working men were suspicious of having
their husbands socialize with other women. Many female workers viewed
unions as "male" institutions.

The gender discrimination of the AFL was not so characteristic of the
more radical unions. Like the Knights of Labor, the Industrial Workers of
the World (IWW) did not exclude women. Initially focusing on unskilled,
mass-production industries in the West and the South, like copper and coal
mining, IWW picket lines often included nonworking wives, who battled
the police with brooms and buckets. When the IWW extended its operations to the East, the union concentrated on the textile mills, which employed entire families. The AFL refused to organize the Lawrence textile
workers or to support their strike, since they were almost all unskilled
workers, but the IWW took a leadership position in the strike.

Similarly, the activism of Socialist women was central to the garment
strikes of 1910. Socialist women were led by a strong Woman's National
Committee, while neighborhood locals gave them community access to
garment workers, many of whom were young immigrant Jewish women
who had been radicalized in Eastern Europe. Both the IWW and the socialists, however, emphasized class struggle above gender concerns, while
male members exhibited gender chauvinism. Such attitudes were particularly true of the IWW, which never outgrew the masculine culture of western mining in which it had first taken root.

An exception to the weak showing of women in labor unions was the
union organized by the telephone operators of the Bell System, which controlled many of the nation's telephone exchanges and was the largest employer of women in the early twentieth century. Many of the telephone operators were native-born women who had been to high school and had
participated there in extracurricular organizations and student government
associations. Through this participation they had gained self-confidence
and had learned management skills. Thus they were able to construct a
union that was composed of women and that women led. In no other industry in the nation during this era were women able to build a national,
woman-led organization.

THE CONSUMERS' LEAGUE AND THE WOMEN'S TRADE UNION LEAGUE

The sexism of male unions, in addition to middle-class reformism, resulted in cross-class alliances of women to improve conditions for working women across the board. Two major Progressive organizations grew out of this impulse. The first, the Consumers' League, emerged in 1890 in New York and then in 1899 on the national level. It was formed to improve working conditions for department store saleswomen through consumer boycotts; it later became a leader of the movement for protective legislation for working women. The second, the Women's Trade Union League (WTUL), was founded in 1903 at a convention of the AFL. Its goal was to educate and organize both middle-class and working-class women to support better conditions for laboring women, especially for women working in factories.

The WTUL remained an amalgam of workers and the well-to-do. Among its early state and national presidents were Margaret Dreier Robins, a wealthy New York philanthropist, and Mary Anderson, a daughter of Swedish farmers who immigrated to the United States on her own in 1886. She worked as a dishwasher in a boardinghouse for lumberjacks in Michigan, then as a domestic servant, and finally as a stitcher in a shoe factory before becoming a salaried organizer for the WTUL in 1911. She became director of the Women's Bureau in the Department of Labor between 1920 and 1944. The WTUL was key to organizing the huge strikes by female garment workers in 1910, and its organizers played a major role in organizing the telephone operators nationwide. Indeed, it built a social community among those women, one that included dances, parties, and programs of education. It also persuaded a number of local unions of telephone operators to work for women's suffrage and world peace.

Yet even with funding from the AFL, the WTUL was short of money, and its successes were limited. In local chapters, middle-class members, called "allies," often stressed cultural uplift and bourgeois values. Socialist members of the WTUL felt alienated from moderates. By 1913 these differences, plus the WTUL's difficulty in organizing women outside the garment trades and the telephone operators, led it to focus on campaigning for special legislation for working women. Still, for a decade and more it brought women of differing social classes together behind the cause of the advancement of women in the workplace.

THE NEW SENSUALITY

By the 1890s a new, modern society was emerging in America. This society was more secular, more commercial, more urban. Department stores and beauty parlors appeared. Publishers like Joseph Pulitzer and William Randolph Hearst launched sensational daily newspapers (the "yellow journals"), which focused on celebrities and scandals. There were dance halls, amusement parks, and the movies, which began in 1906 by playing in small theaters called nickelodeons in immigrant neighborhoods. From the 1890s to the 1910s, the Gibson Girl was the model for women; by the 1920s the flapper would take over.

For the most part, these institutions of pleasure were designed for young, urban, working-class men and women. They were an expanding group of consumers eager to establish personal autonomy, and they had limited space at home for courtship. Some of them had left rural families to move to cities, where they lived in single rooms in cheap boardinghouses. Middle-class reformers considered the young women among them, outside family control, to be a major social problem. They called them "women adrift" and persuaded state legislatures to create special women's reformatories to deal with those who broke the law. Katharine Bement Davis's Bedford Hills reformatory was one such state institution.

Many of these young women went to dance halls and amusement parks after working hours to meet men. For some, sex was the next step. Investigators for the Massachusetts Vice Commission, one of many such urban commissions formed in this era, reported that in 1914 in every Massachusetts city young women loitered around dance halls, waiting to be picked up by men. Many of these women, the investigators found, were willing to have sex with them. Yet the women were incensed by the offer of payment, for that meant prostitution, and they did not consider themselves prostitutes. Other vice commissions in other cities found a similar situation.

Nonetheless, prostitution flourished in the first decades of the twentieth century, and the occupation attracted modern young women with loose sexual morals. In addition, the extremely low wages and seasonal unemployment of much unskilled labor for women made the higher pay of sex work, whether in a brothel or on the streets, attractive to some female workers.

The attitude of the women in the Massachusetts dance halls reflected the freer morality that was emerging in the United States in the 1900s and that appeared first among young working-class women. By 1912, it was evident among their middle-class peers. In that year began the so-called dance craze. All over America, dance halls were thronged with people dancing the bunny hug, the turkey trot, and the tango—dances previously identified with the working-class dance halls and black dives. And like so much American popular music and dance in the twentieth century—from ragtime and jazz early in the century to rock 'n' roll and hip-hop in its later years—African Americans had created it. By the 1920s the "dance craze" would widen into the flapper phenomenon, as women across the nation challenged Victorian mores with short, uncorseted, straight dresses showing legs, short hair, and makeup on their faces, cigarettes in their mouths, and freer sexual behavior in general.

THE SUFFRAGISTS

By 1900 the suffrage movement, which had existed since a female suffrage amendment was first introduced into Congress in 1869, had fallen on hard times. No vote on the amendment was taken in 1869 or in the years after. Campaigns for passage in the states also had limited success. Between 1896 and 1910 referenda on the suffrage amendment were held in only six states and it was defeated in all six. In 1910 women had equal suffrage in only four states—Wyoming, Utah, Colorado, and Idaho—where successful women's suffrage campaigns had been waged in the late nineteenth century.

Three major factors were responsible for catalyzing the suffrage movement out of its doldrums in the 1910s. First, new leaders, some of whom had lived in England, where suffragists employed militant tactics, contributed new ideas and energy. Second, the majority of female reformers came to agree that votes, rather than moral arguments, swayed politicians. Third, the Progressive reform movement came to regard female suffrage as part of their program, and the suffrage movement gained strength from an identification with the popular reform movement.

Suffrage Deceived

The failures of the suffrage movement in the 1900s were partly due to a suffrage strategy that didn't seem to work. Elizabeth Cady Stanton and Susan B. Anthony, who led the women's rights movement from its inception, died in the 1900s, and new, more moderate leaders took over. Anna Howard Shaw, president of the National American Woman Suffrage Association (NAWSA) between 1904 and 1915, and her associates followed established paths, circulating petitions and holding regular conventions. They avoided any militancy, such as street demonstrations, however, that might associate them with radicalism. They made no alliances with working-class groups. Such moderation in the second generation of leaders, however, often occurs in the development of organizations devoted to social change.

These failures were also partly due to a strong antisuffrage opposition. Local antisuffrage groups, often headed by socially prominent women, appeared in the late nineteenth century. In 1911 they united to form the National Association Opposed to the Further Extension of Suffrage to Women. This organization claimed a membership larger than that of the NAWSA. It was financially and socially supported by three powerful groups: the liquor industry, fearful that women's suffrage would bring prohibition; the political bosses, afraid that women with the vote would vote for reform politicians; and the Catholic Church, with its belief that women's primary place was to remain in the home.

The arguments of the antisuffragists were appealing not only to traditionalists, for they used the same arguments about women's moral superiority that was present in suffragist rhetoric. The rough world of politics, they believed, was no place for women, whose moral superiority should be exercised in the home—or in reform activities. Politics was a male preserve, central to the male public sphere. It thrived on underhanded practices and barroom deals; most polling places in this period were set up in saloons and barbershops. (They were moved to schools and churches once women could vote.) Antisuffrage arguments played on conservative fears: if women could vote and hold office they would leave the home, destroy the family, and take power away from men.

The antisuffragists were not always conservative on issues other than women voting. Many were social reformers, active in reform organizations. Those involvements gave them a further argument against women's suffrage. They reasoned that, without the vote and consequent party affiliations, women could more effectively influence legislators because their motives could not be questioned. However naive such reasoning may seem in today's political climate, the argument was convincing to women's organizations like the General Federation of Women's Clubs, which did not endorse women's suffrage until 1914.

Suffrage Achieved

By 1910 new, often younger, women took over leadership of the women's suffrage movement. A number of them, such as Carrie Chapman Catt and Alice Paul, had lived in England and observed the militant suffragist tactics there, which included direct confrontation through civil disobedience. They brought new ideas and energy to the movement. Appearing first in New York, they revived flagging organizations. They introduced the suf-

© Hulton-Deutsch/Corbis

Suffrage Rally at the U.S. Capitol. In 1913 Alice Paul introduced variations on the militant suffrage tactics used in England into the American movement and focused on
congressional passage of the amendment. As a result parades and rallies became common suffrage events. Men sometimes supported the women's actions by marching and
demonstrating along with them, although there were instances of violence on the
part of male bystanders against women in the parades.

frage parade—an innovation that gained national attention. In the meantime, social reformers who believed in the priority of reform conceded that
votes, more than moral arguments, swayed politicians. Progressives accepted
female suffrage as part of their program. Between 1910 and 1914, six additional states gave the vote to women: Illinois, Washington, California, Arizona, Kansas, and Oregon.

Carrie Chapman Catt and Alice Paul were also important to the new
suffrage strategy. Catt had been president of the NAWSA between 1900 and
1904, but she had resigned and moved to England to become president of
the new International Woman Suffrage Association. By 1915 Catt returned
to the United States, and she was reelected president of the NAWSA. Alice
Paul, who had also been living in England and participating in the English
suffrage movement, founded the Congressional Union in 1913. (In 1916 she
reorganized it as the Woman's Party.) Both Paul and Catt used the new techniques of parades and rallies. Catt concentrated on passage of the suffrage
amendment in state legislatures, while Paul focused on Congress, where the
suffrage amendment had been dormant in both houses since 1893.

By 1916 many women's organizations across the nation were united

© Bettmann /Corbis

Suffrage Rally on the Capitol Steps. Women marching in the suffrage parades sometimes wore white, along with purple, as a symbol of the suffrage movement. Alice Paul inaugurated her campaign for direct, militant action with a large suffrage parade in Washington, D.C., coinciding with the inauguration of Woodrow Wilson as president.

around suffrage. Jane Addams, active in the NAWSA, described the extent of the coalition, as women realized the importance of the vote to all of their reform goals. She wrote that the NAWSA was joined by:

> a church society of hundreds of Lutheran women; . . . by organization of working women who had keenly felt the need of the municipal franchise in order to secure . . . the consideration which the vote alone obtains for workingmen; by federations of mothers' meetings, who were interested in clean milk and the extension of kindergartens; by property-owning women, who had been powerless against taxation; by organizations of professional women, of university students, and of collegiate alumnae; and by women's clubs interested in municipal reforms.[9]

Women and World War I

During World War I women served the nation. The federal government formed the Women's Committee of the Council for National Defense, and Anna Howard Shaw and Carrie Chapman Catt served on it. A small number of women joined the Allied Expeditionary Force overseas as telephone operators, clerical workers, and nurses, while volunteers went abroad to work for the YMCA and the Red Cross. Once the United States joined the war effort in 1917 and men began joining the army in larger numbers, female workers in the United States took over male jobs, such as operating machines in factories. The media made heroes of some of them, like the women in Cleveland, Ohio, who took over driving the streetcars when male drivers joined the armed forces. Yet the U.S. participation in the war lasted for only eighteen months. Once the war ended and the men returned home, the women returned to their regular jobs. Still, the nation thought that women deserved recognition for their efforts on behalf of the United States in the war, and some Americans regarded suffrage as an appropriate way of honoring them.

The Final Victory

Even after women's contribution to the American effort in the war, women's suffrage was not easily achieved. In 1916 the campaign for the prohibition of the sale and consumption of alcohol, led by the WCTU, triumphed when the Prohibition Amendment was passed. Its passage, which indicated that conservatism was strong within the nation, both encouraged the suffrage forces and led many to fear that the general public might confuse the two causes, thus creating further difficulties to passage of the suffrage amendment. Indeed, success in the suffrage struggle required four more years.

By 1917 suffragists organized a round-the-clock picketing of the White House. President Woodrow Wilson had them arrested and jailed. The national press coverage they received embarrassed the administration by exposing the harshness of their treatment, including force-feeding when they refused to eat. The Supreme Court quickly ruled the action a violation of their civil rights, and they were released. Even the picketing did not bring an immediate congressional victory. Congress did not pass the suffrage amendment until 1919, after numerous additional state victories. Finally, on August 18, 1920, with its passage by the state of Tennessee, the Nineteenth Amendment, giving women the right to vote, became law in the United States.

NOTES

1. Alice Hamilton, *Exploring the Dangerous Trades: The Autobiography of Alice Hamilton* (Boston: Little Brown, 1943), 269.
2. Mary Earhart, *Frances Willard: From Prayers to Politics* (Chicago: University of Chicago Press, 1944), 194.

3. Ida A. Harper, "Women in Municipal Governments," in May Wright Sewall, ed., *The World's Congress of Representative Women: A Historical Resume for Popular Circulation of the World's Congress of Representative Women, Convened in Chicago on May 15, and Adjourned on May 22, 1893* (Chicago: Rand McNally, 1894), vol. 2, 453.

4. Blake McKelvey, *American Prisons: A Study in American Social History Prior to 1915* (Chicago: University of Chicago Press, 1936), 214.

5. Robert L. Duffus, *Lillian Wald, Neighbor and Crusader* (New York: Macmillan, 1939).

6. Josephine Goldmark, "The World's Experience Upon Which Legislation Limiting the Hours of Labor for Women is Based," in Josephine Goldmark, *Fatigue and Efficiency: A Study in Industry* (New York: Russell Sage Foundation, 1917), 1.

7. Glenda Elizabeth Gilmore, *Gender and Jim Crow: Women and the Politics of White Supremacy in North Carolina, 1896–1920* (Chapel Hill, N.C.: University of North Carolina, 1996), 178.

8. Theresa Wolfson, *The Woman Worker and the Trade Unions* (New York: International, 1926), 110.

9. Jane Addams, *Twenty Years at Hull House* (1910; Urbana, Ill.: University of Illinois Press, 1990), 103.

1896 1926

Thirty Years of "Progress"!

3

Freedom or Disillusionment?

The 1920s

The revolt of youth that had emerged in the pre–World War I era took center stage in the 1920s. This was "the roaring twenties," "the great spree," the "age of excess." With prohibition in force, illegal speakeasies appeared, and young women and men went to them to drink liquor, smoke cigarettes, and dance the two-step and the Charleston to a hot jazz beat. (There were ten thousand of these hidden, often underground, places in New York City alone.) In parked automobiles and other private spaces, young people engaged in "petting parties."

The Gibson Girl as the symbol of the "New Woman" was replaced by the "flapper," complete with short skirts, bobbed hair, and bound breasts. She looked like a preadolescent girl—or a young boy; she symbolized the fixation with youth as the ideal that would increasingly characterize modern America over the course of the twentieth century. The flapper was a product of the rising popularity of places of commercial leisure, of the success of women in gaining the vote, and of the national sense of emotional release from the horrors of World War I. In that war new weapons like machine guns, bombs dropped from airplanes, and poison gas caused horrible

Opposite: John Held Jr.'s answer to the Gibson Girl in a 1926 issue of *Life* magazine

injuries and many deaths. As an iconic figure, the flapper found freedom in personal behavior, not in women's rights activities.

Despite the rebellion of youth, political and social conservatism was strong in the 1920s. At the beginning of the decade, the Bolshevik takeover of Russia incited a national paranoia about internal subversion. During the "Red Scare" of 1919 and 1920, the federal government prosecuted and deported radicals, including Emma Goldman. (The American Civil Liberties Union (ACLU) was founded in 1920 as a result of government incursions on free speech during the Red Scare.) Throughout the decade the Ku Klux Klan flourished, prohibition was in force, and immigration from Eastern Europe and the Mediterranean region was severely restricted by federal statute. Big business was dominant; the presidential administrations were Republican, pro-business, and conservative. The labor union movement declined, and political radicalism was in retreat. Americans seemed even more dedicated than before to making money and having a good time.

Personal income rose; between 1919 and 1929 the gross national product increased 40 percent. The middle class swelled in size, and many of the "new immigrants" of the pre–World War I era (or their children), who by now had become citizens and homeowners, began to move upward in the social order, achieving the "American dream" of upward social mobility. At schools like the City College of New York, they were able to get college degrees. Farmers moved to the cities, and the census of 1920 showed that for the first time in U.S. history, the urban population was larger than the rural one. Yet sectors of the economy were in recession throughout the decade, including farming and some industries. These problems foreshadowed the stock market crash in 1929 and the Great Depression of the 1930s.

ANTIFEMINIST UNDERCURRENTS AND FEMINIST CONSERVATISM

The mood of the country was not reform-minded in the 1920s, for business seemed to be providing material prosperity to all. Americans were dazzled by mass-produced consumer goods: automobiles, radios, and, for women in particular, washing machines, vacuum cleaners, and electric kitchens—major aids in caring for homes and families. Buying on the installment plan was first introduced in auto sales in 1915, and it soared in the 1920s among the middle class. Chain stores and supermarkets appeared; the first suburban shopping center, the Country Club Plaza, was built in Kansas City in 1923. The mail-order catalogue for the Sears, Roebuck Company, which Sears had introduced in the 1890s, already had a large circulation when the company opened its first retail store in 1925. By 1928, it had opened 254 stores across the nation.

Per capita output of cosmetics increased threefold in the 1920s. For young working women and college women, "putting on a face" became a morning ritual. Using cosmetics had previously been associated with prostitutes, and respectable women avoided using them. But that was no longer the case. Small gold and silver, enameled and painted "compact cases," containing rouge, lipstick, and powder, were all the rage. Using cosmetics also became a sign of "Americanization." Some immigrant women painted their faces as a badge of belonging—and sometimes to get a job. Indeed, the amount and type of cosmetics used was often a marker of social class and occupation. The wealthy wore natural rouge and lip tints. Office workers often tried to look "tasteful" and to conceal that they were "working girls" by toning down the amount and color of the makeup they wore. Older middle-class women slowly adopted the bright red lipstick and glossy nail enamel that their "flapper" daughters often wore when they dressed up. Those products were introduced in the 1920s.

The fashionable sheath-like flapper dress was constructed from two pieces of material that were sewn together at the shoulders and side seams. Given its simple, nonconfining construction, it seems liberating, although women bound their breasts to achieve the straight look that was in vogue. Hair was cut short, but perming it at beauty parlors, using the Nessler electrical waving machine, was popular. Dieting became a fad, since flapper fashions required a slim body. Calorie counting became voguish, and diet products abounded. The weight scale became a popular item in the new indoor bathrooms that appeared as a feature of middle-class homes in the 1920s.

By the mid-1920s, it was a matter of belief—proclaimed by the media and accepted by many individuals—that women had achieved liberation. Suffrage had been won. Scores of female college graduates appeared in major cities every year to become secretaries, copy editors, and management trainees in department stores. Female sports stars, like Helen Wills in tennis and Gertrude Ederle in swimming, were challenging the belief that women could not excel in athletics. Over the course of her career, Wills won seven U.S. singles crowns, eight Wimbledon singles titles, and four French singles championships. In 1925 Ederle became the first woman and the sixth person to swim the English Channel. She broke the record established by a man by two hours, and she was welcomed home by a ticker-tape parade in New York City attended by an estimated two million people. Journalists Jane Grant and Ruth Hale formed a Lucy Stone League in New York City to encourage married women to use their maiden names. They followed the example of Lucy Stone, the nineteenth-century suffrage leader, who kept her maiden name after she married reformer Henry Black-well. Even feminist Suzanne LaFollette wrote in 1926 in her book about the situation for women in the United States that the women's struggle "is very largely won."[1]

The premise that women had achieved liberation gave rise to a subtle antifeminism. By the late 1920s, articles appeared in popular journals contending that in gaining their "rights," women had given up their "privileges." The articles pitied working women for not having the "delightful" experiences of "taking an hour to dress," of "spending the day in strictly feminine pursuits," of "actually making the kind of cake that [now] comes from the bakery."[2] The press sometimes described the pre–World War I women's rights advocates as physically unattractive and antimale, just as the media of the 1970s and after would describe "second-wave" feminists of the 1960s and 1970s as unattractive and antimale. And in the 1920s—as in the recent era—many individuals accepted the media stereotype of the looks and attitudes of feminists of an earlier generation.

The antifeminist argument of the 1920s was appealing to young women. Playwright Lillian Hellman, who came of age in the decade, wrote that the young women of her generation took the emancipation of women for granted and weren't especially concerned about women's rights:

> By the time I grew up the fight for the emancipation of women, their rights under the law, in the office, in bed, was stale stuff. My generation didn't think much about the place or the problems of women, were not conscious that the designs we saw around us had so recently been formed or that we were still part of that formation.[3]

Advertising spread the message that women had gained political and social emancipation by insinuating that their true freedom lay in buying the items the advertisers were promoting. Expanding dramatically in volume in the 1920s, advertising continued to find the major market for its products in women. The clothing and cosmetics industries advertised their way to a phenomenal growth. Advertisers secured endorsements from socialites and movie stars in their ads for the products they were selling, while those ads made clear that looking right and shopping were to be women's most important concerns. Advertisers often connected their product to the appeal of the body of the female models in their ads, thus applying the adage that "sex sells," while turning women into both consumers and objects of consumption. Blatant sexuality, however, was downplayed in the ads of the 1920s, and a "romance formula" that focused on the emotional attraction between a man and a woman was often applied. According to this formula, women should transform their bodies through the use of products whose "magic" would enable them to attract and then keep a man. Ads for skin creams, lotions, and cosmetics in particular used this formula, as they promised to keep a woman eternally young so that she would always be attractive to a man.

SEXUALITY

In the 1920s the notion that sex was a necessity for both men and women was widespread. Before World War I, some feminists and doctors had downplayed Victorian prudery to promote the idea that women were capable of enjoying sex; now marriage manuals describing erotic techniques were available. The theories of Sigmund Freud, popular in the 1920s, validated their message, for he argued that unconscious drives, especially sex, dominated human behavior. In order to be contented, humans needed to satisfy their sex drive. Films made sex a stock device, and leading ladies on the screen capitulated to "Latin lovers" like Rudolph Valentino, while Gloria Swanson luxuriated in exotic bathrooms in baths that coyly hid her naked body. Sex-story magazines like *True Confessions*, written for an audience of working-class women, used romance and sex in their stories to gain huge sales.

Lesbian subcultures appeared in cities like San Francisco and New York, while in Harlem and Greenwich Village bisexuality was in vogue. Some well-to-do Anglo-Americans went to Harlem for sex circuses and mixed bars catering to blacks and whites, heterosexuals and homosexuals. Experiencing what they saw as "the primitive excitement of Africa," white sophisticates, looking for sexual thrills, acted out their desire for "the primitive and the exotic."[4] In New York, drag balls were held in upscale ballrooms such as the one in the Savoy Hotel and in the huge Madison Square Garden. Both women and men cross-dressed at these events.

"FLAMING YOUTH"— NEW LIBERTIES, NEW REPRESSIONS, AND OLD ATTITUDES

The "Sexual Revolution" of the 1920s expanded women's options and increased their freedom, but there were costs. Given the emphasis of the new sexuality on heterosexuality, limits were put on romantic behavior between women, and the Victorian approval of romantic friendships among women largely disappeared. Women still lived together in long-term arrangements, but the term "Boston marriage" to describe these relationships became quaint and out-of-date. Indeed, some historians contend that the sexual revolution of the 1920s enforced a "compulsory heterosexuality." Moreover, the new sexuality for women challenged the beliefs of women's rights advocates of the pre–World War I period about women's moral superiority and their call for men to give up the sexual "double standard" for women's "single standard." Now it seemed that women were joining the sexual world of men.

Moreover, Freud's ideas about sexuality were as constraining for women as they were liberating. For Freud believed that women were inevitably dissatisfied because of their desire for the male sex organ—Freud called this supposed desire "penis envy." According to Freud, women could ultimately satisfy this longing only through motherhood—particularly through having a male child. Even though he trained a number of important female psychoanalysts, including his daughter Anna Freud, he believed that professional women for the most part were acting out an inappropriate form of their "penis envy."

Furthermore, the extent to which the sexual revolution of the 1920s ended older, more repressive attitudes about sexuality is debatable. Aside from undergarment ads, advertisers didn't use nudity in advertisements. Skirts had been raised and sexual emancipation proclaimed, but to show the back of a woman's leg was still considered risqué. Romance, not sex, was the magic promised by the fantasy world of advertising, while in the world of Hollywood films the word "it" became the euphemism for "sex" or "sexy." A series of sex scandals in Hollywood brought the creation of the Motion Picture Producers and Distributors of America in 1922, formed by the major studios to head off state and federal censorship of films. Its moral code was modest until 1930, when an official list of do's and don'ts was published. In 1934 a strict morals code was enforced, including prohibitions on explicit sexuality, interracial romance, and the depiction of homosexuality.

Surveys of sexual attitudes done during the 1920s point to a limited change in behavior. In 1929 Katharine Bement Davis published an acclaimed study of the sexual behavior of 2,200 women from across the nation, mostly college-educated and middle class. Davis found that only 7 percent of the married women in her sample admitted to having had heterosexual intercourse before marriage, while 10.5 percent of the unmarried women admitted to having had sex with a man. Moreover, 80 percent of both groups were opposed to premarital sex.[5] Judge Ben Lindsey of the juvenile court in Denver, Colorado, renowned for his work among teenagers, reported that the sexual behavior of the young people he saw wasn't that different from the behavior of their elders. In his opinion, both generations were rebellious and restrained at the same time. He did think, however, that before World War I young men had sex with prostitutes, while after the war they were able to turn to female schoolmates. However, in his opinion, no more than 10 percent of Denver's young women—even after the war— were sexually permissive.[6]

The situation in Butte, Montana, is telling. Before World War I, the copper industry dominated the city. With large numbers of unmarried, young male workers, it produced a masculine culture of saloons, gambling, and prostitution. After the passage of the Prohibition Amendment, het-erosocial speakeasies opened and quickly became popular, as even young women in Butte adopted freer behavior. Young women and men danced and listened to jazz in the speakeasies; they drank liquor and smoked ciga-rettes. Young women in Butte dressed like flappers. In 1917 there were no beauty parlors in the city; in 1931 there were twenty-eight. Butte was a small city, with closely knit neighborhoods and a strong Catholic Church. Most young women lived at home with their parents. They combined the modern and the traditional. They went to the nightclubs on the weekends, but they also attended Sunday church services and religious and family events.

Mexican American young women in Los Angeles and young ethnic women in Chicago (Slavs, Italians, Jews, and Greeks) also combined the traditional and the new in their behavior. In Los Angeles, the Spanish-language *La Opinion*, the major newspaper of the Mexican American com-munity, featured sketches of the latest fashions and advertisements about cosmetics. There were many beauty contests, sponsored by patriotic socie-ties, newspapers, and even churches and labor unions. But Mexican Amer-ican girls mostly lived at home; chaperonage was strict; and they worked at young ages to contribute to the family income. In Chicago, ethnic young people formed clubs that met in neighborhood buildings. In their clubs they danced the new dances, listened to the new music, engaged in courtship be-havior, and discussed politics and jobs and the latest fashions in dress and be-havior. But they also lived at home and attended Sunday church services and religious and family events.

Young women in general adapted the new behaviors to their own needs. Novelist Mary McCarthy, raised by a strict Protestant grandfather and a Jewish grandmother, was forbidden to date until she was eighteen. She dis-obeyed this rule only once. In a secret journey with female friends to a distant state, she had a passionate, although unconsummated, affair with a married man, who gallantly preserved her "virtue."[7] Indeed, sexual eman-cipation in the 1920s most often led to marriage. Divorce statistics contin-ued to rise, but the number of marriages was high, and the median age of first marriage for women remained at about twenty-two. Some historians contend that the real sexual revolution during the 1920s occurred among married women, who began to demand sexual fulfillment in marriage. One participant in the youth culture of the 1920s later remembered that she and her friends debated free love and companionate marriage. They bobbed their hair and carried hip flasks. But the rebellion stopped there. Ten years later, these "rebellious" women were respectable citizens, caring for homes and children. They "worried about the interest on the mortgage; [and about] making poor Aunt Ida feel she really isn't a burden."[8]

CONSERVATISM AND EUGENICS

The liberal sexual attitudes of the 1920s existed alongside a social conservatism that influenced even social reformers. Birth control advocate Margaret Sanger, a radical before World War I, gave up marches and demonstrations to focus on her organization, the American Birth Control League, and on lobbying legislatures and medical groups such as the American Medical Association. She established birth control clinics staffed by female doctors, and she supported the freer sexuality of the decade (for which birth control was essential). In her speeches and writings, however, she employed eugenic arguments about the inferiority of people of color to argue that ethnic and working-class women should have access to birth control in order to reduce the large numbers of offspring they were having, especially since the rates of reproduction among middle-class whites were dropping.

Female reformers like Jane Addams and Florence Kelley were attacked as communists by ultraconservative organizations, such as the American Legion and the DAR. Jane Addams was accused because of her pacifism; Florence Kelley because she campaigned for an amendment prohibiting child labor that the extreme right viewed as part of a communist plot to undermine the family. Army officials created the infamous "spiderweb chart," which linked the major women's reform organizations together as a "pink sisterhood," supposedly controlled by the Bolsheviks in Russia. Moreover, "patriotic groups," backed by employers, charged supporters of special legislation for working women with being "unAmerican."

One powerful ultraconservative organization during the 1920s was the Ku Klux Klan. It had appeared briefly in the South after Reconstruction as a group aimed at curbing black independence in local communities. Reconstituted in the early twentieth century, it expanded greatly during the super patriotism of World War I. Its members marched in parades in white robes and hoods, and they burned crosses at rallies. The 1920s Klan was not only antiblack but also anti-Semitic and anti-Catholic, and it was strong in the Midwest and in Southern California, not just in the South. It drew its members from religious fundamentalists who disliked cities and romanticized small-town life. It had a female membership of about 500,000. The role of its women members was to organize "poison squads" to spread slander about the groups it disliked and to form consumer boycotts against their businesses.

Like the female antisuffragists before World War I, the women of the Klan were not always conservative on women's issues; they supported equal legal rights for women and equal pay for them in employment. And they found personal fulfillment in working with other women. According to historian Susan Blee, these Klan women "recalled their years in United States history's most vicious campaigns of prejudice and hatred primarily as a time of solidarity and friendship among like-minded women."[9]

The eugenics movement, which influenced Margaret Sanger, was also powerful during the 1920s. Following Social Darwinist arguments, its proponents viewed the "white race" as threatened by the large numbers of immigrants with dark skin from Eastern Europe and the Mediterranean who had come to the United States before World War I. So determined were the eugenicists to separate the "white" population from these Mediterranean and Eastern European populations that they defined what we would call separate "ethnicities" or "nationalities" as separate "races." At the same time they hoped to create a better future through selective breeding. Colleges introduced courses on eugenics, and "better family" contests were held at state fairs. The eugenics argument was a major force behind the Immigration Act of 1924. That act established national quotas for immigration that were heavily weighted toward people from Northern Europe and that virtually eliminated immigration from Eastern Europe and the Mediterranean.

Eugenic ideas also led to the compulsory sterilization of some unmarried women receiving state mothers' pensions. The argument was that poverty was connected to immorality and that both were inherited traits that were passed on to children and that on these grounds the states should stop women on welfare from giving birth. By the 1920s twenty-three states had enacted compulsory sterilization laws, and in 1927 the U.S. Supreme Court upheld them. By 1960 over sixty thousand eugenic sterilizations had been performed nationwide on women who were poor and without husbands. On Native American reservations, such operations were performed on as many as 25 percent of fertile women. Most women who were sterilized were told that they were undergoing an appendectomy. The abuse did not decline until the 1970s, when feminists protested against it and raised a public outcry.

As for the eugenics movement, it was discredited in the United States with the rise to power of Adolf Hitler in Germany. Hitler preached the superiority of a Germanic "Nordic" race with fair skin and hair and blue eyes and employed eugenic ideas as a rationalization for the extermination of

© Bettmann./Corbis

Flappers. The precursor of more recent dances, such as swing and hip-hop, the Charleston originated in black dance halls in the South after slavery, and first reached a large public through the all-black Broadway show, *Runnin' Wild,* in 1923. Note short skirts, bare legs, and "cloche" hats.

Jews and homosexuals in Germany and the countries he conquered. Such extreme actions seemed to indicate how far the eugenics argument might go, and thus they undermined the entire movement.

WOMEN AT WORK: PROGRESS AND SETBACKS

During the 1920s the proportion of women in the workforce increased, as it would throughout the twentieth century. Twenty-three percent of American women were employed in 1920 and 24 percent in 1930. Yet the percentage rise was only 1 percent, and the additional two million women who entered the workforce reflected general population growth. At the height of women's employment during World War I, only 5 percent of female workers had not been in the labor force before the war. What seemed to be

Women's KKK. Masked and robed women in Atlanta, Georgia, in 1922. They are members of the Dixie Protestant Women's Political League, an organization closely modeled after the Ku Klux Klan.

new employment usually involved women already in the workforce being promoted to higher-paying, higher-skilled jobs during the war. When the men returned home, they took over these jobs and the women lost them. In Cleveland, the women who became streetcar operators were heroes for a time, but they were laid off when male operators returning from the war went on strike against their continued employment.

Married Women at Work

During the 1920s the percentage of married women in the workforce continued to rise, as it had earlier in the century. The percentage increased from 5.6 percent in 1900 to 10.7 percent in 1910 to 11.7 percent by 1930. Moreover, the percentage of professional women who were married also rose— from 12 percent in 1910 to 27 percent in 1930. Many of these women worked, however, because of economic necessity or increased consumption desires on their part. "The two-car family," noted psychologist Lorine Pruette, "demands the two-wage family."[10] In the case of working-class women, a number of factors decreased options for working at home and brought more married women among them into the workforce. Immigration restriction reduced the pool of male boarders to whom they might rent a room in their homes, while new "antisweating" ordinances in many cities ended industrial homework done in small workshops in tenement districts where people lived. Moreover, many states, responding to the national demand for an amendment prohibiting child labor, began strictly to enforce state laws restricting child labor that were already on the books. Some mothers went to work outside the home to replace the income lost from children now unable to work.

The increasing participation of married women in the workforce was a major long-term trend in the employment of women. It challenged the traditional belief that linked women with the home and defined masculinity in terms of a man's ability to provide unaided for his family—the so-called breadwinner ethic. But it was not always easy for married women to work. Popular magazines featured "confessions" by self-styled "ex-feminists" who found caring for a home while working outside of it difficult. These women often complained that their husbands refused to help with household labor. The women themselves, however, sometimes regretted having no time for pleasurable domestic activities. Many women wanted not only careers but also, as one "ex-feminist" put it, "the rich domestic life of husband, home, and babies that my mother's generation enjoyed."[11] It was difficult for them to combine the two roles of career woman and housewife and to perform both of them successfully.

Professional Women

The popular evidence of women's emancipation in the 1920s—women at work, freer sexuality, looser clothing—masked the discrimination that still existed. Except for their movement into clerical work, women did not improve their position in the labor force. Although the number of women holding professional jobs increased in most professions, they still held jobs that were less prestigious and were lower-paid than those of men. For example, women received about one-third of the nation's graduate degrees each year, but only 4 percent of the full professors in U.S. colleges and universities were women. In medicine, the proportion of women to men declined. Even the expanding fields of business administration and advertising offered limited opportunities for women. In business, women were rarely promoted above clerical work. In advertising, although many women were employed as copywriters, it was hard for them to rise any higher through the ranks. M. Louise Luckinbill, a secretary at the Schultz-McGregor Advertising Agency in New York City, declined a promotion to a vice presidency because businessmen "would throw up their hands in horror at the idea of a woman being . . . vice-president of an [advertising agency] which served them."[12]

Successful businesswomen continued to market products designed for women, especially in the clothing and cosmetics industries. Helena Rubinstein, who began by marketing the beauty cream her mother had made in her home and parlayed it into a cosmetics empire, was one of a number of such women. Yet Rubenstein recalled in her autobiography that "it was not easy being a hard-working woman in a man's world." She became a tyrant at work, indulging in legendary rages. She married a count, lived in luxury, and was known as "madame." For "added courage," as she put it, she wore elaborate, expensive jewelry. To Rubinstein, the quest for beauty, central to her business and her personal life, was important in women gaining self-confidence. It was, she wrote, a "force . . . to make you feel greater than you are."[13]

Artists and Writers of Achievement

In the 1920s acclaimed female writers and artists appeared. Gertrude Vanderbilt Whitney, who possessed great wealth, was both a sculpter and a major patron of the arts. When the Metropolitan Museum of Art refused her offer to build a wing to house her collection of modern art, she donated the money to build the Whitney Museum.

Ruth St. Denis, Isadora Duncan, and Martha Graham were key figures in the emergence of "modern dance," which utilized natural body movements and soft shoes in place of the rigid poses and toe dancing of classical ballet. African American jazz dancer Josephine Baker became the toast of Paris after appearing in one of the popular black revues that originated on Broadway and toured Europe in the1920s. Baker became the emblem of the driving energy of jazz throughout Europe, but she never became a star in the United States. When she returned to New York City in the late 1920s to appear in the renowned Ziegfeld Follies, she had difficulty finding a hotel in white Manhattan that would rent her a room.

Poet Edna St. Vincent Millay became a symbol of emancipation for women in the 1920s. Her poetry was featured in popular magazines, and she was renowned for her bohemian lifestyle in Greenwich Village. The famous line from her poetry about her candle burning "at both ends" that would not "last the night" became a slogan of independence and pleasure for young women. Willa Cather continued her distinguished career as a writer of frontier fiction and a critic of technology. Dorothy Parker was a leader of the New York City intellectuals and wits who gathered for lunch and conversation at the famed "round table" at the Algonquin Hotel. Renowned for her one-liners, she was famed for the remark she presumably made to a young man who told her that he couldn't bear fools. "That's odd," she said to him. "Your mother could."

In Harlem, Regina Andrews made the 135th Street Branch of the New

Zora Neale Hurston. An eminent folklorist, anthropologist, and writer, identified with the Harlem Renaissance and famed for her novel *Their Eyes Were Watching God.* In the 1930s she served as editor for the Federal Arts Project in Florida of the Works Progress Administration of the New Deal.

Jessie Redmon Fauset. A member of the Harlem Renaissance who wrote realistic novels about the dilemma of people of mixed blood and light skin who attempt to "pass" as white. As literary editor of the *Crisis,* the magazine of the NAACP, she encouraged young black writers to pursue their creative talents.

York Public Library a gathering place for African American intellectuals. Jessie Fauset, as literary editor of the *Crisis*, the magazine of the NAACP, encouraged young black writers. Both Andrews and Fauset thus contributed to the Harlem Renaissance—the outpouring of writings by black authors in the 1920s and 1930s living in Harlem, which had become the African American intellectual and artistic center for the nation, just as Greenwich Village was a center for artists and writers in general.

The major female writers of the Harlem Renaissance—like Nella Larsen and Zora Neale Hurston—wrote about the double discrimination involved in being both black and female, as even male leaders of the Renaissance sometimes disregarded them. In her novels *Passing* and *Quicksand*, Larsen created women who attempt to "pass" as white and who lose themselves in the process. Hurston, however, was more optimistic. In "How It Feels to Be Colored Me," she praised her childhood free of racism in the all-black town of Eatonville, Florida, where her father was a preacher and a town leader. Hurston came to New York City in 1925 and studied anthropology at Columbia University with Ruth Benedict and others. Between 1927 and 1932 she journeyed through the South as an ethnographer, studying African American folkways. In 1937 she wrote *Their Eyes Were Watching God*, which drew on her experiences in Eatonville. It is considered today to be one of America's greatest novels.

Many female artists and authors experienced difficulties because of their gender. Zora Neale Hurston died a pauper and was buried in an unmarked grave in Atlanta, until writer Alice Walker tracked the grave down in the 1970s and identified it. In the 1920s painter Georgia O'Keeffe began her distinguished career, which spanned six decades. Gaining recognition for her work, however, was not easy. Her friendship with, and eventual marriage to, Alfred Stieglitz, the famed photographer, was important in securing New York shows for her and in attracting the attention of critics. Her work, however, was often judged more in terms of her gender than her art. Critics were confounded by her canvases with huge flowers resembling female genitalia, for the paintings violated the canon that women should produce small and delicate paintings.

Despite the all-woman bands that toured in this period as well as a tradition that identified amateur music with women, major symphony orchestras included few female musicians, and the field of conducting was closed to them. When conductor Antonia Brico returned to the United States after an acclaimed European debut, few orchestras engaged her. In order to be able to conduct, she ultimately founded her own orchestra of female players. What woman, it was said, possessed either the authority or the musicianship to mold eighty or more instrumentalists into an effective ensemble?

MEXICAN IMMIGRATION: WOMEN, WORK, AND ACCULTURATION

The 1920s seemed to be a time of economic prosperity. Sectors of the economy, however, were depressed; 50 percent of farm and industrial workers earned survival wages. This group especially included African American and Mexican workers. Initially, both seemed to profit from the immigration restriction of the 1920s, which cut off immigration from Eastern Europe and the Mediterranean and created labor shortages. African Americans moved North in larger numbers, attracted by the Northern need for labor and by the destruction of Southern cotton crops by an insect called the boll weevil. Despite the availability of jobs, however, exploitation and a system of de facto segregation awaited them in the North.

In the case of Mexican farmworkers, powerful farmers and industrialists in the Southwest and the West secured an exemption from the immigration restriction laws so that they could continue using Mexicans as cheap labor, in the so-called bracero program. Among Mexican migrants, entire families continued to pick crops at piecework rates and live in substandard housing provided by their employers. Owners in Texas preferred Mexican to Anglo-American tenants because their wives and children would work in the fields, while white tenant farmers' wives refused to do so. According to historian Rosalinda Gonzalez, the independence that employment outside the home often fostered in women did not occur in the case of women who were picking crops in Texas because of their isolation from mainstream society and the slave-like conditions of their work.

Large-scale farmers throughout the Southwest still preferred to hire families rather than single workers. Before World War I the growers of sugar beets in the South Platte Valley of Colorado, who operated large "factory-like" farms, had employed families from Germany. When the war and the anti-German sentiment that accompanied it cut off that labor source, the owners hired single Japanese and Mexican men—called "solos." They finally turned to Mexican families, who could easily be exploited as noncitizens with limited opportunities for employment and who could be used as a wedge against Anglo-American workers and potential unionization.

Large numbers of Mexicans migrated to the United States in the 1920s. Their migration to Los Angeles was so sizable that its barrio became the largest Mexican community in the world outside Mexico City. "Americanization" campaigns targeted the new immigrants to Los Angeles. Anglo-American teachers were sent to Mexican women in their homes to instruct them in "American" foodways and standards of nutrition. Reflecting capitalism's need for cheap labor, Mexican women were encouraged to work as laborers for clothing manufacturers and as domestic workers in Anglo-

American homes. At a time when the federal government considered an annual income of $800 to be the subsistence minimum for a family, many Mexican families made less than $100 a year. In 1930 only 2.6 percent of Mexican American women held clerical jobs. Such jobs were better paid than factory or service work—and Anglo-American women dominated them.

Growers and manufacturers actively recruited Puerto Ricans and Filipinos to come to the United States because they were nationals whose citizenship status allowed them to freely enter the country. The largest Puerto Rican *colonas* (neighborhoods) were in New York City, where many Puerto Rican women took in piecework in their homes, while others worked as domestics. They were shocked by the rigid color division between blacks and whites in the United States, for the Puerto Ricans in their homeland culturally identified a number of additional types, including browns and Indians. A focus on a variety of types of colors of human skin was characteristic of Latin American cultures in general.

Single men continued to compose the majority of Filipino immigrants. Still few in number, they nonetheless spread from Hawaii throughout the United States. They became, for example, the main labor source for the asparagus growing industry in Stockton, California. Given a shortage of domestic workers in California, they became house servants for the well-to-do in San Francisco and Los Angeles. Due to the miscegenation laws that existed in many states of the continental United States, in addition to the tendency of Filipina women to remain in the Philippines, they formed familial relationships among themselves when on the U.S. mainland. They sometimes paid prostitutes or women who danced in dance halls money to give them female companionship.

WORKING WOMEN

During the 1920s, most unskilled laborers experienced financial difficulty. Wage increases went to skilled laborers. The income of many unskilled workers, which included the majority of female workers, hardly rose at all. And the position of these women relative to male workers worsened. The differential between the hourly wages paid to unskilled male and female workers rose from 6.3 cents in 1923 to 10.2 cents in 1929.

Within unskilled employment, non-Anglo women encountered the greatest discrimination. Over 70 percent of all Asian women workers and over 90 percent of all Latina and African American workers worked as domestics or in agriculture, while less than 40 percent of white female workers were so employed. In the 1920s factory work began to open up to nonwhite women, but pay differentials still existed. In Texas, for example, white factory women were paid about $7.50 a week, while Mexican American women earned about $5.50 and blacks earned $3.75.

Working-class mothers who worked away from home faced special difficulties. For the most part, they left young children with relatives or neighbors, and their older children often fended for themselves after school. Charitable organizations ran most of the nursery schools for lower-income working women, but these working mothers were often suspicious of the schools because they thought that welfare workers too often took children away from the low-income families who were their clients for no justified reason and placed them in asylums and foster homes. Moreover, many social workers opposed establishing childcare centers and nursery schools because they wanted the money to be used to expand county and state relief programs to mothers with children so that the mothers wouldn't have to work and could stay at home to raise their children. Such programs, indeed, were widely underfunded.

LABOR UNIONS
IN A CONSERVATIVE ERA

These conditions of low pay and little relief for working mothers partly resulted from the disarray of the union movement, which might have worked to alleviate the situation. However, union membership plummeted in the 1920s, and there was limited strike activity. Yet workers were consistently threatened by unemployment and chastened by the defeats that unions suffered in a series of major strikes after the end of World War I. An unsuccessful strike by telephone operators in New England in 1921 resulted in the destruction of their union, with its large female membership. After the strike, the telephone company fired union members and introduced a direct dialing system that reduced the number of workers it needed to employ. Telephone operator unions were undermined throughout the nation.

Even the ILGWU fell on hard times. The advent of flapper fashions was accompanied by a rise in demand for ready-to-wear clothing for women. This was a boon to the garment industry, but individual companies became dependent on the caprice of fashion. When an individual dress style failed, the company that had created it and the workers who had made it suffered. Such insecurity made organizing workers in the industry difficult. Also difficult for the ILGWU was the appearance of a determined communist faction among its membership in the 1920s. The communists in the union challenged its moderate leadership over control of the union. Instead of concentrating on organizing workers and on strike activity, the union spent the decade engaged in infighting. Its membership dropped from 250,000 to 40,000 over the course of the decade.

In many areas of the country, large corporations succeeded in replacing trade unions with company unions that were controlled by management. The federal government, dominated by pro-business Republicans in the 1920s, sided with employers. Female workers, as well as men, were reluctant to challenge employers, who promised a welfare capitalism under which employers would assume responsibility for the welfare of their workers. Efforts to do so, however, were actually limited.

Unions sometimes formed coalitions with business in the 1920s. In Seattle, "business unionists" controlled the AFL unions. They promoted the idea of harmony between labor and capital, made deals with owners, and did not encourage strike activity. They served on committees of the Chamber of Commerce, and they participated in organizing fairs sponsored by both employers and employees. (Chambers of Commerce are organizations of businesspeople in many cities that promote a favorable social and economic climate for business.) The major goal of the Seattle unions was to persuade consumers to buy products with a "union label," which certified that union members had made them. It was not an ineffective strategy, although it required the kind of close cooperation with the owners of industries that could easily undermine union independence.

The Consumers' League and the Women's Trade Union League, Progressive organizations focused on improving the conditions of labor for women working in factories and in service jobs, continued in the 1920s, but problems beset them. The WTUL was no more successful in organizing workers than the unions were. It spent its small budget mostly on lobbyists for special legislation for working women. The Consumers' League also focused on such legislation. The 1923 Supreme Court decision in *Adkins v. Children's Hospital*, however, hampered the work of these groups. In this decision, the court reverted to the common law principle of freedom of contract between employer and worker to rule that federal minimum-wage laws violated such freedom. They rejected the argument that employers had unfair advantages in such bargaining situations, given their access to money, trained lawyers, and private police forces that could be used to break strikes.

WOMEN'S ORGANIZATIONS
IN THE 1920S

During the 1920s most major women's organizations continued in operation, and several new ones appeared. In 1919 the National Federation of Business and Professional Women's Clubs (BPW) was founded under the auspices of the YWCA. The next year the League of Women Voters, the Women's Bureau in the Department of Labor, and the Women's Joint Congressional Committee (WJCC) were formed. The WJCC lobbied for social welfare issues before Congress. Older organizations like the Women's Trade Union League and the National Consumers' League declined in membership, but some women's organizations expanded in size. By 1930 the YWCA had 600,000 members, while the National Congress of Parent-Teacher Associations had a million and a half members. Historian Nancy Cott contends that "the greatest extent of associational activity in the whole history of American women took place in the era between the two wars."[14] The situation seemed promising for women.

The Progressive coalition of settlement-house and social workers, coordinated through the Children's Bureau in the Department of Labor, continued to exist. Reformer Miriam Van Waters in Los Angeles drew on its expertise and influence to persuade the recently established juvenile courts there to initiate more humane treatment of delinquent girls. She persuaded the California State Federation of Women's Clubs to lobby the state legislature for social welfare bills, until the Federation took a conservative direction in the late 1920s and withdrew its support. Van Waters became superintendent of a girls' reformatory in Los Angeles and then one in Massachusetts. At both institutions she drew on settlement house practices to establish women-run institutions providing loving care, vocational training, and a sense of community among the inmates and their teachers and guards. Such policies contrasted to those in the many girls' reformatories of that age that were run like prisons.

Yet there were problems for women's organizations. After the passage of the suffrage amendment, Anna Howard Shaw told Emily Newall Blair, a young suffragist: "I am sorry for you young women who have to carry on the work for suffrage was a symbol, and now you have lost your symbol."[15] Subsequently, the women's movement divided into four groups—social reformers, pacifists and internationalists, professional women, and supporters of an Equal Rights Amendment. Although these groups sometimes formed coalitions around issues of joint interest, they often disagreed over policy and remained separate from each other.

Women's Organizations in Transition

With suffrage won, the NAWSA was disbanded, and a new organization, the League of Women Voters, was created in its place. The League, which was bipartisan in political orientation, supported municipal reform, women's legal rights, tighter consumer laws, a child labor amendment, and the extension of state pensions for indigent mothers. Its major program nationwide, however, was voter education about political issues and process.

When the turnout of women in the elections of the early 1920s was low and their voting patterns similar to those of men, League leaders decided to concentrate on educating women for responsible citizenship. (In fact, voter turnout in general—both male and female—was low during this period.) Yet the League's focus on education too often produced study rather than action, slowing down any focus on reform initiatives.

The League was activist, however, in a number of locales. In the state of Connecticut, the state league led a coalition of women's organizations that lobbied the legislature for an extensive reform agenda, including birth control. Republican businessmen, however, controlled the legislature, and they regularly defeated the women's program. In Chicago, the League worked with the Chicago Women's Club and the Women's Civic Club to pressure the city government into providing better health care for women and children and passing laws to protect female workers. According to historian Maureen Flanagan, however, Chicago women failed to change a city organized on a male model of competitive individualism into one organized on what she calls a female model of social interdependence.

In some instances, women successfully challenged male politicians. In Ohio, Florence Allen won a seat on the state supreme court in 1922 by mobilizing former suffragists to support her campaign. They wrote publicity, scheduled meetings, and distributed campaign literature for her. (In 1934 Franklin D. Roosevelt appointed Allen to the Circuit Court of Appeals—the highest court below the Supreme Court.) In 1928 Ruth Hanna McCormick of Illinois won her deceased husband's House of Representatives seat by reconstituting the network of state Republican women's clubs she had organized for his successful House race in 1924. They carried out her campaign.

It wasn't easy to form coalitions of women in the 1920s. Many former suffragists were exhausted. The League of Women Voters complained of a dearth of able women willing to become leaders of local chapters; only a small number of the members of the suffrage organizations that had successfully fought for the women's suffrage amendment joined the League. The new Women's Bureau in the Department of Labor was poorly funded, and it became primarily a fact-finding service, concerned with women's employment. Its long-term head, Mary Anderson, came from the Women's Trade Union League. She swung the important support of the Women's Bureau behind the campaign for special legislation for women.

Moreover, the coalition of women's organizations that had supported women's suffrage also fell apart. Alice Paul's Woman's Party rejected the League of Women Voters' program of social reform and education as well as the campaign for special legislation for working women to focus on attaining an Equal Rights Amendment (ERA). This amendment, they believed, was the easiest way to abolish the many laws still on the books that discriminated against women. As well, it was a matter of simple justice for women. The ERA was first introduced in Congress in 1923. Its brief text stated that "men and women shall have equal rights throughout the United States and every place subject to its jurisdiction." Most women's organizations, however, including the League of Women Voters, opposed the ERA on the grounds that women in industry needed protective legislation.

While women's organizations like the League of Women Voters maintained a reform profile in the 1920s, others involved in the prewar Progressive movement turned away from social activism. Members of local women's clubs, for example, now often discussed fashions and gardening at their meetings rather than civic improvement. Or they played the card game of bridge, which was a national craze in the 1920s. An ex-president of a suburban club in the Midwest bemoaned the change from politics to pleasure. Her clubhouse had once echoed with brilliant speeches, but now, she wrote, "it rings with such [bridge] terms as 'no trump' and 'grand slam.'"[16] In line with the growing conservatism, the national office of the General Federation of Women's Clubs sponsored programs on home economics.

Some former suffragists focused on pacifism and internationalism as their primary reform interest. Carrie Chapman Catt established the National Conference on the Cause and Cure of War, and Jane Addams supported the Women's International League for Peace and Freedom (WILPF). The outbreak of World War I had angered many women's rights advocates, and some blamed it on male aggressiveness. Echoing the pre–World War I arguments of women's rights leaders about women's moral superiority, some contended that women as mothers had a "peculiar moral passion against both the cruelty and the want of war."[17] Female pacifists and internationalists in the 1920s had some success. The WILPF, for example, was a major force behind the decade's disarmament and peace conferences. It was also influential in pressuring the United States to sign the 1927 Kellogg-Briand Pact, an international agreement that outlawed war as national policy.

Professional women, for their part, focused on equal pay and equal employment opportunity in their own professions. In 1919, the National Federation of Business and Professional Women's Clubs (BPW) was formed. Composed primarily of teachers and clerical workers, its goal was gender equity in these professions. But it was difficult to implement such a policy. Women's efforts to simply maintain the status quo in male-dominated professions often absorbed all their energy. In "feminized" professions like nursing and librarianship, male supervisors often blocked women's advancement. Ellen Richards's American Home Economics Association developed a traditionalist wing, and domestic science departments in the state colleges of the Midwest often taught little more than household management skills. Most of their graduates became teachers of domestic science in high schools and colleges. Some, however, became social workers and settlement-house workers.

With regard to social workers and settlement-house workers, community chests were established in many cities in the early 1920s to coordinate charitable giving, and they often became the major financial backers of the settlement houses. Conservative businessmen hostile to social change often controlled the community chests. In their movement North, African Americans from the South often settled in the formerly Jewish, Italian, and Slavic neighborhoods that the settlements had first served. As these ethnic groups became more affluent, they moved away from the areas of urban poverty in which they had first settled. The change in the ethnic composition of the areas the settlement workers served created challenges for them due to their own racism and cultural conventions of newcomers that differed from their former clients. Moreover, the field of social work was going through the process of becoming a profession. That process involved a focus on issues of standards, training, and pay for the social workers that drew attention away from clients and their needs. As social workers pursued the goal of gaining increased status, according to historian Kathleen Jones, they separated themselves from their low-income clients and blamed the mothers they saw for the problems of their families rather than the economic system or the environment of poverty in which their clients lived. Still, the idealism of the founders of the profession continued. Some of these women now taught in schools of social work and inspired a new generation of social workers toward idealism about their work.

In 1920, a number of women's organizations formed the Women's Joint Congressional Committee (WJCC). These organizations included the League of Women Voters, the BPW, the General Federation of Women's Clubs, the National Congress of Parents and Teachers, and the National Council of Jewish Women. They were led by Julia Lathrop, head of the Children's Bureau, who had begun her career as a reformer at Hull House. The WJCC worked for improved education, the Child Labor Amendment, and, reflecting the goals of the internationalists, U.S. membership in the World Court. Its greatest success was the 1921 Sheppard-Towner Act, which provided matching federal grants to states to set up maternity and pediatric clinics to care for pregnant women and infants. The act was intended to reverse the shocking reality that the United States had one of the highest infant mortality rates in the industrialized world.

The Sheppard-Towner Act: Successes and Failures

The Sheppard-Towner program was administered by the Children's Bureau, and three-quarters of the directors of the state programs were women.

The programs employed over eight hundred public nurses, all of them women. These nurses traveled from county to county, working with local doctors and women's groups to organize health conferences to examine mothers and their preschool children. The nurse might then make follow-up visits to monitor the health of these individuals. Or she might attempt to persuade local communities to set up their own clinics.

In 1927, however, Congress refused to reallocate funding for the program. Part of the difficulty was the lack of a women's voting bloc in Congress, which might have insisted on continuing it. In addition, the American Medical Association (AMA) lobbied to end the program, because the male members of the AMA in Sheppard-Towner areas disliked losing patients to the visiting female nurses. Most important, furthering social welfare was not a government priority in this conservative decade. Even the efforts to secure amendments to the Constitution restricting child labor and outlawing lynching—measures that seem hardly controversial—were unsuccessful.

THE NEW HEROINES

In the 1910s Jane Addams was celebrated as a secular saint by a generation of humanitarian Americans. The heroines of the 1920s, however, were women of individual achievement, often career women. In 1928 twenty-seven-year-old Margaret Mead published her first book, the best-selling *Coming of Age in Samoa*. It was a study of adolescence on Samoa, and it ratified the trends of the age by arguing that sexual freedom existed on Samoa and that it was a major factor in the success of adolescence and of the society there. Now in the public eye, Mead began her career of anthropological travels and commentary on public events that would continue for the next fifty years. Pilot Amelia Earhart and movie actress Mary Pickford were other female models in the 1920s. So was the "flapper," a ubiquitous figure who emerged as a major type of young woman in films. On the one hand, they seem emancipated; on the other, they indicate the limits of feminist liberation in that era.

Amelia Earhart's early career was divided between social reform and flying. After graduating from Barnard College, she became a settlement worker in Boston. Meanwhile, she learned how to fly. She searched out female instructors, because she found male pilots insulting and overprotective. In 1927, Amy Phipps Guest, a wealthy flying enthusiast, suggested to Earhart that she make a solo flight across the Atlantic, as Charles Lindbergh had done the year before. With Guest's financial backing, Earhart made the flight, although a male pilot was at the controls of the airplane, and she

Margaret Mead. In 1929 with several of the children she interviewed in Peri Village, on the island of Manus off the coast of New Guinea, for her study of childhood socialization, *Growing Up in New Guinea*.

Aviatrix Amelia Earhart Boating with Duke Kamanamoku. The famed pilot, paddling in 1935 in Honolulu harbor in a native canoe with Duke Kamanamoku, as she waited for favorable flying conditions to make a trans-Pacific flight from Honolulu to Oakland, California. Kamanamoku was a former swimming star and mayor of Honolulu.

served only as navigator. Earhart's life was a testimony to women's abilities. But she was shy and self-effacing. She was popularly known as "Lady Lindy" because she looked a lot like Lindbergh. Indeed, it was alleged that she had been chosen for the flight because of that resemblance. She belonged to the Woman's Party, but her feminism was modest. Flying was her real love.

Earhart's last flight, on which she disappeared over the Pacific, took place in 1937. On that flight, she was attempting to become the first female pilot to fly around the world. After her disappearance, there were many other female flyers, but as aviation became professionalized, male pilots came to dominate it. In 1931 an innovation was added to commercial air flights that indicated the future position of women in aviation. Airline stewardesses, then required to have a nursing degree, were introduced on commercial flights to attend to the needs of passengers. Male doctors had nurses and businessmen had secretaries; now pilots also had female helpers.

Mary Pickford, another heroine of the 1920s, was a virginal child-woman. She was "America's Sweetheart," its "Little Mary." The golden-haired Pickford played adolescents on the verge of maturity, although she was sometimes portrayed as athletic or as a working woman. As a person she was tough and shrewd; she was the first movie star to demand and receive the high salary that became standard in the industry for its major performers. She was less successful in convincing the public to accept her as other than the personification of girlhood—a role she came to hate. When in the late 1920s she cut off her long blonde curls, she almost lost her audience.

The movie flapper began her career before World War I as the "vamp," appealing to the nation's new fascination with sexuality. She can be traced to burlesque and vaudeville, to featured performers like Little Egypt (Farida Mazhur), who had shimmied her way out of the Egyptian village at the Columbia Exposition of 1893 onto the vaudeville stage as a popular performer. As often happened, World War I accelerated a cultural trend already underway before it began. At first the vamp was simply a seductress. But with the rise of the youth cult and the appearance of censorship codes in the early 1920s that restricted sexuality on the screen, she became the "flapper."

The vamp first appeared in 1915 in the movie *A Fool There Was*. It starred Theda Bara, who became famous overnight for her sultry sensuality, although her melodramatic poses seem almost silly today. She was born Theodosia Goodman in Cincinnati, the daughter of a tailor. Press agents transformed her ordinary American background into an Oriental saga, in which Egyptian cutthroats supposedly kidnapped her when she was a child and raised her. After the war, the mantle of "sex queen" passed to Gloria Swanson. She was more sophisticated than Bara, but she was also a seductress. The flapper was different. She was the playful flirt. She smoked and drank, but she was honest at heart and destined for marriage. In the person of screen actress Clara Bow, she exhibited "it." That word encapsulated the frenzied flapper behavior of the 1920s. It both stood for sex and obfuscated it in a world still influenced by a Victorian past.

Another screen image for women existed. In prewar screen serials, the main characters had often been a woman who could solve any predicament. The most famous serial was *Perils of Pauline*, which starred Pearl White. Pauline could ride and shoot a gun as well as any man; she rescued women in distress and prevailed over the villain. According to historian Karen Mahar, the disappearance of Pauline from the screen partly resulted from the "masculinization" of the film industry in the 1920s. Between 1906, when moviemaking began, and the mid-1920s, hundreds of women worked as film directors, producers, screenwriters, and editors. In the 1920s, however, studio executives introduced modern business practices, putting men in control of all aspects of filmmaking. By the late 1920s, women, aside from actresses, had largely disappeared from important positions in the industry.

Indeed, a new emblem for women in the 1920s was the "beauty queen." In 1920, hotel owners in the beach resort of Atlantic City, New Jersey, devised a scheme to lengthen their summer season by hosting a beauty contest late in September, after most vacationers usually went home. This contest was to crown America's reigning beauty, its "Miss America." (She would, predictably, be fair-skinned for many decades.) Beauty contests would soon appear throughout the nation, in festivals, among ethnic groups, and for high school homecoming queens. Movie producers would hold them in various locations as a way of promoting films, with the mythology that any young woman could enter these contests and become a star. Beauty contests would become a major institution of the culture of women in modern America over the course of the twentieth century.

NOTES

1. Suzanne LaFollette, *Concerning Women* (New York: Albert and Charles Boni, 1926), 10.

2. Elizabeth Onatavia, "Give Us Our Privileges," *Scribner's* 87 (June 1930): 593–94.

3. Lillian Hellman, *An Unfinished Woman: A Memoir* (Boston: Little Brown, 1969), 35.

4. Lillian Faderman, *Odd Girls and Twilight Lovers* (New York: Penguin, 1992), 68.

5. Katharine Bement Davis, *Factors in the Sex Life of Twenty-Two Hundred Women* (New York: Harper & Bros., 1929), 248.

6. Ben B. Lindsay and Evans Wainwright, *The Revolt of Modern Youth* (New York: Boni and Liveright, 1925), 66–67.

7. Mary McCarthy, *Memories of a Catholic Girlhood* (New York: Harcourt Brace Jovanovich, 1957).

8. Maxine Davis, *The Lost Generation: A Portrait of American Youth Today* (New York: Macmillan, 1936), 25–26.

9. Kathleen M. Blee, *Women of the Klan: Racism in the 1920s* (Berkeley: University of California Press, 1990), 1.

10. Lorine Pruette, "The Married Woman and the Part-Time Job," *Annals of the American Academy of Political and Social Science* (1929): 302.

11. Worth Tuttle, "Autobiography of an Ex-Feminist," *New Republic*, 22 (April 14, 1926): 218ff.

12. *Women of Today* (Philadelphia: John B. Winston, 1926), 235.

13. Helena Rubenstein, *My Life for Beauty* (London: Bodley Head, 1964), 22.

14. Nancy Cott, *The Grounding of Modern Feminism* (New Haven, Conn.: Yale University Press, 1987), 97.

15. Emily Newell Blair, "Wanted—A New Feminism," *Independent Woman* (Dec. 1930): 499.

16. Anna Steese Richardson, "Is the Women's Club Dying?" *Harper's*, 69 (Oct. 1929): 607.

17. Marie Louise Degen, *The History of the Women's Peace Party* (Baltimore: Johns Hopkins University Press, 1939), 20.

4

Women in the
Depression and War Era
1930–1945

The Great Depression dominated the 1930s. By the winter of 1932–33, thirty-eight states had closed all banks, local governments could not meet relief payments, long lines stretched outside Red Cross and Salvation Army food distribution centers daily, and thousands of homeless families lived in makeshift shacks. Twenty-five percent of the workforce was unemployed in what was the highest rate of unemployment in the nation's history. In addition, many employed workers had suffered pay cuts. Although women remained in the workforce, many were demoted to lesser positions. Women of color were especially hard hit by layoffs and firings. In addition to unemployment, the rise of the authoritarian systems of fascism and communism in Europe, with their expansionist aims, engendered fears that capitalism was breaking down and that the United States was threatened by external and internal forces. In such a situation, scapegoats are often found. In this case women were blamed for having caused the Depression, while homophobia became more virulent.

Extensive legislation to alleviate the economic situation was passed during the presidency of Franklin Delano Roosevelt, from 1933 to 1945, in the

Opposite: A 1936 movie billboard in Atlanta, Georgia: Women controlled by violence

longest presidential administration in the nation's history. What came to be called the New Deal was designed to end the Depression and to aid the unemployed. The many New Deal programs included women, both as administrators of the programs and as beneficiaries. Eleanor Roosevelt, Franklin's wife, became an advocate for women both within the administration and to the nation. Labor unions grew rapidly, and they made greater efforts to organize female workers. Finally, World War II, in which the United States was involved between 1941 and 1945, opened up greater employment opportunities to women, as World War I had twenty years earlier. Once again it seemed that war might bring women liberation.

During the economic downturn of the 1930s, the youth rebellion of the 1920s took a back seat. By the end of the decade, however, high school attendance soared and a new generational consciousness emerged among young people. By the middle of World War II, the word "teenager" was coined, as it became apparent that young people constituted a rising consumer and cultural force in American life.

FEMINISM AND WOMEN'S ORGANIZATIONS

Women's organizations continued their efforts to extend women's legal and political rights. In 1936 their national leaders discussed joining together around promoting a charter of women's rights devised by Margaret Anderson, head of the Women's Bureau in the federal government. This initiative failed, however, because women's groups were divided over special legislation for working women and the Equal Rights Amendment. Women's organizations did form coalitions on the state level to lobby successfully against state bills prohibiting the employment of married women who were not heads of households. State branches of the National Consumers' League successfully lobbied for the passage of protective labor legislation for women at the state level. Many female activists continued to work for pacifist groups like the Women's International League for Peace and Freedom. In 1931, at the age of seventy, Jane Addams won the Nobel Peace Prize.

Given the Depression, however, many women's organizations focused on social issues. That was evident in a new consumers' movement, led by the American Home Economics Association, which focused on securing guarantees of the safety of consumer products and on lowering the escalating costs of housing and food. Moreover, in both large cities and small towns, impoverished women on occasion took the situation into their own hands by boycotting food stores charging high prices and demonstrating against evictions for nonpayment of rent. Black mothers in Cleveland hung wet laundry over utility lines to force the local power company to stop shutting off electricity in the homes of families who had not paid their bills. To protest the high price of meat, Polish housewives in Chicago doused thousands of pounds of meat with kerosene and set it on fire. Such women also created barter networks and lobbied governments for controls on food prices and rents.

SOUTHERN WOMEN AND
THE ANTILYNCHING MOVEMENT

Both black and white women were central to the antilynching movement that emerged in this era, particularly in the South where the lynching of black men (and sometimes women) by self-constituted vigilantes as a means of social control remained a major problem. The Jim Crow laws were still in force in the South, as well as the mythology that black men were sexual predators who threatened white women and that black women were naturally promiscuous. At the end of World War I, in response to race riots that occurred in many cities in which whites inflicted violence in black communities, a Commission on Interracial Cooperation had been formed by a number of organizations, including the NAACP and the Urban League. It held conferences during the 1920s to promote interracial harmony, find ways to create better conditions for African Americans, and identify potential leaders. In 1922 the NAACP and the National Association of Colored Women formed a women's group called the Anti-Lynching Crusaders to mobilize support for an amendment to outlaw lynching. In 1930 Jessie Daniel Ames, a widowed mother of three who operated a telephone exchange in Texas, brought these groups together to form an Association of Southern Women for the Prevention of Lynching.

With the onset of the Depression, the number of lynchings increased, and the Association leaders launched an educational campaign directed to churches and women's organizations. They sent out speakers, passed out pamphlets, and lobbied state legislatures. They collected forty thousand signatures on an antilynching petition. By 1933, partly due to their efforts, the incidence of lynching began to decline. Although Congress never passed the antilynching amendment, by 1942 Ames's organization was disbanded. Yet before its demise, it contributed to ending a brutal form of violence, and it persuaded white Southern women to actively protest the cultural mythology that black men threatened them sexually, that white men were guiltless of any sexual crimes, and that black women were promiscuous temptresses. The women's antilynching association was also an important forerunner of the organizations that would spearhead the civil rights movement of the 1950s and 1960s.

ELEANOR ROOSEVELT

During FDR's presidency, Eleanor Roosevelt became a leading spokesperson for American women and an exemplary role model for them. Through her radio broadcasts, her weekly newspaper column, her books, and her speeches, she influenced public opinion. Like the women's rights advocates of the 1900s, Eleanor felt that women possessed a morality lacking in public life and that they should strive to reshape society and the government accordingly. Women had "understanding hearts," she wrote in 1933 in her book, *It's Up to the Women*. Men, however, had "ability and brains." In a crisis men too easily concluded "that they must fight." Women's pacifism was needed to moderate male aggression.[1] Eleanor was born in 1887, and her attitudes reflected her upbringing by a Victorian grandmother and her early experience of marriage to Franklin Roosevelt, her cousin, who was dominated by his mother. For the first fifteen years after her marriage in 1905, Eleanor was a dutiful wife. She bore six children, deferred to her mother-in-law, and performed the duties of a political wife, while her husband served as Assistant Secretary of the Navy from 1913 to 1920 and ran for vice president on the unsuccessful Democratic ticket of 1920.

Two events revolutionized her life. The first was her discovery in 1917 that her husband loved another woman; the second was his crippling attack of polio in 1921. (Eleanor was then thirty-seven.) These experiences gave her the strength to defy her mother-in-law, to persuade Franklin to return to public life after his illness, and to take on a leading public role in her own right. Choosing to participate in women's organizations, she became active in the League of Women Voters, the Consumers' League, women's groups in the Democratic Party, and especially the Women's Trade Union League. Female reformers came to know Franklin through her and to counsel him about labor and social welfare, especially when he served as governor of New York State between 1928 and 1932 and also during his presidency.

Transforming herself in her late thirties and early forties was not easy for Eleanor, who was shy by nature. The media continually depreciated her looks. She found experts in politics and speechmaking to coach her, learned through hard-won experience, and developed into a skilled politician. She became an unofficial adviser to FDR on domestic matters, and she traveled around the country for him, reporting what she saw to him. For emotional support, she turned to other women, acting in line with the culture of romantic friendships between women of her youth. Like Jane Addams and other female reformers in her circle, she turned to a woman for affection.

Her special friend was Lorena Hickok, a journalist who covered the White House for the Associated Press.

Under FDR's New Deal, a host of agencies were created to achieve economic recovery and further social change. Among the measures FDR's administration designed in 1933 to aid the unemployed were the Federal Emergency Relief Administration (FERA), the Civil Works Administration (CWA), the Civilian Conservation Corps (CCC), and the Public Works Administration (PWA), a major federal public works program. Never before in the history of the United States had so many government agencies been created in such a short period of time. The National Recovery Administration was also established that year, and it oversaw meetings between representatives of labor and management in each industry to draft production codes. In 1935 the Works Progress Administration (WPA), another public works project, was established. The National Youth Administration (NYA), which provided work for nearly a million students, was established under its auspices. Its Federal Theatre, Art, Music, and Writers' projects gave work to unemployed writers and artists.

Eleanor was not involved in the central planning for these projects, aside from the Federal Theatre Project (the government's first subsidy to the arts), and the building of fifty communities in rural areas for the indigent, which were funded under the NRA. Eleanor took particular interest in Arthurdale, in West Virginia, settled by impoverished coal miners, who had previously lived in substandard housing. Now they had well-built houses, with grass yards and white picket fences. Indeed, Eleanor became an advocate for those groups—African Americans, the poor, and women—whose interests were often overlooked even in the New Deal administration. She monitored and supported proposals submitted by women to government agencies, and she lobbied for the inclusion of women in New Deal programs. In an incident famous in the history of race relations, when the DAR banned the famed black contralto Marian Anderson from performing in their auditorium in Washington, D.C., Eleanor arranged for Anderson to give an outdoor concert on the steps of the Lincoln Memorial. Seventy-five thousand people attended the concert.

Under Eleanor's influence, Franklin appointed a number of women to government office. These included the first female judge on the Circuit Court of Appeals (Florence Allen) and the first female ministers to foreign countries: Ruth Bryan Owen, daughter of William Jennings Bryan, to Denmark; Florence Jaffray Harriman, widow of railroad magnate Edward H. Harriman, to Norway. Women from the Consumers' League and the Women's Trade Union League were appointed to every New Deal agency concerned with social welfare. Frances Perkins, a former settlement worker and lobbyist for the New York Consumers' League, became Secretary of Labor—and the first woman in a presidential cabinet. These appointments

Eleanor Roosevelt. In her role as the president's wife and promoter of worthy causes, Eleanor opens the Grandmother's War Bond League Campaign. This campaign was one of the drives to sell war bonds that were popular as a way to finance World War II and to encourage public support for the Allied efforts.

reflected not only Eleanor's influence but also women's domination of the profession of social work, from which many New Deal welfare bureaucrats were recruited.

By the end of the 1930s, polls showed that Eleanor was very popular. After FDR died in 1945, there was talk of her running for president. Like other female reformers of her time, who had decided after World War I that

Mary McCleod Bethune. Second from the right, with Marian Anderson and three ship-yard workers, Bethune was a prominent black educator, president of the National Association of Colored Women, and founder, in 1935, of the National Council of Negro Women. She also served as director of Negro Affairs under the National Youth Administration during the New Deal. In a legendary event in the struggle for black rights, Eleanor Roosevelt arranged for famed African American singer Marian Anderson to perform at the Lincoln Memorial after the DAR refused to permit her to appear at their Constitutional Hall in Washington, D.C.

world peace was their priority, her interest turned to internationalism, especially to the United Nations, which was founded at the end of World War II. In 1946 she served as the U.S. representative to the United Nations General Assembly and from 1947 to 1952 as U.S. representative to the United Nations Human Rights Commission and its Economic and Social Council.

THE WOMEN'S NETWORK
AND NEW DEAL PROGRAMS

In addition to Eleanor Roosevelt, central New Deal female administrators joined together informally with female leaders in the Democratic Party to create a "network" on behalf of women. In addition to Eleanor Roosevelt and Frances Perkins, the network included Mary Dewson, head of the Women's Division of the Democratic Party, and Ellen Woodward, head of Women's and Professional Projects of the WPA. Others were in the Women's and Children's bureaus of the Labor Department. They continued in the 1930s the "dominion of women reformers" that Robyn Muncy identified as existing in the Progressive era. A number of them, in their fifties and sixties, had been part of the earlier group.

On the periphery of the women's network was Mary McCleod Bethune—the most important African American female leader during this decade. The daughter of slaves, Bethune began her career teaching at Lucy Laney's Haines Institute in Augusta, Georgia. Laney inspired her to found the Daytona Normal and Industrial Institute in Daytona, Florida, in 1904. It became Bethune-Cookman College in 1929. By then a prominent educator, Bethune became president of the National Association of Colored Women. In 1935 she founded the National Council of Negro Women, a coordinating group for twenty national and ninety-five local organizations, representing 850,000 African American women. Appointed director of Negro Affairs under the National Youth Administration, Bethune founded the Federal Council on Negro Affairs. This organization was dubbed the "black cabinet," for it safeguarded African American concerns in the New Deal administration just as the women's network looked out for women.

In 1933, Eleanor Roosevelt and other administration women worked with the Women's Trade Union League, the League of Women Voters, and the National Consumers' League to call a White House Conference on the Emergency Needs of Women. In its discussions and reports, it publicized women's economic problems and set priorities for relief. The earliest relief agencies in 1933—the FERA and the CWA—-included women in their programs. By 1935, WPA rolls included 350,000 women, about 15 percent of the agency's total employment. Under FERA and later under the National Youth Administration, job-training camps were set up for unemployed young women that paralleled the Civilian Conservation Corps (CCC) camps for young men. The 1935 Social Security Act provided old-age pensions as well as federal funding for state and local aid-to-dependent-children programs and for state programs for maternal and pediatric care reminiscent of the 1920s Sheppard-Towner clinics.

Attempting to awaken the nation to the severe poverty among farmers, the Farm Security Administration employed photographer Dorothea Lange to record the grim conditions of farm life in the South and the West. Most of the WPA employment projects for out-of-work artists and writers also employed women. Although women were not often hired for the Federal Music Project (renowned for transcribing folk music), they were central to the Federal Art Project and the Federal Theatre Project. The Federal

Art Project commissioned murals in post offices and other public buildings, while the Federal Theatre Project attempted, through its productions, to make theater accessible to all social classes. It was known for its "Living Newspapers," in which actors improvised scenes from current events featured in the newspapers. The Federal Art Project employed Louise Nevelson, who became an eminent painter and sculptor, and Zora Neale Hurston, who was an editor for the project. The Federal Writers' Project employed Tillie Olsen, a socialist and feminist known for her essays and fiction, including the short story collection *Tell Me a Riddle*.

By encouraging social relevance in the work of its employees, the Federal Writers' Project furthered the writing of the proletarian novel, the major genre of fiction in the 1930s. Writing in this vein focused on the struggles of the working class to survive and form unions in a terrible economy. Among the major proletarian writers of the 1930s were Tillie Olsen as well as Mary Heaton Vorse, whose *Strike!* is a fictionalized account of a textile strike in Gastonia, North Carolina, where Vorse worked as an organizer for the Amalgamated Clothing Workers of America. Meridel LeSueur also wrote articles and short stories in the proletarian genre, in which she described radical farmers' strikes and picket lines, as well as women working in strike kitchens and living on welfare.

THE NRA AND NEW DEAL
DISCRIMINATION AGAINST WOMEN

The National Industrial Recovery Act (1933), under which the NRA was established, mandated that the codes for each industry contain maximum-hour and minimum-wage provisions. In 1938, after the Supreme Court declared the NRA unconstitutional, Congress passed the Fair Labor Standards Act, which reaffirmed legislation mandating the maximum hours for interstate industries that employees could be required to work and the minimum wage below which their earnings could not fall. State legislatures followed suit for intrastate commerce.

Such legislation represented a reversal in the way the federal government viewed workers. For all workers, the old common-law doctrine of the inviolability of contract between the individual worker and his or her employer—which had often been used by the courts to declare unions illegal—was overruled, and labor unions were approved. For women, the New Deal legislation brought into question the campaign for special legislation for women, which had divided organized women for over a decade. For such legislation as the Fair Labor Standards Act guaranteed better workplace conditions and higher wages to both men and women. By 1933, even the Women's Trade Union League reversed its historic stand to join other women's groups in advocating general labor legislation for minimum wages and maximum hours, not just legislation for women. The way was now open for women's groups to unite in support of the Equal Rights Amendment, although support for special legislation for women would continue for some time.

The unequal treatment of women, however, had not been ended. Gender discrimination was the rule in most New Deal work programs—as was discrimination against minorities. The WPA and other work-relief agencies barred women from construction jobs—the major employment they offered—and relegated them to sewing tasks and other traditional women's work, with lower wages. The reforestation and service projects for young men under the CCC were also closed to women. The welfare aid for mothers under the aid-to-dependent-children provision of the Social Security Act of 1935 was not always beneficial to the women who qualified for it. Once it was available, some local WPA officials fired women with children from higher-paying WPA jobs and demanded that they go on welfare.

Moreover, many of the codes drawn up by the NRA permitted industries to pay less to female workers than to men employed in similar jobs. In general, the minimum wages established by NRA codes did increase women's wages. Yet fully one-fourth of these codes contained some measure of wage discrimination, particularly the codes written for industries that employed large numbers of women. This had, of course, long been the unofficial practice. The Fair Labor Standards Act of 1938 exempted from its provisions many job categories, like domestic service, in which women were clustered. The argument was that such marginal work might disappear if wages were raised. Still, the lack of regulation invited exploitation.

Furthermore, despite the protest of women's organizations, the federal government ruled that only one member of a family could work in the federal civil service. The intention was to create more jobs for heads of families, but the ruling resulted in the resignation of thousands of women with civil service jobs, who usually earned less than their husbands.

CHANGES FOR THE
WORKING WOMAN

Until the late 1930s, unemployment figures were higher for men than for women. That situation occurred primarily because the consumer-goods industries and the clerical occupations, which employed large numbers of women, were initially less affected by the economic downturn than occupations in which men were the majority of employees. However, unemployment figures, which include only individuals actively seeking work, may not provide an accurate statistic. When finding employment seemed impossible, women may have left the workforce more readily than men, since they more easily turned to domesticity than did men, thus exiting from the unemployment rolls more frequently. The number of day-care centers in the nation decreased in the 1930s: from eight hundred in 1930 to six hundred in 1940. This decrease made it even more difficult for mothers to leave the home for work. Unmarried women also had problems finding jobs. According to one observer in 1934, there were 75,000 homeless, single women in New York City.[2] A large number of teenage girls joined the unemployed men who roamed the nation—the so-called tramps, notorious for jumping on freight train boxcars and riding them from area to area. Some of these girls resorted to prostitution to make a living. Older women, often the women with the least resources, were also hard hit by the Depression. Many companies refused to hire women over thirty-five years of age.

Even women who were employed faced major problems. In many occupations, women's wages were cut and advancement for women became even more limited than before. Stenographer's jobs paid $40 a week on average in 1929 and $16 a week in 1933. Men entered the feminized professions of teaching, librarianship, and social work in larger numbers than ever before. During the 1930s, the number of male librarians grew from about 9 percent of the profession to 15 percent, while the number of male teachers increased from 19 percent of teachers to about 24 percent. The number of male social workers grew from 20 percent of social workers to over 35 percent. Moreover, men continued to hold most of the high-level administrative positions in all these fields.

With regard to male-dominated professions like medicine and law, the percentage of women remained stable. But women were often demoted from high-level positions and replaced by men. In business, positions held by two women were sometimes combined into one, and the new post was given to a man. In university teaching, the number of female faculty declined.

Laws prohibiting married women from working especially affected female schoolteachers. By 1940, only 13 percent of elementary and high school districts in the nation hired married women as teachers and only 30 percent retained women who married after they were hired. A 1930 Gallup poll found that nearly four out of five Americans felt that wives should not work if their husbands were employed. Among women, the figure was 75 percent. Indeed, writers in newspapers and magazines sometimes proposed that women had caused the Depression by going to work and taking jobs away from men. Or it was alleged that by leaving home, women had weakened the moral fiber of the nation and brought on the economic crisis. Such scapegoating—finding an innocent target, often a minority group, on which to blame social ills—has not been an uncommon phenomenon in the American past.

AFRICAN AMERICAN
AND HISPANIC WOMEN

The Depression was especially severe on African American women. Employment on federal work-relief projects was often closed to them. Traditional discrimination in employment still permeated the work sphere. A Women's Bureau study in 1938 found that only 10 percent of African American working women were employed in manufacturing—only a 7 percent gain over the statistic for 1890. Downwardly mobile white women pushed women of color even out of domestic work. In 1930 42 percent of black women were employed; by 1940 only 39 percent were. In 1935 42 percent of the nonwhite population of New York City was on relief. Even disadvantaged whites were better off than African Americans: in 1939, the median annual earnings for nonwhites were 38 percent of those for whites. In many cities, black women's only hope of employment was to gather on street corners where white women drove by offering a day's housework, often at very low wages. In New York City such locations were called "slave markets."

Hispanic women also encountered severe social and economic problems in this time period. In 1935 in Chicago, 32 percent of Mexican Americans were unemployed in comparison to 47 percent of the black population and 11 percent of all foreign-born residents. Among Hispanic female heads of households in Chicago who had worked at some time in the past, only 25 percent were actively seeking work and almost none found employment. In San Antonio, Texas, the labor of humans became cheaper than that of machines. The Southern Pecan Shelling Company there scrapped its machines and employed Mexican families as laborers. In that city the NRA code for pecan shelling was never put into effect.

Moreover, the economic downtown brought an official move to repatriate Mexicans living in the United States back to Mexico. About 500,000 individuals of Mexican descent left the country, and immigration authorities staged raids in which children who had been born in the United States and thus were U.S. citizens were swept up and taken over the border. In 1940 the Mexican American population in the United States was about half what it had been in 1930.

UNIONS IN AN AGE OF DEPRESSION

As the economic situation worsened, one promising avenue of relief for workers appeared. Massive unemployment and new government sympathy to labor produced a stronger labor movement. The International Ladies' Garment Workers Union (ILGWU), which by 1930 had nearly ceased to exist, underwent a transformation. The passage of the NRA prompted union leaders to call a series of successful strikes. Throughout the clothing industry, hours were reduced, and wages were increased by as much as 50 percent. During 1934 union membership increased from 45,000 to over 200,000.

The formation in 1935 of the Committee for Industrial Organization (CIO) by a faction within the AFL leadership was important for female workers. (In 1938 the name of the CIO was changed to the Congress of Industrial Organizations.) The CIO abandoned the skilled-craft orientation of the AFL to focus on all workers in an industry—unskilled as well as skilled. Under its leadership, mass-production industries like auto and steel, which employed small numbers of female workers, were finally organized. Inroads were even made in the textile industry, located largely in the traditionalist South, in which 40 percent of the workers were women. Through effective and often bloody strikes, as well as through the mediation of the National Labor Relations Board, employers were forced to recognize worker demands. In 1939 and 1940 black and white female workers in the textile mills of Durham, North Carolina, came together in strike activity to force the largest textile mill in the South to sign its first contract with its workers.

Women were involved in many of these strikes in the 1930s. In the famed 1937 "Memorial Day Massacre" at the Republic Steel plant in Chicago, police fired without provocation into a demonstration of 1,500 strikers and sympathizers. About 15 percent of the demonstrators were women and children. Ten workers were killed, and women were indiscriminately beaten. Films of the event show Lupe Marshall, a social worker at Hull House, being beaten and arrested. In the strike in Flint, Michigan, in 1936–37, which finally brought the unionization of a significant proportion of the automobile industry, women formed an Emergency Brigade and armed themselves with clubs and blackjacks. They broke windows to keep strikers from being gassed inside the plants, and they took injured pickets to the first-aid station. In a confrontation at one of the plants, a diversion by women was crucial to the successful takeover of the plant by the strikers.

Because factory women were clustered in the mass-production industries, the new labor movement became valuable to them. The CIO cannot be credited with any extensive pro-woman sentiment. In many industries, however, the CIO had to include female workers in its organizing efforts in order to gain a majority position. Few women became officers in the new labor organization. Nor was the new union organization among female workers extensive. The CIO was no more willing to support the Women's Trade Union League than the AFL had been. In 1947 the WTUL was dissolved.

In her study of the labor movement in Minneapolis during the Depression, Elizabeth Faue contends that laboring men in the milling, lumber, iron-processing, and food-processing plants that dominated industry there felt their masculinity challenged by unemployment, for it threatened the breadwinner ethic, crucial to their sense of self. Thus they emphasized masculine solidarity in their pamphlets and meetings, symbolically excluding women from their group. Faue is also critical of the workplace orientation of the CIO—and, by implication, of most labor union organizing. In Minneapolis, she argues, a community-based labor movement arose outside the AFL and the CIO that drew from all the trades in the city and that revitalized party politics. In her opinion, the increasingly bureaucratized national unions, focused on organizing individual industries and with limited interest in community organizing or in women contributed to the decline of the labor movement after World War II.

An important exception to the lack of union interest in working women can be found among Mexican American unions in the Southwest. Important here was the CIO's United Cannery, Agricultural, Packing, and Allied Workers of America (UCAPAWA). This union dated from 1937, and it was centered in the food-processing industry. Because 75 percent of the workers in this industry were women, UCAPAWA was a women's union. "Women organizing women" was its slogan. Forty-four percent of its local union offices were filled by women.

THE IMPORTANCE OF
THE COMMUNIST PARTY

The Communist Party had a major impact on unionization in the 1930s, as it did in other areas of American life. With the breakdown of capitalism in the 1930s, the Communist Party experienced a growth in membership.

It was especially strong in Hollywood, where labor unions had been organized at all levels of the movie industry. Believing that labor created the real
value of products (not the capitalist principle of the law of supply and demand) and wanting to create an egalitarian state, Communists were successful union activists and organizers. The contrast between the apparent
economic success in Russia and the failure of the world capitalist system increased their appeal. The "common front" with other leftist groups that the
world Communist Party called for in the 1930s encouraged communist organizations in the United States to work with other leftist groups. Thus the
division in the labor movement in the 1920s over communist politics that
was evident in the ILGWU did not continue in the 1930s.

Many writers and artists were inspired by the Depression toward a new
realism in their work as well as a focus on the rural poor and the working
classes. Dorothy Parker, for example, famed for her sophisticated wit in the
1920s, went to Hollywood in the 1930s to make money writing movie
scripts. She declared herself a communist, wrote articles and signed petitions on behalf of the communist left in the Spanish Civil War of 1936, and
was blacklisted (declared unemployable) during the anticommunist purges
of the film industry in the late 1940s.

Communists were receptive to women and people of color, and they
encouraged the discussion of women's issues in their meetings and publications, although their primary focus was on the politics of class. In fact,
they were one of the few Anglo-American reform groups of the era to wel-
come blacks as members and to realize the severe oppression of women
of color. Communist publications used the terms "triple burden" and
"triple oppression" to characterize the status of black women, who were
exploited, in the view of these publications, in terms of their race, class, and
gender.

By the late 1930s, however, disillusionment with the Communist regime was spreading, even among Communist Party members. By that time
it was known that Joseph Stalin, the Soviet Union's dictator, was purging
from the Communist Party in the USSR anyone who disagreed with his
position and he was imprisoning and executing his opponents. To cover his
crimes, he staged phony trials in which individuals were accused of treason
and sentenced to death or to exile in Siberia. Millions of individuals were
dealt with in such fashion during his regime. In 1939 Stalin signed a non-
aggression pact with Hitler, severing his ties to the Allied forces who were
fighting against the German dictator. As a result of Stalin's actions, Communist Party membership in the United States plummeted. Concurrently,
the organization's influence was significantly reduced among American intellectuals and labor groups in general.

The Radio Show. A West Virginia coal miner and his wife spend an evening listening to the radio, the major form of family entertainment in the 1930s.

SEXUALITY AND SECURITY

Contraceptives and abortion were increasingly available in the 1930s, but their availability probably did not lead to an increase in sexual promiscuity. Studies of sex in the 1930s showed that premarital intercourse among young people was common but that it was expected to lead to marriage. A 1936 *Fortune* magazine survey of college campuses found that the depressed economy had replaced liquor, sex, and religion as the dominant issue among the students and that most female undergraduates wanted to marry immediately after graduation. In this time of economic insecurity, the family could become a bulwark of stability. The number of divorces decreased in the early 1930s, but so did attendance at public events, except for the movies. In part, people were staying home and staying married because they could not afford to do otherwise. The radio had become a popular form of home entertainment, which families listened to together in the evenings. Moreover, the extended family group often became more cohe-

© Bettmann /Corbis

The famed married acting team, Alfred Lunt and Lynn Fontaine, starred with Noel Coward in his sophisticated comedy of London high life and sexual experimentation, *Design for Living*, in 1932. The "sexual revolution" of the 1920s continued to have impacts on the "legitimate" stage during a period when the Depression turned the public focus away from sex to economic survival.

sive: families with a stable income often gave money to indigent relatives and shared living space with them.

Nevertheless, severe economic adversity could hit families hard, some times undermining their cohesiveness.

Marriage and Family in an Insecure Age

Despite attempts to prohibit married women from working, their employment increased during the Depression—from 11.7 percent of married women in 1930 to over 15 percent in 1940. Thus the trend toward the employment of married women that had begun early in the century continued. Many women worked because of economic need, although most families tried to retain the consumption standards they had set during the affluent 1920s. The automobile, for example, had once been viewed as a luxury, but it was now considered a necessity by many. Due to compulsory education laws that were widely enforced and state laws prohibiting child labor, families were less able to put their children to work. Wives, not children, had to supplement the family income more readily, just as in the 1920s and before.

Contrary to reactionary predictions that working wives would destroy the family, it often became stronger during the decade. Gallup polls found that most married women still defined domesticity and motherhood as their primary responsibility. In this time of economic insecurity, the family assumed a new importance. The home was one place where the individual could find emotional sustenance.

Severe economic adversity, however, could undermine traditional family roles. Sometimes wives could find jobs when husbands could not, increasing women's power in families. One psychiatrist who observed long-unemployed miners in Pennsylvania found that the structure of their families had shifted. The men hung out on street corners and dreaded returning home, blaming themselves for failing to fulfill the "breadwinner ethic." Within their culture, both a jobless man and his family considered him worthless. Wives punished their husbands by belittling the men.[3] In John Steinbeck's *Grapes of Wrath* (1939) the Joad family is torn apart by the process of their migration from their farm in Oklahoma to California and by the difficult conditions of picking crops for migrant families there. It is Ma Joad, the mother and doyenne, who holds the family together by her resilient strength and unfettered spirit.

Given women's increased authority in the family and in response to the economic uncertainties, the birth rate dropped during the 1930s. More couples were using contraceptive measures, and by 1940 every state in the nation, with the exception of Massachusetts and Connecticut, had legalized birth control. At the beginning of the decade, there were twenty-eight family planning clinics in the nation. By 1941 there were 746, and almost one-third were receiving government assistance. Still, in her history of birth control, Andrea Tone contends that through false claims the makers of Listerine advertised their product so successfully as a birth control douche that it became the most widely used product in the nation for that purpose. Yet in addition to the fact that Listerine is not effective in preventing conception, it can inflame sensitive vaginal tissues.

As for abortion, in many states physicians referred patients seeking abortions to abortion specialists, mostly women practicing on their own. Yet in California a criminal syndicate, copying the practice in the liquor industry under prohibition, gained control over abortionists throughout the state through the threat of legal exposure. Once in control, they raised prices and decreased the safety of the procedure in order to make more money. Yet it was not until the 1940s that cities and states began strictly to enforce the antiabortion statutes. That enforcement began the era of self-inflicted "coat hanger" abortions and of "back alley" abortionists.

With regard to the younger generation, Americans of the 1930s were concerned that young people would not be able to find jobs and that they might become permanently embittered. A national movement arose to persuade them to remain in high school, and National Youth Administration funds were used to pay both boys and girls wages for after-school jobs so that they would not drop out. As a result, by 1940 half the nation's seventeen-year-olds were high school graduates, which was double the number just a decade before.

Lesbians and Gays: Oppressed Minorities

During the 1920s, with its climate of sexual freedom, lesbians and gays had been by and large left alone. The 1930s, however, brought extensive repression. Local statutes widened the sodomy laws, which criminalized behavior, not identity, to include vague definitions of "perverse" sexual identity. Laws were passed to prohibit the open depiction of homosexual behavior on the Broadway stage, and the moral code of conduct established for the movies forbade any depiction of homosexuality. Police regularly raided gay bars and arrested individuals for alleged homosexual offenses. Many bar owners made regular payments to the police, and blackmail was a common problem for affluent gays and lesbians. In New York City vigilante groups organized campaigns against "perverts." By 1936 electric shock therapy and prefrontal lobotomies were being used to "cure" homosexuality—even by respected doctors and psychologists.

In 1939, in response to a number of murders of children sensationalized by the newspapers, a national "sex crime panic" broke out and lasted for several years, even though there was no evidence that the incidence of sex crimes had increased. Its premise was that psychopathic men roamed the country, looking for children to molest and kill, and that many of these men were homosexual in orientation. The panic resulted in the passage of "sexual psychopath" laws by state legislatures under which law enforcement agencies could place homosexuals in state mental institutions with minimal evidence. In Inglewood, California, a mob pulled a "pervert" suspected of having killed a child out of jail and lynched him, even though his connection to the crime had not yet been proven.

Sigmund Freud's theory that most individuals had a homosexual side did not entirely disappear in the 1930s. A similar argument was advanced by Margaret Mead, in her *Sex and Temperament in Three Primitive Societies*, a best seller of 1935. In that book, based on research among three tribes in

New Guinea, Mead argued that gender was a social, not a biological, construction and that a bisexual orientation was not uncommon among human beings.

POPULAR CULTURE

In line with the economic insecurity of the 1930s, an older look for women replaced the flapper ideal, with longer skirts, girdles, and a more defined bosom. "Glamour," indicating an older, more knowing sexuality, became the watchword of the age. Strong women became standard figures in movies, comics, popular literature, and the new "soap operas" beamed on the radio. Hollywood genres like the women's film and screwball comedies appeared, as women continued to constitute a majority of cinema audiences. Black women in entertainment took on new roles as blues and jazz singers, while their image in the movies continued to be primarily as mammies, faithful servants to white families.

Fashionable Appearances and Contradictions

By 1929 among all women, working or not, a return to tradition was evident in their choice of dress. Women no longer wore the short-skirted and flat-chested frocks of the 1920s. Although clothing remained loose, hemlines dropped, and waistlines and bosoms reappeared. Indeed, to look just right, well-groomed women again donned some form of figure-molding undergarment. The brassiere became de rigueur, and Maidenform, its leading producer, introduced the modern system of separate sizing for chest width and breast cup.

Hair became longer, and mouths, noses, and eyes larger—a look achieved through makeup, although cosmetic surgery was becoming increasingly popular to attain the ideal appearance. With the onset of the Depression, the theory of psychologist Alfred Adler that the basic human motivation was an "inferiority complex" came into vogue. Cosmetic surgeons, who mostly reshaped noses and ears and did face-lifts, used Adler's theory to argue that surgical measures to create an idealized body provided the best way to overcome that complex. Women portrayed in advertisements and in the movies, however, look older, more confident, and more "glamorous." Advertisers introduced more sexuality in their ads. Scantily clad women had previously appeared only in lingerie ads, but by the late 1930s nude and partially nude women were being used in advertisements to sell even household products like towels and soaps.

Strong Women: Soaps, Sleuths, and Scarlett

In 1933 men began to read the new mainstream men's magazine, *Esquire*, which featured stories and articles by well-known male writers like Ernest Hemingway and F. Scott Fitzgerald along with drawings of erotic young women by Alberto Vargas and George Petty—the Vargas and Petty girls. Millions of wall calendars decorated with these drawings were also sold. Such drawings turned women into objects for men's viewing pleasure, but this was also an era when strong female figures appeared throughout popular culture. In 1930 Chicago radio station WGN introduced the first soap opera, the domestic melodramas aired for women during the day that feature the ongoing lives of families in one community and that have remained very popular—first on radio and then on television—throughout the twentieth century. They were called "soaps" because detergent commercials provided their financial support. Female writers such as Irma Phillips created the "soaps." Their plots often portrayed strong women struggling to keep intact a community that unreliable men threatened to undermine, while a clever seductress tried to lure away their boyfriends and husbands. There were three soaps on the radio by 1931; thirty-one by 1936; and sixty-one by 1940.

The popular female fictional characters Nancy Drew and Blondie also appeared during this decade. Nancy Drew was an independent young detective created by Carolyn Keene, and she solved crimes and investigated mysterious situations in a series of novels that became favorite reading for adolescent girls in the 1930s and in the coming decades. Blondie was the daffy, although capable, housewife in the comic strip *Blondie*. Blondie dominated Dagwood, her worried, frail husband, who was often confused and incompetent. In the 1940s a series of popular Blondie and Dagwood films were produced.

The most popular comic-strip heroine of the era was Little Orphan Annie, a girl about eight years old who lived in an orphanage and was adopted by the fabulously wealthy Daddy Warbucks. With a combination of mature intelligence and childlike innocence, Annie solved problems that baffled adults. The child film star Shirley Temple, one of the most popular screen actresses of the decade, played a similar character in her many films.

There was also Scarlett O'Hara, the most famed fictional character of the age, in Margaret Mitchell's epic *Gone With the Wind*, published in 1936. Set in the South during the Civil War and Reconstruction, the work resonated to the economic and social problems of the 1930s. During the narrative, Scarlett casts off traditional womanhood and her role as a "Southern belle" in the face of economic and social chaos. Identifying with her self-made immigrant father, she becomes a successful businesswoman and the financial support of a family nearly destroyed by the war and its aftermath. Of indomitable spirit, she is calculating and ruthless. A nation of women trying to keep families afloat during the Depression adored her.

Imagining Movies: West, Westerns, and Censorship

An influential model for women in the 1930s was the movie star. In a time of economic want, people lived their lives vicariously through films. Greta Garbo was the rage; then Marlene Dietrich and Joan Crawford. When Jean Harlow bleached her hair to a hyperplatinum blonde color in 1930, she started a national fad that would punctuate Hollywood imagining and American culture for generations.

The films of the 1930s continued trends from the 1920s. The "flapper" character disappeared, but the sophisticated vamp remained. Scenes in which hundreds of chorus girls, dressed in scanty costumes, danced in unison, kicking their legs high, were popular in musical films. Western films employed the American myth of the lone gunman in frontier towns vanquishing rustlers, bandits, or Indians and restoring order to the community. Women in Westerns were virtuous schoolteachers who tried to domesticate the cowboy (or adventurer heroes). Or they were prostitutes "with hearts of gold" who understood the untamed bravado and sexual nature of the male protagonists. During the 1930s, however, a strict censorship code was in force. The film industry had established its own censorship board in the 1920s, but a number of films in the early 1930s that were considered highly sensual brought down the wrath of religious groups. (In *Red Dust,* for example, Jean Harlow flirted with Clark Gable while naked in a bath after having seduced him.) A new code, written in 1934, decreed that endings had to be happy, adultery had to be punished, and that neither sexual intercourse nor homosexuality could be depicted.

Mae West, according to some, was as responsible for the code as Jean Harlow. Large and buxom and with bleached-blonde hair, she mocked contemporary standards of female beauty. In voice and movement, she exuded sexuality, and no man could resist her. No man could manipulate her, either. A range of men from Cary Grant to W. C. Fields chased her; and to Grant's question, "Haven't you met a man who could make you happy?" her answer was classic West, "Sure, lots of times." She was strong and confident, always in command. She wrote much of her dialogue herself, and her sardonic, salacious lines were so cleverly worded that, for a time, they slipped by the censorship board.

Most movie plots, however, continued to deny authority to women. In gangster films, a favorite genre of the 1930s, gangsters mistreated their girlfriends. In the "woman's film," female self-sacrifice was a major theme, as the heroine came to terms with illness or stifled her "illicit" sexuality to take up domesticity or child-rearing. Bette Davis, for example, fights blindness in *Dark Victory* (1939) and gives up her lover to raise his child in *Now, Voyager* (1942).

The Code's restrictions on sexuality, however, encouraged the development of one of Hollywood's most imaginative genres, the "screwball comedy." In that type of film zany behavior and sparkling repartee between the hero and the heroine substituted for sex. Yet in most screwball comedies a strong man teaches a professional woman or a wealthy woman that marriage to a virile man is what mattered most. In *Take a Letter, Darling* (1942), Rosalind Russell quits her career as head of an advertising agency to travel around Mexico in a trailer with Fred MacMurray. In *Lady in the Dark* (1944), Ginger Rogers relinquishes her position as a magazine executive to marry her assistant, Ray Milland, after her psychoanalyst convinces her that she can only be fulfilled through marriage. Spencer Tracy and Katharine Hepburn waged the war of the sexes in eight films; in most, the battle is charmingly intense until Hepburn gives in during the last scenes.

Yet despite Russell's and Hepburn's capitulation, their forceful personalities dominate their films. That is often true even of the woman's films, in which actresses like Bette Davis and Joan Crawford transcend the roles of suffering women, or vamps, or working women yearning for husbands that they were given to perform. Such female stars fought the male studio heads to carve out their legendary careers, and the strength they gained through such struggle is evident in the strength of the characterizations they created in their films. They also were role models for working women, who were the main audience for the movies in this era.

Race and Popular Culture

The complexities of the movie image of white women in the 1930s were largely abandoned in the case of women of color. Indeed, Hollywood often assigned dark-haired Anglo-American women like Dorothy Lamour or Ava Gardner to portray such women when the character was beautiful or exotic. Rita Hayworth, born Margarita Carmen Cansino, underwent plastic surgery to have her Latin features restructured into those of an Anglo-American glamour queen. In keeping with the persistent racism of the age, black women in films were usually servants, often "mammies." They were simple in intellect, loyal to white employers, and they had large, round bodies. Hattie McDaniel was the most famous movie mammy; she won an Academy Award for her portrayal of the character in the film version of *Gone with the Wind*.

Another type of African American entertainer was popular in the 1920s

Mae West. Known for her sensuality and her bawdy wit, Mae West was a Hollywood box-office favorite in the 1930s, even though the enforcement of strict moral codes of behavior under the Hollywood Production Code of 1932 put a brake on her sexual double entendres and her seductive behavior. Alone among Hollywood stars, she controlled her productions and wrote much of her dialogue.

Billie Holiday. Known as "Lady Day," she has been hailed as the most influential female jazz singer of all time. Renowned from the 1930s through the 1950s for her vocal style and her dignity, she was often the victim of discrimination, and in her later years she suffered from alcoholism and drug addiction.

and 1930s. In roadhouses and nightclubs, black female vocalists bellowed and crooned jazz and the blues—the shouts, laments, and ribald songs that grew mostly out of the tragic reality of the African American experience. Ma Rainey established the genre in the 1900s. Bessie Smith continued the type in the 1920s. Ethel Waters and Ella Fitzgerald carried it into the 1930s.

Many of these women came from poverty, sometimes through a period of prostitution. Dressed in satins and spangles, they mocked mainstream standards of beauty by often being overweight. They exhibited a nouveau-riche prosperity, while they sang songs of sexuality, despair, and female strength that contrasted with the idealized love refrains of Anglo-American popular music. Whites sang songs like "You're My Everything." African American blues singers sang "Don't Fish in My Sea," or "Sweet Rough Man," or "Freight Train Blues," with its lines: "When a woman gets the blues she goes to her room and hides / When a man gets the blues he catches the freight train and rides."

WOMEN AS PART OF THE WAR
EFFORT DURING WORLD WAR II

Both World War I and World War II brought about major changes in the female workforce. Although few additional women entered the workforce during World War I, more than six million women went to work for the first time during World War II. The U.S. participation in World War I lasted eighteen months; World War II, and the need to employ women, lasted for four years, from 1941 to 1945. The proportion of women in the labor force increased from 25 percent in 1940 to 36 percent in 1945. This increase was greater than that of the previous four decades combined.

To persuade women to fill the jobs vacated by men, the molders of public opinion created "Rosie the Riveter." Large and muscular, Rosie wore coveralls and carried a wrench in her hand: she could do any job. The media encouraged women to at least raise a "victory garden" at home or work as a Red Cross volunteer. Farmwomen were encouraged to leave home to become "tractorettes"—operators of heavy farm machinery—although farmers resisted hiring unattached women as workers.

Government policy backed the employment of women. During the war years, the federal bureaucracy hired four times as many women as men. The War Manpower Commission, established to find ways to utilize labor resources more effectively, sponsored vocational-training programs for women in high schools, storefronts, and on job sites. State governors and legislatures suspended protective legislation for women so that heavy labor and other jobs considered manly would be open to them. The War Manpower Commission repeatedly urged a policy of equal pay for women. The government opened day-care facilities for working mothers: by 1945 100,000 children were enrolled in such facilities. By the end of the war, 26 percent of wives were working for pay outside the home, and young single women moved across the nation to take up jobs in the new war factories, many of them on the West Coast.

Women served Civil Defense organizations as vehicle drivers, observers watching for enemy planes, and air raid wardens. They also enlisted in the armed forces. Women's separate services included the noncombatant Women's (Auxiliary) Army Corps (WAC), the Navy WAVES (Women Accepted for Voluntary Emergency Service), and the Marine Corps Women's Reserve. Women joined the WASPS (Women Air Force Service Pilots) and the Women's Reserve of the U.S. Coast Guard. By the end of the war, thirty-five thousand women had served in the armed forces, including four thousand African American women.

World War II also resulted in a significant expansion of lesbian and gay communities. Although homosexuals were forbidden to enlist in the military, it was easy for them to fool the draft boards that monitored enlistments. Young gay men and lesbian women met each other both socially and romantically in the armed forces. After the war many relocated to cities like New York and San Francisco, where gay and lesbian communities already existed, greatly increasing their self-determination and revitalizing their cultural heritage.

WOMEN TAKE ON MALE ROLES

Women assumed many male roles during the war. Philip Wrigley, owner of the Chicago Cubs, organized the All-American Girls' Baseball League in 1943 because he feared the demise of professional baseball when four thousand male baseball players were drafted. The league didn't expand beyond the Midwest, but by 1948 it had ten teams and an attendance of nearly one million at its games. Even the field of entertainment was affected by male performers entering the military. With few men at home to play musical instruments, "all girl" bands toured the nation's ballrooms, theaters, and military installations, and they sometimes went abroad to entertain the troops overseas. They drew recruits from girls who played instruments in high school bands. In colleges and universities, with male students at war, women were added to the ranks of cheerleading squads. These women formed the basis of what would become the "pom-pom" squads of sexualized young women kicking their legs and showing off their bodies at athletic events.

Women's fashions, reflecting wartime shortages in fabrics and women's assumption of men's roles, became spare and masculine. Suits and even dresses had padded shoulders and tailored lines. Hair was long and often arranged in buns and chignons or upswept with rolls and combs. Powerful women in popular culture appeared, especially in the comic strips. There was Sheena, Queen of the Jungle, and Miss Fury, the female counterpart to Batman. She was created by Tarpe Mills, one of the day's few women cartoonists. The most popular independent woman in cartoons was Wonder Woman, who first appeared in 1941. She came to the United States from Paradise Island, an "enlightened land of women." Her mission was "to save the world from the hatred and wars of men in a man-made world."[4]

Film Noir and Anxious Roles

During the war, Hollywood made films that focused on the bravery and superiority of American soldiers in battle. They also produced escapist entertainment, such as musicals. Or they featured a wife or sweetheart who went to work and took over a male role while waiting for her man to return from the war. With many male film stars in the armed forces, female film stars became more popular and powerful than ever before. They became national heroes as they raised millions of dollars in war bond drives, danced in canteens for the USO in Hollywood with ordinary soldiers, and toured home and overseas bases entertaining servicemen.

Women's assumption of male roles with men overseas, however, produced anxiety. That was reflected in "film noir" movies, a brilliant Hollywood genre that dated from the beginning of the war and continued through the 1950s. Hundreds of these films were made. French critics coined the name film noir because of the bleakness of the movies, reflected in the use of black-and-white film and scenes that were often shot at night or in shadows. The camera focuses on dark, evanescent phenomena— crowds, smoke and steam, rain splattering off streets, faces seen behind venetian blinds and in mirrors. In these movies the universe is corrupt, and humans are evil, beset by desolation, brutality, and alienation. Luxurious and decadent mansions are often the settings for the stories, as are elegant gambling halls and nightclubs. Sometimes the films are set in run-down urban areas: these films depict the underside of the American dream.

The male protagonist is sometimes an ordinary man haunted by existential fears or lured by evil. Often he is a jaded detective, tracking down crooks or murderers—or the ubiquitous communists that became a fiction of the American imagination after World War II. Most often the detective is a "hard-boiled" antihero. His clothes are unpressed and his face unshaven, and he speaks the knowing slang of the streets. When he needs to he engages in fistfights, and he usually wins. Nuclear families are rarely depicted in these films, and romance is usually an illusion.

The women in film noir films are powerful femmes fatales, narcissistic and amoral, but so beautiful and sexual that the male protagonists cannot resist them. They have waves of hair and large lips, with lots of makeup on their faces indicating artifice and sensuality. They are often wealthy— sometimes married to men they despise—or they are nightclub singers. They often lure the male protagonists into larceny and murder, as in Billy Wilder's *Double Indemnity* (1944). In that film Barbara Stanwyck convinces a young insurance salesman to kill her husband for his money. In Orson Welles's *Lady from Shanghai* (1948), Rita Hayworth lures a young seaman, played by Welles, into killing her husband's associate. Even the hard-boiled detectives have difficulty resisting the lure of these women, as Humphrey Bogart struggles with his desire for the tainted Lauren Bacall in *The Big Sleep* (1946). The film noir films seem to reflect a fear that in taking on male roles during the war, women were a danger both to men and to the nation's future.

Limitations During the War

Women entered the armed forces and increased their participation in the workforce during World War II, but discrimination against them was still in force, both in the military and in the workforce in general. Women who were WASPS mostly ferried planes from factories to air bases. African American women were restricted to the lowest grades of the Women's Army Corps, and they were excluded from the Navy, the Coast Guard, and the WASPs. In all the armed forces, women were forbidden to engage in combat or to command men. They were also forbidden to marry or to have children. Americans observed women in military uniform—a traditional symbol of masculinity. There were fears that such masculine dress—and their masculine behavior as soldiers—might encourage women in the military to become lesbian.

Although women at home were courted to join the workforce during the war, they were hired primarily in clerical and factory jobs. Some opportunities opened in medicine and law, but women rarely moved permanently into professional careers. Women were not hired for high-level positions in business or in government. A shortage of teachers and school administrators occurred not just because men went to war but also because industry and business, lacking administrative talent, lured male teachers into executive positions with higher salaries than they could make in education.

With regard to government directives that women's wages should be the same as men's, lax enforcement allowed employers to violate them with impunity. Women's Bureau studies showed that the 100,000 children enrolled in federal day-care centers constituted only 10 percent of the children who needed such care. Female leaders charged that the government dismissed their recommendations. The War Manpower Commission, for example, which was composed of men, shunted women into a Woman's Advisory Committee that was rarely consulted.

The concern for women lacked impetus because they were not expected to continue working after the war ended. In the advertising designed to attract women into the workforce, factory labor was often described as akin to housework. Women, it was said, could adapt to factory machines as easily as to electric cake mixers and vacuum cleaners. The implication was that the transition back to domesticity would be equally easy. Typical of the national attitude, federal funds for day-care facilities were cut off in 1946.

Along with Rosie the Riveter, the "pinup" became an important symbol of women in this period. Many soldiers openly collected suggestive photographs of their favorite movie actresses in bathing suits. The movie studios sent out such photos upon request for free. Magazines produced for the troops, like *Yank*, included pinup photos, and the army provided

"Rosie the Riveter." The acclaimed woman at work who was the symbol of women helping the national effort during World War II. In this case the "riveter" is an arc welder at the Bethlehem-Fairfield Shipyards in Baltimore, Maryland, in 1943.

Nurses. In addition to joining the WACS, WAVES, and WASPS of the American forces during World War II, U.S. women also served the Allied armies in other ways. In this photo three American nurses recruited for the Free French Army Service treat a wounded French soldier in France in 1944.

soldiers and sailors with free subscriptions to *Esquire*. The most famous pinup was Betty Grable, blonde and blue-eyed. She was one of the highest paid Hollywood actresses in the 1940s. One army unit voted her "the Girl We'd Like to Fly with in a Plane with an Automatic Pilot." Marilyn Monroe, raised in Los Angeles in a series of foster homes after her mother was committed to a mental institution, worked in her late teens on the assembly line in an aircraft factory, while the husband she had married at the age of sixteen, in her sophomore year of high school, was overseas. A photographer for one of the magazines for soldiers first "discovered" her when he was looking for beautiful women in the factories to photograph. Finding her an extraordinary model, luminescent in front of the camera, he recommended her to a local modeling agency. That success launched her career and gave her the impetus to divorce her husband. In her experiences during World War II Monroe symbolized women as "Rosie the Riveter," as "wife," and as "pinup," and those symbols marked the polarities of women's situation in modern America as wife, worker, and iconic and manipulated object of desire for men.

But Marilyn's career was never easy. She seduced and manipulated agents and producers to obtain her first roles, and the major roles among them were in film noir movies in which she played the classic evil temptress. In *Don't Bother to Knock* (1952) she is a psychopathic babysitter; in *Niagara* (1953) she is a wife who attempts to murder her husband with the aid of her boyfriend. Even when her career was established, she fought movie executives to get the roles and the recognition that she wanted. She was often later cast as a "dumb blonde," and she was trivialized by the press as someone whose only talent lay in her curvaceous body. For her part, she wanted to be recognized for her intelligence and her determination as a career woman and an actress.

WORK AFTER THE WAR

When the war ended, many women happily left jobs in factories and offices to return to the marriages and homes denied them during the war years. Yet a Women's Bureau study in 1944 showed that 80 percent of the women employed during the war wanted to continue in their jobs. After all, many women had moved into high-paying skilled labor positions. The manpower crisis had especially aided African American women; the number of black women who worked as servants fell from 72 percent to 48 percent of black women at work, while the proportion of black women working in factories grew to nearly 19 percent.

Cutbacks among female workers, particularly in industry, began as soon as peace was declared. In the period of conversion from wartime to peacetime production, businesses and factories did not need as many workers. Yet large numbers of women were laid off in comparison with men. For example, in plants making aircraft engines, women had made up 39 percent of the workforce, but they comprised 51 percent of those laid off. In keeping with these trends, the percentage of women in the labor force in general dropped from 36 percent in 1945 to 28 percent in 1947.

After 1947, the number of working women began to rise. By 1951, the proportion reached 31 percent. Yet women in manufacturing who had held skilled jobs during the war did not regain them. Without equal rights legislation on the books, there was little they could do. State protective labor laws for women had been suspended only temporarily during the war years, and once reinstated, they were interpreted again as meaning that women were not capable of performing labor defined as "men's work."

In some instances, the unions were willing to aid female members; the movement of women into war industries brought a quadrupling of their membership in the CIO. During the war years, Detroit unions negotiated an equal pay agreement for women with General Motors. But once the war ended, the male-dominated unions acquiesced to agreements with employers that reserved higher-paying positions for men. In the late 1940s, some women filed court suits demanding back pay as a result of these practices. Most of these suits were denied, but thirty-one women in 1948 won a retroactive wage settlement of $55,000 from the Chrysler Corporation because the company had laid them off after World War II in violation of their seniority.

After 1951, the percentage of women in the labor force steadily increased. By 1973 it reached 42 percent. The percentages of employed married women and older women also rose. Many women thus retained their tie to a world outside the home. The experience of war, both at the home front and overseas had lasting effects on women—at least on those who were now relatively permanent members of the workforce.

REBEL YOUTH

Increased high school attendance during the 1930s brought adolescents together, furthering the extent of a separate culture among young people. The opportunities for employment during World War II provided them with jobs and money. Rebellious youths appeared. As in the 1910s and 1920s, dance and dress were central to their expression of self. In 1937 "hepcats" and "jitterbugs" began dancing to the music of "big bands," mostly white, which played a version of African American jazz known as swing. Girls doing the dancing wore tight sweaters and skirts, and they were often called bobby-soxers because of the short, turned over socks they wore. A new behavior appeared among them, as they yelled and swooned at the concerts of singer Frank Sinatra. They exhibited the conduct that teenage girls would later display toward Elvis Presley in the late 1950s and then toward male and female rock stars in the 1960s and after. Their enthusiasm for Sinatra, however, wasn't entirely spontaneous. A clever press agent had thought up the gimmick of paying a large number of girls to display fan hysteria over Sinatra in several of his concerts, and their example sparked many other girls to engage in the same behavior.

The word "teenager" was coined in 1941, and *Seventeen* magazine, the first glamour magazine to be directed specifically toward girls, appeared in 1945. Adults became anxious about defiant young people. "V" (for Victory) girls made themselves sexually available to servicemen at bases in the United States, and that was also troubling. During the first six months of 1943, 1,200 magazine articles were written on the subject of juvenile delinquency, and Congressional hearings on it were held that year.

Of special concern to mainstream Americans was the appearance of young Mexican American "pachuquitas" and "pachucos." The pachuquitas wore short tight skirts, sheer blouses, and lots of makeup. The pachuco young men dressed in "zoot" suits, with tapered pants, wide lapels, and broad-brimmed hats, and they pomaded their hair and slicked it back into a ducktail. The fashion began in Los Angeles and spread east. The styles were derived from the styles of gangsters and jazz musicians, each in their own way rebels against mainstream, middle-class society. Variations on the dress would become standard among rock musicians and their youthful audiences in the decades to come, as young men became molders of the conventions and attitudes of popular youth culture that even young women would follow.

In Los Angeles the pachucos sparked a major riot—the Sleepy Lagoon incident. In that event, soldiers and sailors stationed in the city, who wore crisp uniforms and buzz-cut hair, turned with fury against a group of young Mexican Americans who were violating their codes of race and masculinity through wearing aggressive, yet feminized, dress. It indicated the depths of racism in the United States as well as the disagreements over the nature of masculinity in the decades to follow. The advent of the "zoot-suiters" foreshadowed the emergence of generations of more assertive people of color on the national stage. It also announced that cultural rebellion would be signaled through dress.

Rebellious teenagers, in addition to pachucos and pachuquitas, and V-girls, may have reflected what was an underlying apprehension about the nature of sexuality in wartime America. Although the military authorities took care to issue strong official denials that any fraternization had taken place between servicemen and women abroad, a secret army survey of 1945 indicated that three out of four veterans returned from overseas service more sexually experienced than before they had left. On the island of Oahu in Hawaii, the staging ground for troops being deployed in the Pacific war, military officials set up brothels, staffed by experienced prostitutes. They operated around-the-clock under a system of regulation by which prostitutes were regularly examined for venereal disease. Literally thousands of servicemen lined up day and night to pay for a brief sexual encounter before they journeyed to the field of battle. Once the war began, rates of marriage escalated dramatically in the United States, given the possibility of draft deferments for married men and the imminence of the men's departure and possible death. The age of first marriage dropped and childbirth increased. Once the war ended, however, rates of divorce also escalated, as marriages hastily contracted during the war and women's new independence made both men and women question the choices they had made. Whether or not the rates of promiscuity among women left at home during the war increased, the public and the media thought that they had— and Alfred Kinsey's extensive study of the sexual behavior of women, published in 1953, would lend credence to the notion that the women at home had, in fact, acted on their sexual urges outside their marriages. The war ushered in a fear of all forms of nonmarital sexuality, including a concern about prostitution and "promiscuous" women. Experts warned men to avoid contact with single women for fear of catching venereal diseases. The stage was set both for the return to domesticity and the nuclear family and the sexual conservatism of the 1950s as well as for the sexual rebellion that would also emerge in that decade.

NOTES

1. Eleanor Roosevelt, *It's Up to the Women* (New York: Frederick A. Stokes, 1933), 202–06.
2. Grace Hutchins, *Women Who Work* (New York: International Publishers, 1934), 191.
3. Studs Terkel, *Hard Times: An Oral History of the Great Depression* (New York: Pantheon Books, 1970), 196–97.
4. *Wonder Woman*, with an introduction by Gloria Steinem (New York: Holt, Rinehart and Winston, 1972), unpaginated.

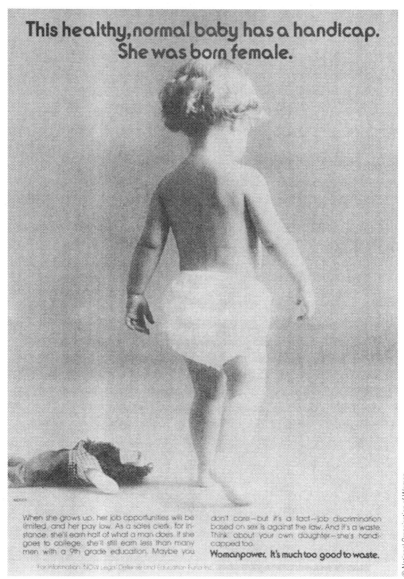

5

A Conservative Era

1945–1960

World War II brought in its wake a gender conservatism that had not been seen since the Victorian era a century before. After four years of wartime instability, both women and men seemed to want to return to a patriarchal order, with women in the home. Behind this desire also lay a national paranoia over internal communist subversion. That mood resulted from the tensions of war, the expansion of the Soviet Union into Eastern Europe at the end of the war, and the fear of the atomic bomb, which the United States dropped on the Japanese cities of Hiroshima and Nagasaki as the war was ending. The Soviets developed atomic capabilities soon after. The paranoia included in its targets homosexuals, women, and liberals. As with the "Red Scare" after World War I, the end of war and the expansion of communism abroad produced an overheated internal reaction. The late 1940s and the 1950s were also an era of affluence. Capitalism seemed triumphant, for big business had operated the factories that produced the weapons and machines to win the war. The New Deal spending hadn't brought economic recovery, but the massive spending during World War II

Opposite: An advertisement sponsored by the Legal Defense/Education Fund of the National Organization for Women (NOW)

stimulated long-term economic growth. Between 1945 and 1960 the gross national product grew 250 percent, and per capita income grew 35 percent. By the mid-1950s, nearly 60 percent of working people had a middle-class income, in comparison with 31 percent in the 1920s. The consumerism of the 1920s returned full force. Historian Lizabeth Cohen contends that in this era of pro-business sentiment "mass consumption became a civic responsibility." Americans believed that buying products would insure prosperity and further democracy.[1]

By the mid-1950s, however, cultural rebellion emerged with the Civil Rights movement, the beat poets, and the expansion of African American rock 'n' roll into the mainstream, especially with the appearance of Elvis Presley. The younger generation continued to exhibit a rebellious streak, and blacks were no longer willing to tolerate oppression. Meanwhile, increasing numbers of women worked outside the home. The stage was set for the appearance of second-wave feminism in the 1960s.

Yet in 1953 Hugh Hefner launched *Playboy,* a magazine for men that focused on sex, with a photograph of a nude woman as its centerfold. Mattell Toys marketed the first Barbie doll in 1959. Both *Playboy* and Barbie symbolized the appearance of a freer sexuality for women, but both also symbolized an increased objectification of women that would remain part of their history in succeeding decades and that would continue to exist to the present.

ANTICOMMUNISM

In 1938 the House Un-American Activities Committee (HUAC) had been founded to investigate presumed internal communist and fascist subversion. During the war years the nation focused on winning the war, and HUAC had a subdued voice. Then in 1947 the Soviet Communists took over much of Eastern Europe, and Secretary of State George Kennan coined the alarming term "Cold War" to describe the ideological and economic competition between the capitalist United States and the communist USSR that had suddenly appeared. (The Union of Soviet Socialist Republics had been established in 1923 by the new Communist regime in Russia from the former Tsarist empire. Disbanded in 1991, it included Russia and what are today fifteen independent nations.) In 1947 HUAC launched an investigation of communism in the Hollywood film industry, and President Harry Truman issued an executive order initiating a loyalty oath program in the federal government. Under the executive order government employees had to swear that they had never participated in a communist organization. That year

Congress passed the antiunion Taft-Hartley Act, which restrained unions in strikes and organizing.

In 1949 Communist forces took over China, and in 1950 Communist North Korea invaded South Korea, resulting in a full-scale U.S. military intervention on the side of South Korea. That same year Senator Joseph McCarthy of Wisconsin held up a piece of paper during a speech before a women's club in Wheeling, West Virginia, and declared that it contained a list of 257 Communists. (McCarthy was later exposed as a fake; the piece of paper contained his laundry list.) Nonetheless, the Senate appointed McCarthy head of his own investigating committee.

As the hysteria permeated the national consciousness, states, counties, and cities set up loyalty programs, and so did corporations, schools, and labor unions. Teachers and government officials were fired for holding liberal beliefs, while by 1960 the FBI had collected files and conducted investigations on over 430,000 individuals. Conservatives gained control of Congress and ended the New Deal agencies. Writers and actors called before HUAC who invoked the first amendment right to free speech and refused to testify about their participation in the Communist Party in the 1930s were jailed for contempt of Congress. Many individuals in the film industry were blacklisted (fired from their jobs and denied further employment in the industry) for refusing to testify. Indeed, only if a witness admitted guilt and named others could he or she be certain of being let off. Playwright Lillian Hellman somehow escaped being cited for contempt, despite her defiant statement refusing to testify before HUAC: "I cannot and will not cut my conscience to fit this year's fashions."

Homosexuals also became targets of the anticommunist crusade. In 1948 Alfred Kinsey, a biologist at the University of Indiana, published an acclaimed study of male sexuality, based on a sample of ten thousand individuals. Widely publicized by the media, the scholarly work became a best seller. Kinsey found a considerable amount of homosexual behavior among the men in his sample. Like Sigmund Freud in the 1900s and Margaret Mead in the 1930s, he argued that human sexual orientation was diverse and that many individuals were bisexual in orientation. Nonetheless, the popular attitude remained that homosexuals were perverted. In the early 1950s the American Psychiatric Association defined homosexuality as a mental disease in its diagnostic manual used by psychiatrists. The definition was not dropped until 1971. Throughout the nation lesbians and gays were arrested, often with little evidence of any wrongdoing. After the murder of a young boy in Sioux City, Iowa, in 1948, the county attorney invoked the provisions of the state's sexual psychopath law to arrest twenty-nine homosexuals and commit them to the state mental institution, even though there was no evidence linking them to the crime. The psychopath law, passed during the sex crime panic of the late 1930s, permitted internment without a trial. Gangs of men went to lesbian bars and beat up women who refused their advances. The police were as likely to arrest the women as the men. Homosexuals were denied jobs in the federal civil service and harassed by the FBI—even when they weren't suspected of communism.

For the first time in the history of the nation, however, lesbians and gays formed organizations in response to the wave of terror against them. In 1950 the Mattachine Society, the first gay rights organization in the history of the nation, was founded in Los Angeles. Its founders took the name from a medieval theatrical order whose members wore masks when they performed; the name symbolized the feelings of many homosexuals that they had to "mask" their true identity in the real world. In 1955 the lesbian Daughters of Bilitis, the first activist lesbian organization, was formed in San Francisco. The word Bilitis came from the name of a lesbian poet who supposedly lived on the island of Lesbos with Sappho in ancient times. In the prevailing climate of oppression, these groups remained mostly small and underground. They did, however, write newsletters that circulated widely among homosexuals, thereby establishing the basis for a national network for lesbians and gays.

WOMEN UNDER ATTACK

Women in general did not escape the era's scapegoating. As early as 1942, in his best-selling *Generation of Vipers,* Philip Wylie accused American women of emasculating their husbands and sons through controlling them at home. Sociologists reported high rates of neurosis among army draftees and alcoholism and impotence among American men in general. Many commentators attributed these problems to women leaving the home for work. In 1956 sociologists Alva Myrdal and Viola Klein in *Women's Two Roles: Home and Work* noted that magistrates, probation officers, and welfare workers blamed mothers, especially working mothers, for the problems of their children. Psychologists found the causes of both schizophrenia and male homosexuality in overbearing mothers.

Freudian Helene Deutsch, in her influential *Psychology of Women* (1945), posited that women were naturally masochistic and that they secretly enjoyed physical abuse. Experts labeled girls subjected to incest as seductive and their molesters as sexually deprived, thus placing blame on the victim, not the perpetrator. Unwed mothers in general were vilified as having been immoral in "getting themselves pregnant," and they were often judged to be mentally ill. Unwed black mothers, however, were condemned as suffering from uncontrollable sex urges.

Nurses and midwives who were abortion providers came under attack, as municipal and state authorities began to enforce the Comstock laws more aggressively than ever before. Abortionists were brought to trial and women who had undergone abortions were forced to reveal the details of their experience before all-male judges, lawyers, and juries. Historian Ricki Solinger contends that these women had to give humiliating (and quasi-pornographic) testimony about their sexual anatomy and the details of the procedures they had undergone. Both they and their abortionists were vilified as psychotic and sadistic. Male doctors who performed abortions were rarely prosecuted. As access to abortion shut down, women were forced to resort to self-inflicted abortions and to find practitioners willing to break the law. These individuals were often poorly trained. The self-inflicted "coat hanger" technique and the "back-alley abortion" now became frequent realities.

DOMESTICITY AND THE FAMILY

After the war, rates of marriage and remarriage after divorce remained high, and the age of first marriage dropped. In 1900 the average age of first marriage for women was 22 years; by 1940 it was 21.5. World War II and the postwar era occasioned the most rapid decrease in the average age of first marriage over the course of the century: by 1962 it was 20.3. Women of twenty-two were considered old maids, and bridal and baby showers were constant, with consumer goods given to the expectant bride or mother to prepare her for her future role and congratulate her on her success. Pink now became the color for girl babies and blue for boys.

In addition, the size of families increased. Families with four or five children were common; the 1950s was a period of family formation unparalleled in the history of the United States since the early nineteenth century. The children of this mass reproduction were dubbed the "baby boom" generation. Two organizations in particular exalted motherhood. La Leche League was dedicated to helping mothers nurse their infants. The Lamaze movement promoted natural childbirth. It combined a humanitarian drive to free women from the pain of childbirth with a fervor to make it the central experience of their lives.

In this era of domesticity, fewer women attended college than had previously. Women had constituted almost half of all college students in 1920, but by 1958 they made up about one-third. By the mid-1950s, 60 percent of female college undergraduates were dropping out of college to marry. Many girls married at eighteen, as soon as they graduated from high school. The 1944 GI bill (Servicemen's Readjustment Act) provided veterans with the funds to attend college, but it also contributed to the decline in the numbers of women attending college. Women who had been in the military were eligible for benefits under the GI bill, but their numbers were small. At the same time many colleges turned down women in general to admit male veterans. Thus the numbers of women attending college declined.

The Back-to-the-Home Movement

After World War II, many Anglo-Americans moved to the suburbs to attain the American dream of home ownership in a rural setting. The federal government encouraged this trend by guaranteeing millions of families with limited incomes housing loans with low down payments and a long amortization, through the Federal Housing Administration and the Veterans Administration. Developers responded to the demand for housing by building multitudes of identical small homes on tracts of land on which farms and forests had previously stood. They constructed instant subdivisions, connected to cities by trains and freeways. The most popular style of home in the subdivisions was the "ranch" design, associated in the public mind with the easygoing lifestyle of the Southwest and Southern California. Built on one floor, the ranch house had a number of bedrooms, an informal "family room," and a formal living room with a large "picture window" to connect the house to the out-of-doors. Suburban shopping centers vastly expanded in number. William J. Levitt, who had built temporary barracks for army troops in the South Pacific during World War II, created the first tract of homes, on Long Island, New York. It was called Levittown. Jews and people of color, however, remained in the cities, since subdivisions like Levittown often had restrictive covenants written into property deeds forbidding sales to them.

It was difficult for women in the suburbs to work outside the home. Jobs were limited away from cities, and domestic help was hard to find. Husbands were away from home longer because they had to commute to work, leaving their wives responsible for the family. Domestic tasks now included the major one of transportation, since schools, stores, and train stations were rarely within walking distance from homes and bus service was often limited or scorned by the new and growing suburban middle class. The "station wagon," which could hold many children as well as groceries and could be used to transport material for home improvements, became suburbia's means of transportation.

New products flooded the market. Frozen foods and TV dinners appeared, as did clothes dryers, disposable diapers, instant rice, and bottled baby formula. All studies showed, however, that no matter the laborsaving devices, the amount of time women spent on housework remained constant. For a compulsion toward ever stricter standards in home cleaning kept pace with the new technology designed to free women from domestic tasks. In 1959, in the model kitchen at the American exposition in Moscow, Richard Nixon engaged Soviet Premier Nikita Krushchev in a famed impromptu debate over the merits of capitalism and communism. At one point in the debate, Nixon proclaimed that capitalism's superiority lay in the suburban home, "designed to make things easier for our women."[2]

Still, suburban housewives got together over "coffee klatches" in their homes. Or they spent time together at local churches or at PTA meetings at local schools. Some of these women had gone to college. They formed a "critical mass" ripe for organizing around initiatives for social change. In 1960 the founders of Women's Strike for Peace, for example, drew members from local chapters of the PTAs and the League of Women Voters. This new peace organization focused on "mothers' issues," such as the dangers to children from the milk they drank because of possible nuclear contamination released into the atmosphere and ingested by cows.

The Evidence from Popular Culture

On a popular level, the new emphasis on domesticity was everywhere. In newspapers and magazines, in radio programs and on billboards, the homemaker replaced "Rosie the Riveter" as the national female model. Advertisers were quick to respond to the expanded market for domestic products offered by the return to a peacetime economy and the appearance of a new affluence. Between 1950 and 1960, advertising expenditures nationwide rose from $5.7 billion annually to $12 billion. The advertisers' model woman in their ads was either a housewife who demonstrated the benefits of the newest home products or a seductress who connected the products to sexuality. Many Hollywood stars, glamorous in the fan magazines of the 1930s, were shown as domestic in the magazines of the 1950s. Joan Crawford, brash and independent in the 1930s and 1940s, was now pictured as doing her own housework and as a devoted mother to three adopted children. Even Margaret Mead emphasized the importance of domesticity and child-rearing for women in her 1949 book, *Male and Female*. Advertisers sometimes depicted women as incapable of doing their housework without the intervention of a male supernatural being, such as "Mr. Clean."

Styles in Dress

Women's dress styles reflected the decade's conservatism. In 1947 Paris designer Christian Dior introduced the "New Look." It featured long, full skirts, held out by crinoline petticoats, with a defined bosom and a tiny

Laundry on the Line. A woman in the early 1950s attaching her laundry to backyard lines with clothespins so that it will dry in the sun, in an era when such domestic tasks became a mark of womanhood and before electric clothes dryers became standard equipment in homes and laundromats.

waist. Not since the Victorian era had women's fashions been so confining. They were also sexualized. Girdles and padded bras were popular, and in the evenings women often wore a "merry widow" waist cincher. Breasts were molded by bras into pointed shapes that resembled the tips of bombs. Shoe styles emphasized spike heels and pointed toes.

Hair was worn short and curled. At first the look was achieved by curling strands of hair around fingers, attaching each roll to the head with a bobby pin, and then sleeping on the pinned hair overnight to curl it. Later in the decade a "beehive look" became the fashion. It was achieved through the use of large round plastic curlers attached to the head with bobby pins. The curlers produced large, smooth curls that could be backcombed, teased, and sprayed with the new hairsprays to achieve the beehive look. By the end of the 1950s the invention and marketing of home hair dryers speeded up the drying process that curled the hair.

Blonde hair became more fashionable than ever before, especially as cosmetic companies produced more effective home hair dyes. Advertising ex-

Marilyn Monroe. In New York City during the all-night shooting of a scene for her film, *The Seven-Year Itch,* Marilyn poses with a wind machine under a grating in the sidewalk producing a breeze to blow her skirt high. The scene was not used in the film, although this still photograph taken during the shoot became one of the most popular pinup photos of the twentieth century.

ecutive Shirley Polykoff launched the vogue for blonde hair in 1956 with her advertising campaign for Clairol hair dyes: "Does She . . . or Doesn't She? Only her hairdresser knows for sure." (The question in the ad, with its sexual innuendo, referred to dying one's hair blonde.) In her autobiography, Polykoff claimed that in 1955 only models, actresses, and members of elite café society bleached their hair, since many Americans considered it immoral to do so. Polykoff circumvented the negative attitudes by creating an aura of respectability in her ads. She used fresh-faced rather than glamorous models, had them wear wedding rings, and posed them with naturally blonde female children. She called her product "Miss" Clairol. Within a short time, Polykoff claimed, the number of women lightening their hair increased from 7 percent of women to over 50 percent.[3]

Movies

The Hollywood movie genres of the 1930s and 1940s continued in the 1950s, including Westerns, crime dramas, women's films, and film noir. However, the attacks on Hollywood as leftist and the prevailing commitment to domesticity made filmmakers cautious. Twenty-eight percent of movies produced in 1947 dealt with realistic social problems, but by 1953 only 9 percent dealt with such issues. Epics dramatizing biblical themes were popular, for they cast an aura of religious respectability over Hollywood. Many science fiction movies were also made, involving attacks by creatures from outer space or by mutants created by atomic radiation. They seemed to reflect Cold War fears that the nation might be invaded by a hostile force.

Romantic tearjerkers and women's melodramas like Douglas Sirk's *Magnificent Obsession* (1954) and his *All That Heaven Allows* (1956) appealed to suburban women. These movies portrayed virtuous, long-suffering heroines whose persistent faith in the American dream was rewarded with romantic love. But the families in films such as *Picnic* (1956) were riven with tensions. They indicated that problems existed in America that were deeper than communism or the Cold War. Many of these films involved a metaphoric search for an ideal husband/father who would stabilize the family, although some male heroes in the films in the 1950s were doomed to despair by a relentless world with which they could not cope.

Popular film actresses Doris Day and Debbie Reynolds, girlish and bouncy, represented a new breed of female film stars who were hyperfeminine and vacuous. Day and Reynolds, however, had a measure of independence reminiscent of the stars of the 1930s and 1940s. The gamine and flat-chested Audrey Hepburn brought the elegance of Paris fashion to the screen, while Elizabeth Taylor, a child star in the 1940s, played dramatic, emotionally charged heroines in the 1950s. There was also a vogue for what film analysts call "mammary goddesses." Those were film stars who, like Marilyn Monroe, had large breasts and flaunted their sexuality in film. The trend toward large breasts became apparent in the 1940s, as large-breasted women came to dominate the drawings in the men's magazines, and film magnate Howard Hughes fought the film censors over the advertising for his movie, *The Outlaw* (1948), which featured actress Jane Russell's large breasts. At the same time, however, Alfred Hitchcock made acclaimed movies that featured cool, mysterious blondes, like Grace Kelly and Kim Novak, who didn't always have the fashionable curves that were in style. From *Rear Window* (1954) through *Vertigo* (1958) to *Psycho* (1960) to *Marnie* (1964), Hitchcock's blondes are sometimes saboteurs and criminals, but they are also often victimized in his films, as though Hitchcock considered his blondes both captivating and dangerous.

Hollywood also made many films in the 1950s extolling the tough male hero, usually as a cowboy or an urban detective. In *High Noon* (1952) and *Shane* (1953), two acclaimed Westerns, the male heroes take on entire communities to right wrongs, showing in the process that they are supermen with the fastest gun around. Marlon Brando, however, dominated the image of men in 1950s films, with his earthy proletarian sexuality, bulging muscles, deep sensitivity, and considerable skill as an actor. Film historian Joan Mellen contends that he seemed to have been created by a homosexual imagination, even as he engaged in "macho" behavior and yet radiated the insecurity that may lie beneath such behavior. By not hiding his feelings, Brando departed from the obligatory suppression of feelings of male film stars like John Wayne.

As a sensitive model for men, Brando was joined by James Dean. Both lived independent lives off-screen, refusing to conform to Hollywood conventions that stars should marry and have families. Both starred in movies about rebellious youth. *The Wild One* (1953), starring Brando, focused on the macho culture of motorcycle gangs. The blue jeans and leather jacket that Brando wore in the film became fashionable among young men. *Rebel Without a Cause* (1954), starring Dean, explored the high school culture of drag racing and traced the antisocial behavior of these teenagers to dysfunctional well-to-do families.

Television

Television had been developed as early as 1939, and by the 1950s it competed with the movies for the nation's viewing audience. In 1950 4.4 million families owned television sets; by 1960 fifty million families owned them. In the early 1950s, known as the "Golden Years" of television, live plays, filmed before television audiences, explored the problems of poverty, class conflict, and racism that lay beneath the surface of postwar optimism. Yet this type of programming largely disappeared as television increasingly came under the control of corporate sponsorship. Shows were soon divided into fifteen-minute segments organized around advertising slots. The live plays of the early 1950s were replaced by game shows, Western and action-adventure dramas, and situation family comedies. In the sitcoms, which glorified the nuclear family and suburban living, middle-class families lived in the suburbs or aspired to live there, and wives were portrayed as domestic beings, while they also were moral and spiritual guides for their families. The emphasis on domesticity for women was pronounced in such long-running, popular TV sitcoms as *Father Knows Best* and *The Donna Reed Show.* Women who worked as secretaries, teachers, maids, and entertainers were not absent from the television shows of the 1950s, but they were depicted as misguided or immature.

Yet in the most popular sitcom of the 1950s, *I Love Lucy,* comedienne Lucille Ball playing Lucy attempted to outwit her Cuban band leader husband, Ricky Ricardo, in every episode. Although she is always defeated, she never gives up trying. And other female comics in sitcoms, such as Imogene Coca, who continued in the tradition of Blondie and Dagwood, were married to inept husbands they regularly had to stop from doing something foolish. These women seemed to indicate the possibility of some independence for women in a decade of domesticity.

SEX AND CHILDREARING

A new emphasis on Freudianism was also central to the return to the home in the 1950s. After World War II, as after World War I, Americans wanted to learn sexual techniques—so long as, in this era, they were confined to marriage. Freudian theorists believed that fulfilling the sex drive was a physiological necessity. But they also argued that true sexual gratification for women lay in motherhood, and they incorrectly claimed that "mature" orgasms for women were not clitoral, but vaginal, produced by male penetration. Marriage manuals continued to recommend that men should be dominant and women submissive in sex. Child-care experts like Benjamin Spock told women that they must stay at home and take care of their children, to make certain they were properly raised.

Adolescent sexuality was a major concern of the 1950s. The "double standard" was in force, and the arbiters of middle-class morality decreed that women must remain virgins until marriage; that before marriage it was a woman's responsibility to restrain male sexuality in intimate encounters; and that having an "illegitimate" child outside of marriage was a disgrace for a woman. Indeed, the "V-girls" of World War II, with their free sexuality, seemed to have provoked a major reaction. "Parking" at night in automobiles in deserted places and engaging in "necking," or intense kissing, with limited petting, was the practice on dates between young unmarried males and females. "Going steady" with one person in high school was the standard behavior, and it was expected to lead to engagement and early marriage.

Historian Elaine May contends that the sexual repression and the "containment" of early marriage in the 1950s was related to the fears of the Cold War and of communism and especially of the atom bomb, which was linked to women's sexuality. The internal "witch hunts" to expose communists and homosexuals decreased with the end of the Korean War in 1953 and the censure of Joseph McCarthy by the Senate in 1954. But the United States continued to engage in a "Cold War" of threats and limited engagements with Russia, and both nations continued to test nuclear bombs. According to May, domesticity as a response to the Cold War included keeping women's sexuality under control. The slang term for a sexy woman was a "bombshell." A painting of Rita Hayworth in a skimpy bathing suit was attached to the hydrogen bomb tested on the Bikini Islands in 1959. The name of the island, "Bikini," was chosen as the name for the revealing two-piece bathing suit designed and marketed that year.

A Sexual Underside

In his study of the sexual behavior of American women, published in 1953, Alfred Kinsey found that 90 percent of the thousands of women he interviewed stated that they had participated in petting before marriage, while half stated that they had engaged in premarital intercourse, and a quarter admitted to having had extramarital affairs. By the mid-1950s, plunging necklines, bare midriffs, strapless dresses, and sheath dresses with tight skirts were in vogue, in addition to full skirts and wasp waists. A purity movement appeared that attempted to tighten the statutes with regard to obscenity in literature, but the courts ruled against the censorship drive. Strict censorship of Hollywood films began to break down. In 1959 the Supreme Court overturned the ruling by which D. H. Lawrence's *Lady Chatterley's Lover* had been declared obscene in the 1920s and removed from libraries and bookstores. The court enunciated a broad interpretation of the right to free speech under the First Amendment, thereby leading the way to the ending of the Hollywood censorship codes in 1968.

Brassiere and girdle ads became bolder, with overtones of exhibitionism. Maidenform's famous advertising campaign, "I Dreamed I Stopped Traffic in my Maidenform Bra," featured female models naked above the waist, except for wearing a bra. Sometimes the ads played with sex. One ad, featuring a model standing next to a bull, had the caption: "I dreamed I took the bull by the horns in my Maidenform bra." By the 1960s the women in these ads were portrayed in male spaces, such as financial offices and pool halls,

Barbie Dolls. A collection of Barbie dolls on exhibit at the Public Library in New York City in 1984. Barbie came in many varieties, but her body was always elongated, with large breasts, a tiny waist, and small, stylized Anglo facial features.

indicating a growing sensitivity to women's increasing participation in the workforce. Women in advertising created the concept of the Maidenform campaign and wrote the ads for it.

The women's magazines in the 1950s aired women's sexual complaints by publishing many articles on "female frigidity." These articles, however, for the most part focused on wives' complaints about their husbands' insensitivity to their sexual needs for foreplay in marital sex. Motivational experts declared that it was the femininity of women in advertisements as well as their sexuality that appealed to the public. Both women and men, the researchers maintained, had a need for reassurance about their sexuality and their sex roles. Given the changes in such roles over the course of the century, women wanted to feel feminine and men wanted to feel masculine. Thus advertisers in their ads portrayed women and men in traditional ways.

Playboy and Barbie

In December 1953 Hugh Hefner, who had been on the staff of *Esquire,* began to publish *Playboy.* Men's magazines such as *Esquire* had included only drawings, not photographs, of voluptuous, semi-naked women, while the women who posed for the pinups of World War II had worn bathing suits. However, Hefner featured a photograph of a nude Marilyn Monroe in the centerfold of his new magazine in 1953. The photo he used had been taken

Playboy Bunnies. Hugh Hefner surrounded by Playboy bunnies in 1963. After launching *Playboy* with its nude centerfold in 1953, Hugh Hefner opened his first Playboy Club, catering to well-to-do businessmen, in Chicago in 1960. The clubs spread to fifteen cities throughout the nation. Their main feature was seminude women with large breasts wearing spike heels and dressed as "bunnies," with rabbit ears and fuzzy tails.

before Marilyn became a star, and she had no rights over it, but it was still considered shocking for a Hollywood star to appear nude. Monroe weathered the storm of criticism. She contended that she had been young when the photo was taken and that she had needed the money she was paid for posing for it. When asked if she had anything on when the photo was taken, she replied with a characteristic quip: "Yes, the radio." Hefner portrayed himself as a rebel in launching *Playboy,* and he contended that his centerfold photos of nude young women were "a symbol of disobedience, a triumph of sexuality, an end of Puritanism." He also positioned his nudes to appeal to men, in line with *Playboy*'s advocacy of an unmarried, self-indulgent lifestyle for men. By the mid-1960s Hefner was worth $100 million.

Marilyn Monroe, *Playboy*'s first centerfold, defined the ideal in female beauty in the 1950s. She was blonde and wasp-waisted, with childlike features and voice. Her movements and speech were sexualized. In her films she often played a "dumb blonde," yet she had an underlying wit and intuitive intelligence that shines through those roles. She led the way, however, to the Barbie doll, invented by Ruth Handler for Mattell Toys in 1959. Before Barbie appeared, most dolls were modeled after babies; Handler decided to create an adult doll for girls. She named Barbie after her daughter, Barbara, and she based her creation on a doll she found in Germany, the "Bild Lilli" doll. That doll had been designed as a lascivious toy for adult men, and it was sold in tobacco shops.

Both Lilli and Barbie were made of plastic, and they had large breasts, a tiny body, long legs, pointed feet, and no genitalia. Barbie was the *Playboy* centerfold come to life. But she was also independent, unmarried, and without children. Her boyfriend, Ken, the bland male doll that Handler also created, was subservient to her. Some analysts contend that the girls who play with Barbie dolls relate to Barbie in a variety of ways. Some girls regard her as a beauty model they should emulate, while others see her as a liberator who enables them to relate positively to their own bodies and to think in terms of being independent in their adult lives. Most girls who play with Barbie dolls own a number of them, and one-third of those girls maim and mutilate their Barbies. Over the years Mattell responded to criticisms of Barbie for being nothing but a sex icon by putting her in professional and athletic dress. Over time Barbie became, for example, an astronaut and a soccer player. Black Barbies and Latina Barbies have been marketed by Mattell, although they have the Anglo-European features of the original Barbie, with darker skin.

Barbie was—and is—very thin, with a look that could be described as anorexic. Anorexia nervosa is the illness caused by dieting to the point that the starvation response of the human body takes over and the individual can no longer eat. It has become epidemic among girls over the past decades. Marilyn Monroe was heavier than Barbie, and by today's standards Monroe looks overweight. Yet in this characteristic, as in others, Barbie pointed the way to the future. Whether or not girls destroyed Barbie or felt liberated by her, she still remained sexualized, Anglo-European, and very thin.

FEMINISM IN THE 1950S

In their study of feminism in the 1950s, sociologists Arnold Green and Eleanor Molnick reported that they encountered few feminists. Those they met felt that it was futile to issue manifestos or form organizations because the majority of Americans had become conservative and conformist.[4] Bold statements did appear. Simone de Beauvoir's *The Second Sex,* with its message that inferiority had been enforced on women throughout history, was published in the United States in 1952. More typical of the feminism of the decade, however, was Mirra Komarovsky's stated purpose for writing *Women in the Modern World* (1953): she wanted to show women how to steer a course between feminism and antifeminism.

This climate produced a call to raise the status of the housewife. Even conservative analysts were aware that many women were discontented at home. The solution of the traditionalists was that women should be educated to find satisfaction in domesticity. "Many a girl marries unprepared either intellectually or psychologically for the lifetime job she is undertaking," wrote a supporter of training programs for future wives.[5] Journalist Agnes Meyer revived the idea of women's superior morality that had dominated the rhetoric of women's rights leaders in the first decades of the twentieth century and had appeared in the writing of Eleanor Roosevelt in the 1930s. Meyer chided women for not organizing on their own behalf. But she wanted women to organize to raise the status of the housewife, not to advance women's rights.[6]

The older women's organizations continued their activities, but many declined in strength. The Women's Joint Congressional Committee, for example, came to serve as an information clearinghouse for liberal organizations, rather than a lobbying group for women's issues before Congress. The Consumers' League was rarely heard from, and the Women's Trade Union League disbanded in 1947. Even the Lucy Stone League, founded in 1921 to encourage women to use their maiden names after marriage, had little impact in the 1950s. "The present young generation is not interested," wrote a leader of the organization.[7]

Disagreement over the Equal Rights Amendment (ERA) continued to hamper united efforts among the women's organizations. The Woman's Party and the National Federation of Women's Clubs supported the amendment, but the League of Women Voters, the Women's Bureau of the Department of Labor, and many women in the labor movement still considered it against the interests of working women. In 1950 and in 1953 the Senate passed the ERA. In both years, however, a coalition of forty-three national organizations, known as the Committee to Defeat the Unequal Rights Amendment, successfully lobbied to attach to the bill riders that exempted state protective laws for working women. The major women's organizations were instrumental in the passage in many states of equal-pay legislation for women doing the same jobs as men. Although the Fair Labor Standards Act of 1938 had established the principal of equal pay, the government and the courts had not applied it consistently.

Women's organizations encountered other difficulties in the 1950s. Anticommunist committees at the state and local levels often investigated liberal organizations and leaders, including women's organizations and their leaders. Even members of the moderate American Association of University Women (AAUW) were brought before such committees. Given this situation, the leaders of most women's organizations hesitated to take controversial stands or to form coalitions with other women's organizations. And there was the mainstream conviction that women ought to stay at home to take care of their families and to raise their children. It was a stance that many members of the women's organizations supported.

Moreover, given the strength of the movement for racial equality in this era, women's organizations were faced with demands that they open their membership to black women. Most did so, but the process often split local chapters. Meetings of organizations like the League of Women Voters functioned as social events as well as policy-making sessions, and some members who were willing to work on public issues with blacks didn't want to interact with them on a more personal level.

The YWCA was in the vanguard among women's groups in integrating its membership and forming interracial coalitions. In 1946 local YWCAs had a combined membership of over 450,000, and by the 1950s they had achieved a significant degree of racial integration. Through speakers and educational forums, they supported the Civil Rights movement and attempted to combat racism. In 1940 three-fourths of all colleges and universities had YWCA chapters. Campus YWCAs mentored and encouraged student activists, both black and white. In 1967, Helen Wilkins Claytor became the first African American president of the YWCA.

Meanwhile, African American women's organizations remained active in seeking rights for blacks. The National Council of Negro Women had over four million members in state and local chapters in the 1950s. By the 1960s it had put into place a range of programs throughout the South. It would be a strong force behind the civil rights movements of the 1950s and the 1960s.

And by 1960, leaders in the mainstream women's organizations, backed by Eleanor Roosevelt, would pressure President John F. Kennedy to appoint a commission to study the status of women. Along with women in the civil rights movement, they would thereby play a role in generating the second wave feminism of the 1960s.

NEW ECONOMIC, DEMOGRAPHIC, AND MEDICAL FACTORS

At the same time that militant feminism was in decline and traditional attitudes prevailed among middle-class Americans, more and more women were entering the workforce. The expanding American economy in the 1950s was capable of absorbing increasing numbers of female workers, largely into low-paying work. In addition, by the 1950s changing patterns in the lives of American women made work outside the home increasingly possible for them. In 1900, the average woman married at twenty-two and had her last child at thirty-two. With a life expectancy of fifty-one years, it was probable that childrearing would take up most of her adult life. By 1950, however, the average woman married at twenty, bore her last child at twenty-six, and had a life expectancy of sixty-five years. Even if she remained at home until her children were grown, she still had at least twenty years of life at home without children. For many women, the alternative was to go to work for remuneration outside the home. The employment figures of married women increasingly reflected this demographic situation. The proportion of married women employed outside the home was about 15 percent in 1940, about 30 percent in 1960, and over 50 percent in 1968.

Medical science was also helping women gain more control over their lives. By 1960, with the marketing of the oral contraceptive for women, birth-control technology made an epic advance. A relatively inexpensive and almost foolproof method of contraception was now available to women, and its popularity was attested to by the sizable numbers of women who began to use it. Women who chose to use the pill finally were free to have sexual intercourse without fear of pregnancy, and they could plan when to have children. The advent of the pill would also contribute to the emergence of the sexual revolution of the 1960s. (Later studies demonstrated a potential danger from cancer in the use of this early pill, composed heavily of the hormone estrogen.)

During the 1950s, it was evident that the experience of the Depression and World War II, with increasing numbers of married women entering the workforce, had eroded the older consensus among Americans that married women shouldn't work outside the home. Marriage rates among professional women also began to rise substantially. In 1940 26 percent of all professional women were married; in 1960, among a sampling of fifty thousand professional women, 45 percent were married. Most significant was the increasing percentage of working mothers with dependent children. In the mid-1950s 25 percent of all women with young children had jobs; by 1969 this statistic had risen to 40 percent. Moreover, between 1960 and 1969, the category of workers that increased most rapidly was that of mothers with preschool children. By 1969 33 percent of these women were employed outside the home.

In a survey of 489 nonfiction articles in eight popular magazines for women, including several for African American women, historian Joanne Meyerowitz found that the domestic ideal existed along with an ideal of individual achievement for women that celebrated public activity and work. The articles Meyerowitz examined often-celebrated individual women. These women included Dorothy McCulloch Lee, mayor of Portland, Oregon, who successfully crusaded against organized gambling and prostitution in her city. Over one-third of the articles on individual women featured unmarried women, divorced women, and women of unmentioned marital status. These articles also defended employment outside the home for women, although the consensus was that women with young children should not enter the workforce. Meyerowitz, however, did not examine the advertisements in the magazines she analyzed. Thus she overlooked their message extolling beauty and fashion and celebrating women as domestic beings in order to sell cosmetics, clothes, and household products and to turn women into model consumers.

THE NEW TRENDS AND THE PERSISTENCE OF DISCRIMINATION

Despite women's increased participation in the workforce, many of the old discriminations against them still existed. In employment pages of the newspapers, separate pages were devoted to jobs for men and jobs for women. Women did not move into higher-paying, skilled-labor or professional jobs after the war. Rather, they clustered in clerical labor. The small gains that women had made in the professions during the war were reversed in the 1950s. Moreover, inflationary cycles created instabilities in husbands' salaries and escalated the costs of such items as cars and college educations. As during the 1930s, many women worked to increase family income. They did not regard themselves as full-fledged members of the labor force, and they did not readily join unions. They accepted part-time work; as late as 1980 only 40 percent of working women were employed in full-time, year-round jobs.

In the mid-1950s tranquilizers were developed in response to what doctors diagnosed as an epidemic of discontent among housewives. Rarely prescribed in 1955, their usage soared to 1.15 million pounds in 1959. By 1960 women's magazines were publishing articles on "The Trapped Housewife." In her 1963 polemic, *The Feminine Mystique,* Betty Friedan called women's discontent as homemakers, "the problem that has no name." Friedan's work would be a major catalyst for second-wave feminism. Until the advent of that movement, however, there was little attempt to raise the issue of women's oppression. It would take the efforts of second-wave feminists to give a name to the problems women were experiencing by having rushed into domesticity without considering its drawbacks.

CONFORMITY AND MALE DISCONTENT

Men as well as women experienced discontent in the 1950s. Their disaffection was especially an outgrowth of the growing size and control of corporations over the economy and the workforce. More and more men worked in large business bureaucracies in which they were molded into a similar image. Between 1940 and 1960 the total percent of the labor force classified as self-employed dropped from 26 percent to 11 percent, and by the late 1950s the top 5 percent of corporations received 88 percent of all corporate income. "The man in the gray flannel suit" became the symbol for what was seen as a new and deadening conformity. Given male discontent, it is perhaps not surprising that eight of the ten top shows on television in 1959 were Westerns, drawing on the old mythology of the powerful lone gunman taming the West.

Yet there was a countertrend toward family "togetherness," in line with the new emphasis on the suburban home. Many commentators noted that fathers were more involved than ever before in diapering babies, feeding them bottles, and spending time with children in general. Gasoline-powered machines for mowing lawns became a major consumption item, as did work benches with tools, along with other products that were marketed as "hobbies" for men. In line with the appeal of the outdoors and the West, barbecuing food outdoors on grills became popular, and men took over grilling the meat that was served.

Despite the evidence of fathers' increased participation in the home, many experts contended that the old divisions in male and female behaviors in the home remained in place. "Wives still have the main responsibility for the home," wrote sociologist David Reisman, with "the husband playing the part of a volunteer aide."[8] Still, by 1957 the birth rate began to decline, and that was an indication of the waning of 1950s traditionalism, at least in the lives of women.

THE YOUTH REBELLION

The consumption ethic of the 1950s affected adolescents as well as their parents. Factory and sales jobs were plentiful, and babysitting provided part-time work for the young. Teenagers were a lucrative market of consumers.

Adolescent girls seemed obsessed with clothes, cosmetics, and boys, while adolescent boys seemed fixated on their cars, which they turned into hot rods and drag racers. In many cities and towns, cruising along streets in the evening became popular, and drag races were held on deserted thorough-fares. Teenagers identified themselves through their music, and by the late 1950s they were spending $50 million on records every year.

Youth alienation had been evident in the 1940s, and it continued in the 1950s. It was apparent in the popularity of male movie stars like James Dean and Marlon Brando. It was also evident in the beat poets, who gained national attention in 1956 with the publication of Allen Ginsburg's poem "Howl." The poem is a diatribe against American capitalism and its mate-rialist consumer culture. It brought a charge of obscenity against Ginsburg and a subsequent trial that he won. The beat poets were colorful and the-atrical in person. Identified with the bohemias of Greenwich Village in New York City and North Beach in San Francisco, the beats were a me-dia sensation. They were also apolitical nihilists with an American sense of adventure as well as aesthetes fascinated by quietist Eastern religions. The anticommunists left them alone.

Novelist Jack Kerouac, who wrote the best-known beat novel, *On the Road,* coined the word "beat." He took it from beatitude, as in Eastern re-ligion. It also referred to the "beat" of a musical line, especially the "off-beat" style of jazz, as well as the phrase "I'm beat"—or worn out. The beat poets were womanizers, and they were sometimes misogynist. Ginsburg was gay. Most of them married, but they had difficulty with commitment and the marriages didn't last. Yet they lived an independent lifestyle, and young women as well as young men identified with it. Rock star Janis Joplin, for example, spent years moving from place to place, imitating Jack Kerouac, who rarely stayed in one location for long.

Then there was Elvis Presley, with his swiveling, eroticized, and femi-nized hip movements, his feminine face and strong, masculine body, and his tight-fitting clothes. Presley first came to national attention in 1955. He patterned his look on Brando and Dean. He sang rock 'n' roll with the verve of an African American at a time when whites didn't buy records cut by blacks. He brought the raucous beat of rock 'n' roll and the haunting rhythm of the blues into the mainstream, while he sang ballads and coun-try music with a sweet, driving spirituality. (Disc jockey Alan Freed coined the term rock 'n' roll; it was a ghetto euphemism for both dancing and sex.)

Teenage girls, who swooned at Elvis's performances, were his major fans. Rock 'n' roll stars were almost all male, and icons like Presley allowed young women to express their sexuality without having to act on it. They could be sexualized, but remain virgins. Eventually sex groupies would appear among them who coveted sleeping with the male rock stars, but that would happen after the sexual rebellion of the 1960s changed the behavior of the young.

The late 1950s and early 1960s also witnessed the popularity of "girl groups," who sang in high voices to a soft rock beat. They were mostly African American, composed of three to four individuals. The young women in the groups looked alike, moved alike, and dressed alike in elegant 1950s styles and beehive hairdos. Their songs were about love and longing, but they expressed the emotions in terms of both conformity and rebellion against romantic conventions that kept women in a subordinate position, always searching for a true love and catering to men. The Shirelles and the Supremes were their most famous representatives. They represented a breakthrough for black women in mainstream music, while they challenged Elvis for popularity, furthered women's rebellion, and honored traditional styles of femininity.

By the late 1950s rebellious young people copied the beats in wearing black clothing, especially black turtleneck sweaters and tights. Beards and long hair for men and long, straight hair for women also came into vogue among them. They went to coffeehouses, where they listened to jazz and poetry. They called themselves "beatniks" and considered dropping out of the mainstream. They also paid attention to the new movements for change in American society, especially the black rebellion that was erupting in the South.

THE CIVIL RIGHTS MOVEMENT

The civil rights movement appeared on the national scene following the 1954 Supreme Court decision in *Brown v. Board of Education of Topeka, Kansas,* which ended racial segregation in the nation's public schools. It gained even more attention through the Montgomery, Alabama, bus boycott of 1955–56, which ended segregation on the city's buses. With the huge protest marches in Montgomery, the nation seemed to be on the verge of a major movement of social reform. Such movements had appeared in the 1900s and the 1930s, and another one of major proportions was soon to appear.

The Montgomery bus boycott began when an African American woman, Rosa Parks, refused to give up her seat on a bus to a white man, as the law required. Parks was a respected leader in the black community and a secretary of the state NAACP. She was arrested and brought to trial. Her gesture provided the test case in court for which the NAACP had long been looking to challenge the Jim Crow laws in the South. Following this incident, black leaders in Montgomery called for a boycott of buses and of white businesses in the city to protest racial segregation. The action was led by Jo Anne Robinson, a professor of English at Alabama State College and the Women's Political Council, the most active African American group in

Montgomery. Martin Luther King Jr., a Baptist minister, emerged as a major black leader during this boycott. The boycott succeeded when the Supreme Court declared against the Montgomery bus segregation law.

In 1960 African American youth in the South began to spearhead the civil rights movement. Four black male college students in Greensboro, North Carolina, refused to leave the all-white lunch counter at the local Woolworth Department Store when the manager asked them to. They inaugurated the "sit-in" movement. College sit-ins swept the South to desegregate lunch counters in drug and variety stores. Also in 1960 Ella Baker, a leader in the national NAACP, was instrumental in founding the Student Nonviolent Coordinating Committee (SNCC). Its emphasis on grassroots organizing and decision making by consensus brought young women into the civil rights movement. It also later influenced the strategy of the second-wave feminist movement in organizing and decision making. Marches, protests, and freedom rides followed the sit-ins, as well as spontaneous demonstrations and actions throughout the South. In the freedom rides black and white protesters organized by the Congress of Racial Equality (CORE) rode together in interstate buses to challenge the segregation of blacks and whites into separate sections on those buses. A massive protest at the Lincoln Memorial in Washington, D.C., in the spring of 1963 and the assassination of President Kennedy that fall also advanced the cause.

In 1964 the civil rights movement scored a major success with the passage by Congress of a comprehensive civil rights act. Under the terms of the Civil Rights Act of 1964, segregation was outlawed in businesses, municipal places, and public accommodations. The act also banned discriminatory practices in employment. To enforce the latter provision, the Equal Employment Opportunity Commission was established, with the power to adjudicate individual cases filed with it and to assess damages in those cases. Moreover, the law could be interpreted to endorse the principle of affirmative action, enunciated by presidents Kennedy and Johnson, under which government contractors and businesses dealing with the government had to give preference to minority applicants when hiring. Most important for women, Title VII of the Civil Rights Act extended the provisions of the act to women. Women in Congress lobbied hard for this measure, but a conservative Southern member of the House of Representatives introduced Title VII not out of feminist conviction, but as a strategy designed to block passage of the entire bill. He reasoned that the men in Congress were so opposed to women's rights that they would vote down the entire civil rights bill rather than pass the amendment. His plan backfired, and the amendment passed together with the bill.

The civil rights protests in the South culminated in the Freedom Summer of 1964, when hundreds of white college students from the North came to Mississippi to work along with African Americans in a voter registration drive among blacks that challenged white supremacist practices in Mississippi in refusing to allow blacks to register to vote. In 1965, partly as a result of the Mississippi Freedom Summer, Congress passed the Voting Rights Act of 1965, which prohibited public discrimination in voting practices.

The Civil Rights movement inspired some of its women participants to found a new women's rights movement. Sometimes male leaders of the groups working in the South relegated women colleagues to housekeeping and clerical chores and expected sexual favors from them. Subjected to such discrimination, some women working for civil rights transferred their allegiance toward founding groups that would advance the women's cause. Moreover, young women activists in the civil rights movement, whether black or white, often were deeply impressed by local black women in the South, often older, who were leaders in their churches and women's clubs. "In every southwest Georgia county," wrote one activist, "there is always a 'Mama.' She is usually a militant woman in her community, willing to catch hell, having already caught her share." These older black women became role models for the younger women. Interacting with them, some women in the civil rights movement were motivated to turn to feminism, once the goals of the movement in the South to overturn segregation in that region were on the road to being accomplished.

NOTES

1. Lizabeth Cohen, *A Consumers' Republic: The Politics of Mass Consumption in Postwar America* (New York: Knopf, 2003).

2. Stephanie Coontz, *The Way We Never Were: American Families and the Nostalgia Trap* (New York: Basic, 1992), p. 28.

3. Shirley Polykoff, *Does She . . . Or Doesn't She? And How She Did It* (Garden City, New York: Doubleday, 1975).

4. Arnold W. Green and Eleanor Melnick, "What Has Happened to the Feminist Movement," in Alvin W. Gouldner, ed., *Studies in Leadership: Leadership and Democratic Action* (New York: Russell & Russell, 1950), pp. 277–302.

5. Helen Sherman and Marjorie Coe, *The Challenge of Being a Woman: Understanding Ourselves and Our Children* (New York: Harper & Row, 1955), p. 17.

6. Agnes Meyer, "Women Aren't Men," *Atlantic Monthly* 66 (Aug. 1950): 33.

7. Doris E. Fleishman, "Notes of a Retiring Feminist," *American Mercury* 68 (Feb. 1949): 161–68.

8. David Reisman, "Two Generations," in Robert J. Lifton, ed., *The Woman in America* (Boston: Houghton-Mifflin, 1965), pp. 72–97.

6

Progress and Backlash

The 1960s and 1970s

The 1960s and 1970s were decades of rebellion. The Civil Rights movement reached a high point with the Civil Rights Act of 1964, and the student movement emerged full blown that year to demand an end to U.S. involvement in the Vietnam War. In 1966 the National Organization for Women (NOW) was founded. It signaled the emergence of the feminist movement to national prominence.

By the end of the 1960s the women's movement gained a mass following, and many new women's organizations were founded. Not since the Progressive Era of the early twentieth century had so large a protest movement on behalf of women's rights been seen in the United States. To its participants, it felt as though a wave had washed over them, carrying them in its wake. To describe their efforts, they took over the word "feminism," used episodically since 1920. Eventually the new term "second-wave" was added to the description, to separate the movement of the 1960s from that of the early twentieth century while still connecting the two movements together. And in the militant climate of the 1960s and 1970s, the women's

Opposite, from top: Coretta Scott King and National Women's Congress delegates; Patricia Ireland, president of NOW

movement was joined by equal rights movements on the part of Native Americans, people of color, and homosexuals.

A resurgent antifeminism, however, appeared in the 1960s, and it grew stronger over the next decades. The antifeminist movement in general was spearheaded by a conservative "New Right," rooted in religious fundamentalism. The "new right" was in evidence as early as 1960 when college students on a number of campuses founded Young Americans for Freedom (YAF), the same year that SDS was founded. YAF supported the Vietnam War, extolled capitalism, and opposed the social programs of the left. The situation resembled the 1920s, when gaining the vote for women had produced resistance to further change. By 1979 the media was declaring the women's movement dead and calling feminists "bra burners" and man-hating lesbians. In the meantime, youth cultures became more alienated and more outrageous, as they produced disco and punk and moved toward a postfeminist and postmodernist stance.

Following the passage of the Immigration Act of 1965, a "new immigration" from Asia, Latin America, and the Middle East occurred during the late 1960s and after. This movement of people to the United States had a major impact on the history of women, for two-thirds of these immigrants were women and children. The mainstream feminist movement of this era didn't deal directly with the new immigrants, but these new ethnic groups added a new element to the fabric of American society.

NEW FACES AND NEW MUSIC

The issue of women's rights was present at the meetings of Kennedy's Commission on the Status of Women, although in a moderate form. It was raised in the Civil Rights movement strongly during the Freedom Summer of 1964 in Mississippi. It surfaced in the student movement in the free speech agitation that fall among the "New Left" at the University of California at Berkeley, when radicals protested against the university policy of prohibiting them to hold rallies in a park adjacent to the university campus. That same year the United States sent military forces to Vietnam. The student antiwar movement erupted in 1965 when President Lyndon Johnson ordered the bombing of North Vietnam. The feminist movement would emerge partly out of these organizations and actions. Moreover, a number of the student radicals were the children of individuals who had been communists during the 1930s. This group would also be represented in the radical feminist movement. They have come to be called "red-diaper" babies.

By the mid-1960s the Civil Rights movement had shifted its attention from the South to the North. In the North they focused on organizing the poor in urban ghettos as a political force. In 1964 Lyndon Johnson had declared a "War on Poverty" to alleviate the growing disparities in wealth between the wealthy and the poor. A provision of the Economic Opportunity Act of 1964 encouraged community organizing in urban ghettos. In doing such organizing in the North, women encountered a number of sexist male coworkers and powerful local women of color, just as they had in the Civil Rights movement in the South. They were again drawn to feminism.

By then new movements in the music and mood of youth were appearing. They underscored the growth of feminist militancy and added to the feminist resolve to work for women's rights. Folk music, which had drawn a devoted constituency since the 1930s from radicals and union organizers, gained a national following with the appearance of new young artists like Bob Dylan and Joan Baez. It became the signature music of the Civil Rights and student movements. Rock music gained momentum when the Liverpool Beatles, with their long hair and sideburns, were a sensation in their tour of the United States in 1964. By 1965 the Rolling Stones and the loud cacophony of acid rock had traveled across the ocean from England to the United States.

By that point, aggressively male rock stars, such as the members of the bands called the Rolling Stones and Steppenwolf, smashed their guitars and strutted and stomped on stage. They indicated that men who were cultural rebels could be as violent and as antiwoman as any males in mainstream society. They also manifested a continuing tension in popular culture between men and women and between machismo, femininity, and feminism. That tension had begun with Elvis Presley and the girl groups, and it would continue to the present.

HIPPIES AND "SWINGING SINGLES"

By the early 1960s the beatniks had turned into hippies, who practiced free love and took drugs. Young people from across the nation flocked to Haight-Ashbury in San Francisco, a low-rent interracial area, where they lived in communal "crash pads," smoked marijuana and took LSD, baked their own bread, and wore Buddhist robes, military surplus uniforms, tie-dyed shirts, Native American headbands, and strings of beads. They were at the vanguard of a new "counterculture" that preached sexual liberalization and rejected the conservatism of the 1950s. The counterculture also generated sexual experimentation, including the practice of couples living together before marriage, which was forbidden behavior among the middle class in

© UPI /Bettman /Corbis

Civil Rights. In Montgomery, Alabama, in 1955, Rosa Parks refused to give up her seat on a bus to a white man. Her legendary action violated the strict Alabama segregation laws and launched the Montgomery bus boycott, one of the opening militant, nonviolent campaigns of the Civil Rights movement of the 1950s and 1960s.

the 1950s. They also occasionally formed clubs for group sex. Another sexual revolution, like the one in the 1920s, was occurring.

By the mid–1960s even unmarried members of the middle class became "swinging singles" by going to singles bars and putting personal ads in the newspapers to meet partners. Helen Gurley Brown predicted the advent of the new sexual mood in her *Sex and the Single Girl* (1962), published a year before Betty Friedan's feminist manifesto, *The Feminine Mystique*. Brown called for young women to have careers, to be adventurous and daring, to take their sexual lives into their own hands, and to use every possible commercial product to make themselves attractive to men. Meanwhile, reflecting both cultural rebellion and the new sexuality, women's skirts were

© FDR Library

Commission on the Status of Women. Eleanor Roosevelt with John F. Kennedy, who appointed her to chair the Commission on the Status of Women, which he created in 1960. The report of the commission was important in launching the women's rights movement of the 1960s and 1970s.

shortened each year, until the hemline was well above the knee. Thus the "miniskirt" came into being. At the same time, long pants, previously considered too masculine for women to wear except in casual situations (or at work during World War II), became an acceptable fashion for women at all times.

THE FORMATION OF NOW

The National Organization of Women was an indirect outgrowth of these developments in radical politics and cultural representations, but its direct antecedent lay in the state commissions on the status of women that had been established after the formation of the federal commission in 1960. In order that each commission could learn what the others were doing and could share ideas, a national conference of the state commissions was held each year, beginning in 1963. In 1966 the Third National Conference of the State Commissions on Women met in Washington, D.C.

The mood among the delegates at that meeting was angry. Most felt that the government was not meeting its obligation to implement the recommendations of the initial report of the federal commission and that federal administrators were not enforcing the existing laws guaranteeing women equality, such as the Equal Pay Act and Title VII of the Civil Rights Act. Meanwhile, women who served on federal agencies concerned with women had communicated the government's failings to, among others, Betty Friedan, who was present at the conference. The consensus among these women was that a new organization was needed to pressure the government on behalf of women the way civil rights organizations, such as the NAACP, had pressured it on behalf of African Americans. From their point of view, older women's organizations, such as the League of Women Voters, were neither sufficiently forceful nor sufficiently progressive on women's issues.

These forces came to a head in a meeting of key legislators and leaders at the conference in Friedan's hotel room, where plans were formulated for the National Organization for Women (NOW). Events seemed to bear out Friedan's judgment that "the absolute necessity for a civil rights movement for women had reached such a point of subterranean explosive urgency by 1966 that it took only a few of us to get together to unite the spark and it spread like a nuclear chain reaction."[1] With the formation of NOW, the new feminism had its official, national birth, and it quickly spread throughout the nation.

THE FEMINIST MOVEMENT
AFTER NOW

Once NOW was founded, other organizations appeared. In 1968 academic and professional women formed the Women's Equity Action League (WEAL) to end sex discrimination in employment and education. The National Abortion Rights Action League (NARAL) was founded in 1969 as the National Association for the Repeal of the Abortion Laws. The name was changed to NARAL in 1973. The Women's Political Caucus was founded in 1971 as a bipartisan group to pressure political parties to support women for office. Job counseling agencies for women, such as Catalyst in New York City, appeared. Courses on women in every field were added to the college curriculum. By the spring of 1972 over six hundred were being offered at colleges and universities throughout the nation. Multidisciplinary women's studies programs were also soon established.

In 1974 clerical workers in Chicago, in their organization Women Employed, and in Boston, in 9 to 5, organized the workplace as a community. They drew on techniques of radical civil rights activists to involve every worker in decision making and in insurgency. Female leaders in the regular unions, often marginalized in the male-dominated AFL-CIO, met through working in NOW and WEAL. The Women's Bureau in Washington, D.C., brought them together for discussions. These discussions resulted in the founding of the Congress of Labor Union Women (CLUW) in 1974. It became a support group for women as well as a training ground for leadership for them. In the 1960s unions in general secured major gains for their members. They were responsible for more than tripling weekly earnings in manufacturing between 1945 and 1970, despite measures such as the Taft-Hartley Act of 1947 that made union organizing difficult. Still two-thirds of American workers remained outside of unions, especially the workers in service jobs and those who were employed part time.

The older women's organizations continued, including the American Association of University Women, the League of Women Voters, and the National Organization of Business and Professional Women. Some increased in membership. This growth resulted partly from the sizable increase in women graduating from college, which had increased in the 1960s after the downward spiral of female college enrollments in the 1950s. Fifteen percent of American women aged eighteen to twenty-four graduated from college in 1950; 25 percent in 1970; and 50 percent in 1980. To appeal to younger women, the older organizations reoriented their programs, sometimes adopting the strategies of lobbying and demonstrations of the new women's organizations.

Throughout the nation, women marched for the repeal of the laws against abortion. In Atlantic City, New Jersey, in 1968 feminists did a "street theater" performance outside the hall in which the Miss America Pageant was held. In their event, staged for the media as well as for participants in the contest and their audience, the feminist women threw artifacts of women's beauty culture that they saw as oppressive—bras, makeup, hair curlers—into a trash can. (The later charge that feminism involved "bra burning" was based on that one event; participant statements differ over whether or not anything was set on fire.) In New York City in 1970 feminists picketed the *Ladies' Home Journal* offices protesting against employment discrimination in the journal's staff and its perpetuation of a traditional image of women in the journal. Feminists throughout the nation began holding small-group sessions, modeled on psychiatric group therapy and the small-group meetings for criticism and encouragement of individuals that communists traditionally held. In feminist "consciousness-raising sessions" women discussed the oppression they encountered in their lives and the relevance of feminism to them. These sessions resembled those of Heterodoxy, the major women's organization in Greenwich Village in the 1920s. They inspired the women who participated in them both to participate in the feminist movement and to establish feminist organizations in their communities.

From 1969 on, many feminist exposés were published. Kate Millett's *Sexual Politics* (1969) became a best seller. It was followed by Shulamith Firestone's *The Dialectic of Sex* (1970), Robin Morgan's *Sisterhood is Powerful* (1970), and Germaine Greer's *The Female Eunuch* (1971). Feminist poetry, novels, and memoirs appeared, beginning in 1973 with Erica Jong's *Fear of Flying* and Sylvia Plath's *The Bell Jar*. Liberation movements have an inspirational quality that often provides rich soil for the nurturing of individual talent. Thus second-wave feminism, like many other revolutionary movements, produced novelists, poets, and philosophers.

Other factors in the late 1960s contributed to the growth of feminism. Increasing militancy in the Civil Rights movement prompted a number of African American organizations to expel white members, thus releasing women to take up other causes. The antiwar protest began to focus on protesting the draft, an issue that didn't directly affect women because they were not subject to conscription. Again, women were drawn to different reform endeavors. With the outbreak of riots in the black ghettos and the increasing violence of the Vietnam War, male radicals began to resemble African American militants in adopting violent rhetoric and a "macho" style, which many women didn't like. At the same time, the radicalism of the 1960s had always included the search for individual fulfillment—through sex, drugs, communal living, and mystical religions. By the late 1960s these strains began to influence all the radical politics of the age, including feminism. "Look to your own oppression" and "the personal is political" became important slogans of the radical left. Internalizing these slogans, many women turned to feminism as their primary political commitment.

DISCRIMINATION AGAINST WOMEN

Feminist scholars in the 1960s and 1970s scoured the past and the present to document the existence of unheeded, but nonetheless real, discrimination against women in all areas of American life. Their conclusions provided another motivation for women to join the feminist movement. In politics, women's participation had been low over the course of the twentieth century. Between 1920 and 1970, only ten women served in the Senate and sixty-five women in the House of Representatives. Most of these women were widows of senators and congressmen. Since 1920 two women had served in presidential cabinets. Frances Perkins had been FDR's Secretary of Labor, and Oveta Culp Hobby had been Eisenhower's Secretary of Health, Education and Welfare from 1953 to 1955. Neither John Kennedy nor Lyndon Johnson appointed a woman to his cabinet. Between 1920 and 1970, three women had been governors, and one woman had served as a state attorney general. Three women had been lieutenant governors. At the state and local levels in 1969 only 4.5 percent of state-elected officials were women. In 1975 the proportion of women in municipal governments was 10 percent.

In employment, feminists also found inequality. In 1940 women held 45 percent of the professional positions in the nation. (This figure included the many women employed as schoolteachers.) In 1967 women held 37 percent of such positions. The percentage of women who were working as domestic servants decreased, as these women moved into clerical work. In the process they created a crisis for employed mothers, who had difficulty finding someone to watch their children while they were at work. All indexes showed that women earned less than men. In 1959 women's earnings were 66 percent of the earnings of men, and by 1968 their earnings were 58 percent of men's earnings. In 1970 the average female college graduate could expect to earn a smaller annual income than the average white male graduate of elementary school.

Poverty among women was on the increase. In 1959 women constituted 26 percent of the total poor, and in 1968 the figure was 41 percent. African American women in particular bore the brunt of poverty. Among families headed by African American women, 50 percent had an income below the poverty line, compared with 25 percent of families headed by white women, less than 25 percent of families headed by African American men, and 7 percent of families headed by white men. Finally, most alimony payments were small, and child support was often not paid. Most banks refused to lend money to women, who were also discriminated against in pension plans, insurance policies, and Social Security payments.

Gender inequity existed in education. The proportion of women to men in college dropped from 47 percent in 1920 to 35 percent in 1958. In 1930 two out of every five bachelor's and master's degrees and one out of every seven doctorate degrees were awarded to women. By 1962 these figures had dropped to one in three bachelor's degrees and one in ten doctorate degrees. Textbooks rarely mentioned women. In children's books, women were depicted in dependent roles, usually as wives or mothers, and powerful women were depicted as evil. Feminists coined the term "sex stereotyping" to characterize the gender traditionalism in this literature.

Hundreds of state laws were still on the books that excluded women from serving on juries and limited their rights to make contracts and to hold property. Prostitution was still thriving, and rape laws in many states made it nearly impossible to convict a rapist. A woman stood one chance in three of being sexually abused by the age of eighteen—usually by a male relative or a friend of the family. When a woman reached college age, the chances were one in five that she would be raped on a date. Nine female employees out of ten had been sexually harassed on the job, and wife battering was not infrequent. Women, however, made up a significant percentage of individuals who battered children.

SEXUALITY AND POWER; WOMEN'S BODIES

In addition to researching and analyzing data revealing discrimination against women, feminists also developed theoretical frameworks to explain women's position. Some feminists contended that female subordination and male power constituted a system of domination they called "patriarchy." They especially found it evident in the sexual objectification and victimization of women. These feminists argued that rape, prostitution, the double standard, pornography, and Freud's theories about women's sexuality were not isolated occurrences. Rather, they constituted a framework of oppression that kept women in their place. Radical feminists referred to the United States as a "rape" culture, and feminists in general began to demand not only economic and legal equality but also control over their own bodies.

That concern produced a variety of specialized organizations. These groups included not only the abortion rights organization but also organizations devoted to women's health issues, such as the Boston Women's Health Collective, which published the best-selling *Our Bodies/Our Selves*. By 1973 over a thousand women's health projects were trying to change sexist medical practices, under which some male doctors treated their female patients like children and didn't pay sufficient attention to their complaints. Shelters for battered wives were founded, and by the late 1970s the phrase "battered women" had entered the language. Feminists held "Take Back the Night Marches" to draw attention to high rates of rape and to agitate for changes in the rape laws that were prejudicial to victims. Rape hotlines, to provide counseling to victims of the crime, were established.

In the late 1970s African American women filed the first cases with the EEOC claiming that the demands for sexual favors in the workplace that they had experienced constituted discrimination under the terms of Title VII of the 1964 Civil Rights Act. Feminists in Ithaca, New York, coined the term "sexual harassment." As a byproduct of the rape movement, an Alliance Against Sexual Coercion was formed in 1976. This group argued that sexual harassment was an attempt on the part of male employers and employees to maintain their accustomed power, as large numbers of women entered the workforce and threatened their authority. In 1980 the EEOC held that sex harassment was a violation of the 1964 Civil Rights Act. They defined sex harassment as including not only outright demands for sex but also innuendos and other sexual conduct that created a hostile work environment for female employees. (In 1986 the Supreme Court upheld the EEOC ruling.) Since 1980, about 4,500 sexual harassment claims have been filed with the EEOC annually, and court cases have been undertaken.

FEMINISM: CULTURAL IMPACTS

In addition to engaging in serious politics, feminists have had a playful, comedic side. Moreover, many feminist comics, singers, and actresses have gained widespread public popularity. Feminist stand-up comics made fun of female issues like menstruation. Helen Reddy became famous with her song "I Am Woman, Hear Me Roar." Holly Near wrote and recorded feminist folk songs, as did such groups as the African American Sweet Honey in the Rock. Rock 'n' roll performers were mostly male, but the raucous Janis Joplin rose to rock's highest ranks, until she died of a drug overdose in 1970.

By 1975 two dozen feminist presses and two hundred newsletters and journals had appeared. *Ms.* magazine, first published in 1972, was a mass-market glossy magazine designed to bring the feminist message to the general public. Its editors tried hard to avoid accepting advertisements that trivialized or objectified women. However, given the financial pressures of mass-market publishing, in which revenues from subscribers are rarely sufficient to pay for the costs of publishing a magazine, that decision proved impossible to maintain.

The title of the new magazine, *Ms.,* was taken from the new formal title for women, Ms., which had been devised to end categorizing women as a married Mrs. or a single Miss and to make their marital status as anonymous as that of men. Until the 1960s, in fact, middle-class married women were referred to by their husband's name, not by their own, as in Mrs. John Smith, rather than Mary Smith. In this case as in many others, feminism had broad impacts on language usage. In formal writing, the word "man" was replaced by neutral words, such as "humankind" for "mankind" and "chairperson" or "chair" for "chairman." The universal "he" to refer to both men and women was replaced by "one" or "they." Or "he" and "she" were used alternately when there were a number of references to men and women as a group in a paragraph. Words like "sexism" and "male chauvinism" were coined. Such usages have continued to the present.

Women's bookstores and banks were founded in the 1970s, and female artists painted feminist works. The most famous was Judy Chicago's "The Dinner Party," a sculptural piece that Chicago did in the late 1970s that was inspired by Leonardo da Vinci's famed "Last Supper" of Christ and his apostles. In da Vinci's work, Christ and his apostles sit around a table, but there aren't any human figures in Chicago's work. Occupying a large room, a large triangular table is set as though for a dinner party. It sits on a white ceramic tile floor. Ceramic dinner plates decorated with flowers and symbols that look like vaginal images sit on embroidered place mats on the table. Chicago designed the plates after the vaginal imagery in Georgia O'Keeffe's paintings. Each plate has a place card in front of it with the name of an important woman from history written on it, and each tile on the floor on which the table stands also has the name of an important woman from history written on it. Chicago oversaw a group of women who did the historical research to select the names. Other women did the weaving, potting, and embroidery—typical women's art—for the place mats, plates, and floor of "The Dinner Party," following Chicago's designs.

In addition to feminist novels, essays, and journals, strong-willed female characters appeared in general literature, even in mass-market books written by male authors like Irving Wallace. Women formed feminist theater troupes and made feminist movies. Female joggers ran the Boston and New

York City marathons. Working with international women's groups, female runners petitioned the Olympic Committee to rescind its stand that long-distance running was too arduous for women and to include a women's marathon event in the Olympics. In 1978 the astronaut program—a bastion of masculinity in its exploration of space and taming of technology—admitted the first group of women to be trained as astronauts. In 1983 astronaut Sally Ride became the first female crew member of a manned space flight. The holder of a Ph.D. in physics, Ride credited the women's movement with inspiring her career.

FEMINIST SPIRITUALITY

Feminist spirituality also was an important part of second-wave feminism. Women in Protestant denominations rewrote the official liturgies of their churches and were ordained as priests and ministers. Buddhism and Hinduism flourished on college campuses, and ashrams and monasteries appeared nationwide. Bat mitzvahs were held for Jewish girls of twelve and thirteen, to celebrate their maturation into women, as bar mitzvahs were held for Jewish boys. Like feminist scholars in the 1900s, feminist scholars in the 1970s searched the ancient past to find evidence of early goddess worship and matriarchal societies. Feminist spirituality groups were founded, and so were witches' covens. Gathering in small groups, feminist witches celebrated the earth and worked for spiritual ends. They also engaged in political activism. They wove a web of string around the Pentagon to protest war, and they established encampments at nuclear power facilities and testing areas, to protest the release of cancer-causing radiation into the air.

Hundreds of communes were founded in the early 1970s, to explore communal lifestyles that rejected the consumerism and materialism of regular society. Some communes practiced sexual freedom, while the inhabitants in others, more conventional, still lived in nuclear families, although they ate together and raised their children together. Some of the communes took up Eastern religions, as the beat poets had. The Lama Foundation, a commune located in the mountains outside of Taos, New Mexico, and still in existence today, became a world ecumenical center. It combined elements of Buddhism, Hinduism, and Sufism in its spiritual practice. Daily meditations were held, and spiritual dancing was practiced. Spiritual leaders from around the world came to teach their doctrines and practices in the summers.

MOVIES AND TELEVISION: A WASTELAND FOR WOMEN

During the 1960s and 1970s, the Hollywood response to feminism was mostly to ignore it. The most pervasive male image of the decade was James Bond, the suave English super spy who engages in stylized violence and whom women can't resist. Intensely racist, most Bond films in this period pitted whites against Asians, with beautiful Asian women especially treacherous sexual beings and antagonists. Clint Eastwood films were also very popular in these decades. Whether Eastwood played a Western gunman or an urban vigilante, he was a super male who killed without feeling and who cared for almost nothing. Along with Charles Bronson, another unemotional vigilante with a gun, Eastwood seemed to appeal to young working-class men who might be laid off from their jobs and to male students alienated from the established culture. Many "blaxploitation" films, featuring African Americans as adventure heroes, were also made in the 1970s. Characters like Shaft and Superfly were violent pimps, renegade cops, and drug dealers who sometimes functioned as Robin Hood figures helping their communities and sometimes as heroes of the underworld. African American Pam Grier, sometimes cast as a police officer, played a female version of these black male characters.

Films centering around male bonding also became a Hollywood staple in this period. The acclaimed 1969 films *Easy Rider* and *Urban Cowboy* showed the corruption and poverty that lie beneath the American dream, but they also glorified male friendship and depicted women as natural victims and sexual temptresses. In the 1970s a group of talented young male directors, including Francis Ford Coppola and Martin Scorsese, expressed their angst and their energy in powerful masculine dramas like the *Godfather* and *Raging Bull,* in which women were largely appendages to the men. Peter Biskind calls them the sex, drugs, and rock 'n' roll Hollywood generation. Hollywood was still an industry run by men. By the mid-1970s a few films that might be described as feminist were made. In *Alice Doesn't Live Here Any More* (1974) and *An Unmarried Woman* (1978), women go off on their own to find themselves, while *The Stepford Wives* (1975) depicts a group of young suburban women who are turned into mechanical dolls by their husbands, who want complete control over them.

The situation on television wasn't much better. The primary depiction of women in the 1960s was as housewives with superhuman powers who served their husbands and lovers, as in *I Dream of Jeannie,* in which the heroine is a beautiful genie confined to a bottle, and *Bewitched,* in which the young housewife heroine is a witch. In *That Girl,* however, Marlo Thomas pioneered in playing an actress who lived alone, although she yearned to be married. By the mid-1970s a greater range of occupational roles for women were shown, and some unmarried career women living alone were portrayed as happy. For the most part, however, men were dominant in interpersonal relations in television dramas and women were objectified even when they played policewomen and spies. In *Charlie's Angels,* for example, three undercover female agents posed as various personalities in tennis shorts and bikinis to solve crimes, showing off their bodies, while they were controlled by the mysterious Charlie, who never appeared in person but instructed them by phone.

MINORITY PROTEST

The Civil Rights movement and the student protest movement of the 1960s encouraged militancy among other minority groups, not just among women. These groups included Native Americans, Mexican Americans, and gays and lesbians. Women as well as men were involved in these movements; they both drew their energy and ideas from feminists and stimulated the growth of the women's movement.

Native Americans

The 1887 Dawes Severalty Act, which enforced a rigid Americanization on native tribes, had been modified under the New Deal to allow more communal ownership of land and the preservation of traditional Indian culture. The federal government, however, still held decision-making power over the Native Americans, and they often gave preference to Anglo-American interests over native ones with regard to tribal lands and rights. During the 1960s, numbers of young Native Americans moved to the cities, where they met with Native Americans from a variety of tribes. Overcoming the barriers of their separate cultures in a neutral setting, they began to form protest organizations and demonstrate for their rights. Among other demonstrations, they occupied Alcatraz in 1969, and in 1972 they went on a "Trail of Broken Treaties" March on Washington.

Native American women were less likely than other women of color to form groups separate from men, partly because women had long been leaders in many Native American tribes. Among Native American women, La Donna Harris, wife of Oklahoma Senator Fred Harris and Comanche by descent, was known for her participation in civil rights and feminist orga-

Seneca Falls Sit-In. Women sitting in at the Seneca Falls nuclear power plant. Such sit-ins, modeled after those pioneered in the labor movement in the 1930s and the Civil Rights and student movements of the 1960s, became popular among radical and spiritual feminists in the 1970s, to protest against the dangers of nuclear war and radiation fallout.

nizations. In the early 1970s, she founded the Americans for Indian Opportunity (AIO), which worked for more Native American input into the policies of federal agencies that oversaw Native American affairs. In 1975 radical Native American women in the American Indian Movement (AIM) formed the Women of All Red Nations (WARN).

Mexican Americans, Hispanics, and Latinos

Individuals of Mexican and Latin American descent, including women, also demonstrated militancy in this period. In 1962 the Mexican American United Farm Workers was formed. Led by César Chavéz, it gained attention for strikes against lettuce and grape growers in California and the formation of national consumer boycotts. It was the most successful agricultural union in the United States. Dolores Huerta, a divorced mother of seven children, and Helen Chavéz, wife of César Chavéz and mother of their eight children, were leaders in the union. Huerta, who cofounded the union with César and was its vice president, defied gender barriers to be-

ACT UP Members Arrested. Lesbian and gay members of ACT UP are confronted by the police. ACT UP, the AIDS Coalition to Unleash Power, was founded in New York City in 1987, and it is committed to direct action to implement medical advances and policy decisions to end AIDS in the United States.

come an organizer, challenging male control of the union. Helen Chavéz integrated family, work, and unionism, often picking crops to help support her family. Historians call this extension of family responsibilities into work and union organization "political familism." Both Huerta and Helen Chavéz drew on family networks for child care.

In 1972 the National Conference of Puerto Rican Women was founded, and in 1974 Mexican American women formed the Mexican American National Association (MANA). By 1990 MANA had members in thirty-six states. MANA's leaders testified before Congress and campaigned for issues ranging from the ERA to a family leave policy. Hispanic women established many local projects, such as the Hispanic Women's Health Center in Hartford, Connecticut, and the East Los Angeles Rape Crisis Center. In San Antonio, Texas, the women-led Communities Organized for Public Service, drawn from Catholic Church congregations, tackled problems ranging from poor schools to unpaved streets. It provided a model for many new female-led community organizations not only among Hispanics but also among African Americans and whites across the nation.

African Americans

Black women's organizations like the National Council of Negro Women and the National Association of Colored Women still worked for the rights of black women. New organizations led by younger women appeared. Many black women were initially involved with NOW, but the refusal of its white leaders to support Shirley Chisholm in her 1972 campaign for the presidency angered them. (Chisholm, who served in the House of Representatives between 1969 and 1983, was the first black woman elected to Congress.) In 1973 they founded the National Black Feminist Organization (NBFO). More radical African American women, who thought that the NBFO was too middle class, formed the short-lived, but powerful, Combahee River Collective. In 1977 the National Association of Black Professional Women and the National Coalition of 100 Black Women were established.

"Black Power" and "Black Is Beautiful" became slogans for African Americans in the 1960s and 1970s. Some black women joined the male-dominated Black Panthers, who employed a militant rhetoric of violence while organizing black communities and providing social services to them. Other women joined the Black Muslims, founded in the 1930s. They were attracted to it in the 1960s by its emphasis on the Muslim values of piety and family togetherness and by the appeal of its major leader in the 1960s, Malcolm X. Men were dominant in Black Muslim families, but women gained self-reliance through their authority in the home and in women's separate organizations.

Lesbians, Gays, and the Stonewall Riot

The Stonewall riot, which occurred in New York City in 1969, triggered activist protests among gays and lesbians. On June 28, police raided a gay bar in Greenwich Village called the Stonewall Inn. Such incidents had occurred for years, even though the owners of gay bars paid policemen not to raid them. This time, however, the police went ahead—and the patrons of the bar, including drag queens and a handful of butch lesbians, fought back. Rioting continued for two nights, with Puerto Rican transvestites and young street people leading charges against rows of uniformed police.

The Stonewall riot became a symbol of the oppression of gays and of their potential to resist. It began the "gay pride" movement. As was the case in many male immigrant cultures, bars were a central feature of gay culture. Lesbian bars also existed, and at some of them lesbians played masculine "butch" and feminine "femme" roles. Yet lesbians were present at Stonewall, and they would play a major role in the second-wave feminist movement.

LEGISLATIVE AND
LEGAL SUCCESSES

The government and the courts responded to women's demands. Once the Civil Rights Act of 1964 included women in its equal opportunity provisions, state and national equal-opportunity commissions pressed sex-discrimination suits filed by women. By 1971 the courts had awarded $30 million in back pay in these suits. In 1970 the Women's Equity Action League brought class-action suits against one hundred universities under an executive order that required federal contractors to file affirmative-action programs with federal investigators, committing themselves to schedules for ending sex discrimination. They mostly won their suits. Title IX of the Education Act of 1972 prohibited sex discrimination in colleges and universities. It led to the enforcement of equity in sports activities and a large expansion in the numbers of female college athletes. In states throughout the nation laws were changed to treat rape victims the same as victims of robbery and assault, with the exception that rape victims' names are generally kept private. Requirements for corroboration of the crime by a witness were dropped, and the examination in court of a victim's previous sex history was ended.

Under pressure from women's organizations, especially NARAL, many states repealed legislation prohibiting abortion. In 1973 the Supreme Court declared abortion to be a private decision between doctor and patient, thereby substantially liberalizing its availability to women (*Roe v. Wade*). In the spring of 1973 both the Senate and the House of Representatives passed the Equal Rights Amendment. By 1975 thirty-two of the required thirty-eight states had passed it. The future looked bright for women's advance.

THE FEMINIST MOVEMENT:
UNITED AND DIVIDED

By the mid-1970s feminism was a powerful force in the nation. Yet like many such powerful movements composed of various groups and individuals with differing interests, dissension appeared in its ranks. Differing feminist ideologies emerged, and lesbians and women of color developed their own agendas. Feminists disagreed over whether women were similar to or different from men. Pornography became a lightening rod in debates on the pleasures and dangers of women's sexuality. At times such disagreements seemed to point toward a healthy maturity for the women's movement. At other times the movement came close to splintering into a pastiche of differing interests.

Marriage and the Family;
"Equality" Versus "Difference" Feminists

By the mid-1970s, feminism had generated groups with differing approaches. Liberal feminists primarily focused on changes in laws, and Marxists focused on economics and wanted to end the class system. Radicals emphasized the physical oppression of women, and socialists attempted to reconcile radicals and Marxists into regarding women's oppression in terms of an interlocking system they called capitalist patriarchy. On questions of marriage and the family, additional divisions emerged. Radicals like Kate Millett argued that women could be free only when communal arrangements replaced traditional marriage and family life. Other feminists were hostile to men and argued that because of their history as oppressors, men should be subordinate to women. Some feminists espoused lesbianism as the most honest female behavior.

More moderate members of the movement shared some, but not all, of these radical sentiments. They were not antagonistic toward men. Indeed, NOW was called the National Organization "for" Women, not "of" women because men were involved in founding it, and they have always been welcomed as members. Moderate feminists (mostly liberal in persuasion) were opposed neither to marriage nor to communal living arrangements; they advocated individual choice in these matters. They did, however, support abortion as well as the establishment of day-care centers. A distaste for domesticity, seen as confining, pervaded their rhetoric, and the professional woman was their ideal. A differing theme in feminist writing focused on motherhood—both as a problem for women and as an enriching experience for them.

Feminist writings celebrating motherhood led to a split in the movement between "equality" feminists and "difference" feminists. Equality feminists saw no difference between men and women. Difference feminists, however, recast old arguments about women's moral superiority into a new structure under which women and men were once again seen as different. Echoing the older point of view, they wanted everyone, both males and females, to embrace the maternal values of gentleness, kindness, and sensitivity to others.

The Sex Wars

Feminists were united in campaigns against rape, wife battering, and sexual harassment. They disagreed, however, about pornography. Catharine MacKinnon, a law professor at the University of Michigan, and her Women Against Pornography connected pornography to rape and wanted it to be made illegal: in fact, they persuaded municipal governments in Minneapolis and Indianapolis to pass ordinances banning the showing or selling of por-

nography in their cities on the grounds that it victimized women. These ordinances, however, were later rescinded. MacKinnon and her group pointed
to the power of a multibillion-dollar international sex industry, controlled
by men. That industry included magazines like *Hustler,* a men's magazine
founded in the early 1960s by Larry Flynt that was even more sexually explicit than *Playboy.* The sex industry also included X-rated movies, massage
parlors, "gentlemen's clubs," and videos. Women Against Pornography contended that in hard-core porn, women are sex machines who cater to men.

MacKinnon's opponents regard the regulation of pornography as a free
speech issue, and they contended that pornography was protected by the
free speech protections of the First Amendment. They viewed it as a legitimate part of sexual pleasure for many individuals, including many feminists.
They pointed out that appealingly aesthetic erotic or lesbian images might
be banned in any sweep against images that were crass or exploitative. Most
drew the line at pedophilia, bestiality, and incest, but they believed that individuals should have the right to express themselves as they chose. Some
feminists who were critical of hard-core porn but were attracted to explicit
sexual imagery created "feminist" porn as a new form of female erotica.

The debates over sexuality and pornography became intense, especially
as some feminist sex radicals argued in favor of sadomasochism as an honest
and pleasurable form of sexual activity and saw "deviant" kinds of sexual
activity as a legitimate rebellion against restrictive middle-class norms. They
sometimes allied with younger feminists who saw liberation for women in
engaging in sexual behavior that matched the assertiveness of much male
sexual behavior.

Lesbians

In the 1970s lesbians emerged as a vanguard within the feminist movement.
They brought both authority and dissension to the feminist coalition. Betty
Friedan worried about alienating the mainstream through identifying feminism with lesbians, calling them a "lavender menace." In 1971, however,
the national convention of NOW voted to acknowledge the inherent feminism of lesbianism.

As the 1970s progressed, lesbians advanced their rights. The Stonewall
riot brought a new dynamism to lesbians as well as to gays, and the successes
of liberation movements in general in this era furthered this momentum.
Many cities passed gay rights bills. At the same time, however, factionalism
appeared within the lesbian movement—as it had within the feminist movement. The major division was between those who contended that lesbianism was biological and those who believed it was a matter of culture and
choice. In addition, some lesbians wanted to retain the older butch/femme
distinctions, while others wanted no gender distinctions in relationships.

Moreover, some older lesbians preferred to keep lesbian identities secret, while others (mostly younger) wanted disclosure.

Women of Color

Women of color added powerful voices as poets and novelists to second-wave feminism. African American writers Toni Morrison and Alice Walker, Asian American writers Amy Tan and Maxine Hong Kingston, and Hispanic writers Julia Alvarez and Sandra Cisneros won major literary prizes, while their books attracted many readers.

Yet women of color were often critical of Anglo-American feminists. They had a legacy of resentment against white women for patronizing them as domestic servants. By speaking for all women, white women made women of color feel invisible. Issues of poverty and welfare were often more important to them than professionalism or career advancement. They found the concept of "patriarchy" problematic, since men of color often seemed more victimized by poverty and racism than white women by sexism. They also differed on issues of sexual victimization. With regard to rape, they were not so willing to condemn men as perpetrators as white women were. White men had raped African American women for several centuries with impunity, but black men, unjustly accused of raping white women, had been lynched. For many black women sterilization abuse was more important than abortion.

Moreover, African American women did not easily condemn the nuclear family. In their culture families had been key to survival. They were outraged by attacks on the African American family as "matriarchal" and dysfunctional, stemming from the famed Moynihan report, *The Negro Family: The Case for National Action* (1965). This report was an agenda paper drafted by presidential staffer Daniel Moynihan for President Lyndon Johnson. It called for re-creating the male-headed family among blacks and enrolling black males in the military as a way of teaching them discipline to stop ghetto violence. Many women of color demanded the right to set their own priorities. Novelist Alice Walker wanted African American activists to be called "womanist" rather than "feminist."

Members of other ethnic groups joined in. In *This Bridge Called My Back: Writings by Radical Women of Color,* Cherríe Moraga wrote of her body as being thrown over a river of history to bridge the gap between women of color and white women, who refused to acknowledge their complicity as oppressors. A movement arose to abandon the term "minority women," with its pejorative connotation of second-class status, and to substitute the term "women of color" for it.

FEMINIST ACHIEVEMENTS AND THE HOUSTON NATIONAL WOMEN'S CONFERENCE

Passage of the ERA by Congress marked one milestone for women in the 1970s. Another was the 1977 Houston National Women's Conference. Composed of 1,800 delegates elected by fifty-six state and territorial public meetings, it was funded by the government under an act mandating the final conference "to identify the final barriers that prevent women from participating fully and freely in all aspects of national life." Women of all races and walks of life were delegates: women of color comprised one-third of the delegates, and nearly one in five was low income.

The National Plan of Action adopted by the conference called for ratification of the ERA, free choice in abortion, extension of Social Security benefits to housewives, and elimination of all discriminations against lesbians. It further recommended federal- and state-funded programs for victims of child abuse, education in rape prevention, and state-supported shelters for battered wives.

A national network of feminist organizations was formed. NOW and WEAL were members, as were the League of Women Voters, the Girls Scouts, and the National Council of Jewish Women. Many new direct action and policy groups, such as the Institute for Women's Policy Research, were included. Most of these organizations had offices in Washington, D.C., and they were linked through a Council of Presidents.

Given the successes of second-wave feminism in forming organizations and generating legislation, why did the ERA fail to achieve ratification at the state level? Some analysts blamed the women's movement for the failure. They argued that its organizing at the grassroots level was weak and that early successes made feminists complacent. Yet the last several years of the ERA campaign witnessed the assembling, under the auspices of NOW, of a sophisticated fund-raising and public-awareness campaign. Between 1977 and 1982 NOW membership rose from 65,000 to 230,000; between January and June of 1982 NOW raised $6 million and brought in more money each month than the Democratic National Committee. In April 1982 pollster Louis Harris reported soaring national support for the ERA; 63 percent of all respondents to his poll indicated their support—a 13 percent increase over the 50 percent of the previous year. Thus, the defeat of the ERA in 1982 cannot be traced solely to weaknesses in the women's movement. Rather, other possibilities must be examined. The most important of these are the backlash against feminism in the 1970s and the growing strength of the New Right.

BACKLASH

In 1991 in her best-selling book *Backlash,* journalist Susan Faludi coined the term "backlash" to describe what she called "the undeclared war against American women." Her term is now widely used to describe currents of antifeminism from 1970 on. Faludi argued that recent decades have witnessed a "powerful counter-assault on women's rights."[2] In fact, Faludi argued that backlash against women had been a constant force in American history, especially during periods of women's advance. Given the success of second-wave feminism, it is thus not surprising that a powerful antifeminism would arise in the contemporary era.

The New Right

Powerful groups opposed the ERA—just as similar groups had opposed female suffrage. The traditionalist Catholic and Mormon churches, both dedicated to domesticity as women's primary role and opposed to birth control and abortion, were influential opponents. The powerful life insurance industry profited from higher charges and lower benefits to women, based on their greater life expectancy than men. The industry was regulated by state legislatures, and it lobbied against the amendment, which might invalidate those differential rates.

More than anything else, however, the ERA encountered the resurgent conservatism of the 1970s. Illinois lawyer Phyllis Schlafly and her National Committee of Endorsers Against the ERA, founded in 1972, led the right-wing campaign against the amendment. They contended that the ERA would enforce the military draft on women, invalidate laws protecting the rights of women at home and in divorce, and make separate toilets for men and women illegal. Ultimately it would undermine American morality and destroy the family. Drawing on the financial resources of right-wing groups and on the fanaticism of their members, members of Schlafly's coalition were effective lobbyists before state legislatures, dominated by males.

Yet the New Right, like the antisuffragists of the early twentieth century and the Ku Klux Klan of the 1920s, was not entirely opposed to feminism. One interview study of evangelical women, for example, found that close to half the informants were in favor of the ERA. The New Right constituted a minority of Americans. New Right ideas, however, resonated powerfully in a nation reeling from the changes brought by the radicalism of the 1960s, the movement of women into the workforce, the ongoing Cold War, a sizable new immigration, and a restructuring of the economy around computer technology and a service orientation. Their romanticization of a "golden age" of supposed cohesive family and religious values harked back to the domesticity of the 1950s and afforded the same security. Within the New Right leadership, economically conservative politicians appealed to the narcissism of the well-to-do and the fears of the downwardly mobile. They were joined by evangelical Christians and conservative think tanks such as the Hoover Institution and magazines like the *National Review*. The power of this coalition was evident in the election of three conservative presidents between 1972 and 1992, beginning with Richard Nixon in 1972 and extending to Ronald Reagan in 1980 and 1984 and George H. W. Bush in 1988.

Pro-Life and Pro-Choice

Women's right to abortion became the major issue for the New Right. Coining the term "pro-life" for their position, they argued that there should be no medical intervention against a fertilized egg from the point of conception. In response, feminists crafted a "pro-choice" position, contending that the state had no right to dictate to a woman how she should use her body. The conservatives had links to the conservative presidents and a large bloc of conservatives in Congress and in many state legislatures. Conservative judges were increasingly appointed to the Supreme Court. Thus they were able to whittle away the right to abortion granted in *Roe v. Wade*.

The 1976 Hyde Amendment, passed by Congress, cut off most Medicaid funds for abortion. (Medicaid is the government program providing medical care for the poor.) Thus abortion became a class issue: middle-class women could afford the procedure, but it was largely closed off to indigent women. Subsequently, hundreds of prohibitive rules were passed in more than thirty states, including laws in thirty-four states requiring minors either to notify their parents about their intentions or to secure their consent. The militant wing of the antiabortion movement in the late 1970s began to bomb clinics, to blockade their entrances, and to threaten the lives of the doctors who performed the procedure. By that point, however, only 10 percent of hospitals in the nation were performing abortions, while the procedure was not being taught in medical schools.

Backlash in the Media,
in Appearances, and in Advertising

Echoing the New Right, the media attacked feminists as ugly, man-hating, "bra-burning" radicals outside respectability. The implication of the writing of many journalists was to separate the gains for women in the 1960s and 1970s from the feminists, who had been responsible for their achieve-

Pro-life and Pro-choice Demonstrators. Pro-life and pro-choice demonstrators confront each other in the debate over abortion rights. Once the Supreme Court legalized abortion in *Roe v. Wade,* a strong antiabortion movement, defining life as beginning at conception and abortion as murder, arose to challenge the National Abortion Rights Action League in court cases, legislation, and demonstrations at abortion clinics and elsewhere. (Note "NARAL" on poster in background.)

ment, and to suggest that feminism was not only unnecessary in the present but that it had never been necessary. In this version of history, exactly who was responsible for women's advance was not made clear.

Despite the strength of feminism, a more rigid standard of physical appearance for women emerged. The vogue of extreme thinness began with the Barbie doll and the English model, Twiggy, who became a media sensation in the 1960s. Her skeletal body and childlike face presaged an era of ever younger—and thinner—models. By the 1960s posing for photographs in fashion magazines and modeling clothes on designer runways had come to represent the height of glamour to young girls. It was a profession to which every girl considered beautiful aspired, even though it required constant attention to body weight and was largely closed to women by the time they reached their early twenties.

The cult of thinness produced a multimillion-dollar dieting industry as well as the life-threatening illnesses of anorexia nervosa and bulimia. A growing emphasis on large breasts produced a lucrative business in surgical

Disco. Like most popular dancing from the beginnings of rock 'n' roll onward, disco involved individual gyrations using all parts of the body to a pulsating musical beat. Many disco artists were African American, including the so-called disco divas, although the disco clubs often drew a mixed race crowd. Shown here is legendary singer Diana Ross dancing in an informal dance hall.

breast implants, while cosmetic surgeons developed ever more esoteric techniques to remove wrinkles, reshape eyes and noses, and inject collagen in lips to make them look fuller. In addition, liposuction was developed. It involves the surgical removal of fat cells through a vacuum suction method to eliminate fatty deposits around stomachs and hips. As life expectancy increased and the population aged, it was clear that a lucrative market existed among aging women for these beauty techniques, most of which are designed to produce a youthful look.

By the 1970s the advertising industry appropriated the rhetoric of the women's movement. Cautious at first, advertisers of beauty products respected the feminist rejection of cosmetics and hair curling by promoting a natural look, while exhorting women not to conceal their femininity. Revlon called its Moon Drops face makeup a "demi-makeup." Max Factor's Geminesee false eyelashes were advertised as looking as though they had always been attached to the eyelids. Sometimes advertisers reversed the genders in their ads, showing women in powerful positions, with men as their inferiors. Still, no matter how advertisers presented women in their ads, their underlying message was that real freedom lay in consumption. Virginia Slims cigarettes played on the goals of 1970s feminists through its name (indicating slimness as well as a rebellion against virginity). Its famed slogan, "You've Come a Long Way, Baby," suggested both freedom for women and infantilization. The glamorous models smoking cigarettes in its ads were portrayed in professional and adventuring situations, as though smoking played a key role in their activities.

DISCO AND PUNK

The radical youth protest rose and fell in the 1970s, while the hedonism of the counterculture continued in a search for pleasure, often expressed in terms of drugs and sex. A new kind of music appeared known as disco, and it soon rivaled rock in popularity. Disco music was designed for dancing, and it was popularized in nightclubs. Its pounding beat was intended to generate an emotional high. It often downplayed performers and focused on disc jockeys, who played records. It reduced the role of the guitar, rock's signature instrument, to a percussive function. It began as a music of African Americans and gays. Male disco singers and dancers often had a feminized side, as does John Travolta in the 1977 movie, *Saturday Night Fever,* which featured Travolta as a disco dancer. Many analysts cite this movie as indicating the height of the disco craze.

Outside the nightclubs, women were important disco singers; some historians contend that they dominated the music. However, they didn't show the independence of female folk-rock artists in the early 1970s, such as Carly Simon and Joan Baez, who played guitars, wrote their own songs, and sang about the problems facing women and society. "Disco divas" were highly sexual, for disco promoters, in addition to the singers' male managers and songwriters and the male-controlled record industry, wanted to appeal to male fans. They wore tube tops, halters, and clingy polyester dresses, while they appealed to male fantasies of women as always eager for sex. Donna Summer's seventeen-minute song, "Love to Love You, Baby," consisted mainly of a writhing beat and orgasmic moans on the part of Summers. It caused a sensation.

In the later 1970s youth subcultures developed new styles of dress and behavior. The new strain of music and dancing known as "punk" began in England and reveled in dress that signified amorality, with body piercing and tattoos, black clothing, and fetishized leather garb that indicated violence and sadomasochism. Punk singers Johnny Rotten and Iggy Pop smashed glass and cut themselves during their performances. Punk women wore ripped fishnet stockings, plastic miniskirts, and garish makeup, both borrowing from the dress of prostitutes and mocking it. On the one hand, punk fashions seem a creative rebellion against conformity and commercialism through style. On the other, they seem to indicate the growth of an extreme alienation among young people, in the face of urbanization, immigration, and structural unemployment, as older industries like coal and steel shut down and scores of jobs were permanently lost in the process.

Punk fashions pointed the way to the postmodernism and postfeminism of the 1980s and after. Did they also indicate the bankruptcy of the radicalism of the 1960s and its retreat into a realm of fashion that the mainstream could co-opt? Did they reflect nothing more than narcissism, as traditional morality declined and consumer culture decreed that buying products to indulge one's self was all that mattered? Were they a true rebellion?

RECENT IMMIGRATION

In addition to the radicalism and feminism of the 1960s, another development that had a major impact on the recent history of women was the new immigration of the late 1960s and after. The Immigration Act of 1965, which established an immigration system based on family preference, abolished the discriminatory quotas based on national origins that had existed since the 1920s and that had favored the immigration of Northern Europeans. Although under the terms of the 1965 Immigration Act only 170,000 immigrants would be permitted to enter the United States each year from the Eastern hemisphere and 120,000 from the Western hemisphere, close relatives of individuals already in the United States were exempt from these quotas. Thus a pattern of family migration was established.

Other special immigration acts granted political asylum to individuals whose lives were threatened under authoritarian regimes. This had been the case as early as 1959, when the successful Communist revolution in Cuba brought thousands of Cubans to immigrate to the United States, especially to Florida and more specifically to Miami Beach. Thousands of Vietnamese were also permitted entry after the U.S. failure in the Vietnam War in 1972. Iranians, both Jews and Muslims, immigrated to the United States after the fall of the Western-oriented Shah of Iran in 1979 and the establishment of a fundamentalist Muslim government. By the 1990s the Muslims would become one of the largest minorities in the United States, with their numbers approaching those of the Jews.

Millions of people of color immigrated to the United States under the family provision of the 1965 Immigration Act, inaugurating a period of "new" immigration as sizable as that of the early twentieth century. These "new" immigrants came from Indochina, Mexico, Central and South America, Korea, Taiwan, India, and the Dominican Republic. And scores of migrants from Mexico and South America entered the United States illegally through its southern borders, fleeing poverty and political persecution.

In contrast to the immigration of the early twentieth century, which had included many single men, this was a migration of families. Two-thirds of these immigrants were women and children. Among them were many professionals. For example, thirteen thousand Korean medical specialists came to the United States in 1965, and a majority of them were female nurses. Still, poverty and acculturation to the society of the United States were major issues for these new immigrants. Even among Asian Americans, considered by many to be a "model minority" because of their education and professional skills, many women worked in low-wage, dead-end jobs on electronic assembly lines and in garment factories. The Organization of Pan Asian Women, formed in 1976, became concerned about mail-order brides, now coming from the Philippines as well as from Japan and Korea. Many of these women had no support system in the United States; they spoke little English; and they lived with the threat of being deported if they displeased their husbands.

The feminists and radicals of the 1960s were mostly from the middle class, and these new immigrants remained within their family groups. With the exception of feminist women in the Latina, Mexican American, and African American organizations and the women in unions who worked to unionize the new immigrants in their places of work, women of the new immigration did not interact with feminists. This does not mean, however, that they did not benefit from legislation that resulted from feminist action, such as the Equal Pay Act and Title VII of the Civil Rights Act, or from the feminist founding of women's health centers and of rape crisis hotlines. Once on the books, this legislation was of benefit to all women. By the 1980s many of their children would begin attending college. Like the immigrants of the 1890s and 1900s, those with modest incomes would begin the process of upward social mobility that has been one of the major features of American life.

NOTES

1. Judith Hole and Ellen Levine, *Rebirth of Feminism* (New York: Quadrangle Books, 1971), 81.
2. Susan Faludi, *Backlash: The Undeclared War Against American Women* (New York: Crown, 1991), xviii.

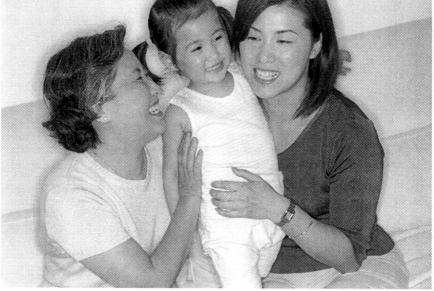

7

The Third Wave

1980–2004

Issues relating to sexuality and women's bodies were at the center of political debate and cultural representation in the 1980s and 1990s. The New Right clashed with feminists over abortion, while a new generation of young women, called "Generation X" and "postfeminist," either rejected feminism or asserted a right to define it themselves, especially with regard to sexual expression. "Third-wave feminism" emerged out of this new generation.

The emphasis in the culture in general on sexuality continued, despite a continuing AIDS epidemic and increases in other sexually transmitted diseases (STDs). Advertisers more and more cast off sexual restraint, and pornography moved out of movie theaters and onto the Internet and videos. Fashions in clothing became more revealing, and topless waitresses, massage parlors, nude strip clubs, and lap dancing gained in popularity. At the same time "sexual harassment" became a major issue, as the Anita Hill–Clarence Thomas stand off in 1991 opened the decade of the 1990s, and the Bill Clinton–Monica Lewinsky scandal in 1998 came at its end. In the former, Anita Hill, a professor of law at Oklahoma University, accused Clarence

Opposite: Three generations of American women

Thomas, a conservative appointee to the Supreme Court, of having sexually harassed her when he was her superior at the Department of Education and then at the EEOC. In the Clinton-Lewinsky scandal, President Clinton's affair with Lewinsky, an intern in the White House, became public knowledge, and the House of Representatives voted a bill of impeachment against him.

Yet organized feminism remained strong, despite the continual media charge that it had died. Forty percent of American women called themselves feminist, and the older feminist organizations continued. New organizations again appeared, while the diffusion of feminism throughout the culture made many feminist organizations and activities that had once been new and shocking seem part of the mainstream.

POLITICS BECOME CONSERVATIVE

The election of Ronald Reagan to the presidency in 1980 marked a triumph for the New Right. Reversing a decade of supporting feminism, the Republican platform on which Reagan ran failed to support the ERA while it called for a constitutional amendment banning abortions and for an administrative policy of selecting judges opposed to reproductive rights. As president, Reagan appointed antifeminists to the judiciary and put them in charge of civil rights enforcement, including appointing conservative officials to the EEOC. Social programs for poor women were cut or abandoned, while Reagan expanded the military.

Reagan was antiunion, preferring to support business over organized labor. Corporations became adept at busting unions by firing workers who joined unions, keeping union organizers away from their employees, and using the Taft-Hartley Act to break strikes. "Right to work" laws that undermined the closed shop were passed in many states. (Under the closed shop, all employees in an industry are required to join a union when 50 percent of the employees vote to do so). These developments, together with industrial restructuring that resulted in significant unemployment, brought a fall in union membership. By the end of the 1980s, less than 17 percent of American workers were organized, half the proportion of the early 1950s.

Rhetoric about "welfare cheats" and the irresponsibility of the indigent became endemic on the part of federal and state officials and others, despite studies showing that most poor people used welfare between jobs as a fallback "safety net," just as many other workers used public unemployment insurance for the same purpose. (Part-time workers and many other low-wage workers are not eligible for unemployment benefits.) The proportion of the population living in poverty rose to 23 percent, and most of the poor were women and children. Homeless people were living on the streets for the first time since the Depression. Ninety-four percent of the new wealth generated during the Reagan economic boom went to the richest 20 percent of individuals in the nation, while half of the new wealth that was generated went to the richest one percent.

In 1982 the ERA went down in defeat as the time limit for its passage by the states expired without the requisite number having approved it. Congress also didn't pass the New Right–sponsored Family Protection Act. That act mandated prayers in public schools and an end to public funding of school textbooks that showed women in other than traditional roles. It also mandated the end of federal laws against child and spousal abuse as well as the federal laws that required equal financial support for men's and women's sports in colleges and universities that received federal funding.

The New Right continued its aggressive attacks on abortion. In 1989 the Supreme Court decision in *Webster v. Reproductive Health Services* upheld a Missouri statute banning the use of public funds or facilities in abortion except to save a woman's life. A 1991 "gag rule" prohibited federally funded clinic counselors from speaking about abortion when advising pregnant women. The antiabortion movement also secured large cutbacks in public funding for family planning services.

In 1981 Reagan appointed Sandra Day O'Connor to the Supreme Court —its first female member. She was a conservative, but she had experienced discrimination as a woman in her life and career. Thus she was more sensitive to women's rights issues than had been expected. She has cast the swing vote on a number of five to four decisions, especially those concerning abortion. For the most part she has upheld the legality of the procedure.

BACKLASH CONTINUES

The backlash of the 1970s became more vituperative in the 1980s. Radio talk-show hosts, such as Rush Limbaugh, used loud tones and harsh, often foul, language to support an aggressive masculinity and to vilify feminists as responsible for the nation's problems. Limbaugh coined the term "femi-Nazi" to refer to supporters of women's rights. But there also existed a pro-feminist men's movement that supported women's rights and called for ending male "macho" attitudes as well as all barriers to gender equality. An opposing (and larger) group of men, however, denied that women were oppressed or that they were less powerful than men. The primary goal of this second group was more rights for divorced fathers, including decreased

child support payments. Poet Robert Bly organized popular wilderness retreats, in which men performed rituals to overcome the damage Bly contended the feminist movement had done to them. At these retreats, men
dressed in animal costumes and beat drums to rediscover "the beast within."

Hollywood continued to denigrate career women and to sexualize
women in general. *Fatal Attraction* (1987), a box office hit, demonized career women and idealized women who stayed at home in the suburbs and
raised children. In that film a maniac career woman goes on a murderous
rampage against the wife and child of the married man who rejected her after a brief affair. *Pretty Woman* (1990), another hit, glamorized prostitution
by having a handsome multimillionaire fall in love with a Hollywood Bou-
levard hooker. The 1980s and 1990s, however, had their share of sensitive
films about gender. In *Tootsie* (1982), for example, Dustin Hoffman cross-
dresses as a woman in order to land a role on a television drama, only to dis-
cover that he enjoys displaying female sensitivity. Yet macho action films
were as popular as ever. Clint Eastwood in detective dramas and Sylvester
Stallone in the post–Vietnam Rambo films took on scores of villains, amid
a bloodbath of violence. Arnold Schwarzenegger did the same in the *Terminator* films, in which he played a partly mechanized being in a future
world dominated by technology.

The National Coalition on Television Violence estimated that horror,
slasher, and violent science fiction films rose from 6 percent of box office
receipts in 1970 to 30 percent in 1985, and the percentages are even higher
today. One TV executive wrote in the *New York Times* that male heroes
were turning violent because audiences were sick of "wimps" and "heroes
who wore their sensitivity on their shirtsleeves." Other analysts contended
that these films reflect the malaise of men living in an economy undergoing
significant structural changes, with the constant threat of unemployment.
Young men are the major audiences for these films and, according to market surveys, they will view them multiple times, thus greatly increasing a
film's profitability.

By the late 1980s video games involving the kinds of combat found in
male action/adventure films had been introduced, and they became very
popular among boys. As has been the case with such movies, the games have
become more violent over time. Recently released games include bodies
that explode when hit by bombs and bullets, with blood, guts, and viscera
flying all around. Although most of the violence depicted in film and television is free of pain, violent video games include the screams of maimed
and dying victims. In a sample of fourth-grade children, 73 percent of boys
and 59 percent of girls reported that their favorite video games were the
violent ones.

THE EMERGENCE OF NEW STYLES

Fashions, Advertising, and Disco

The 1980s saw a return to cinched waists and high heels, while the vogue of miniskirts continued. By the end of the decade, ads in fashion magazines were showing pale and pinched models, who sometimes looked as though they had been beaten. Pornographic and sadomasochistic features in dress, including leather and chains, became popular. The obsession with thinness continued, as high-fashion models wore the smallest possible sizes of clothing. In the 1980s "power dressing" was popular for a time, with padded shoulders and tailored suits. In the 1990s "heroin chic" appeared, and models had dark circles under their eyes and looked wasted and waiflike. Fashion photographers in such popular magazines as *Vogue* employed sadomasochist and brutal imagery in photographing models who were extremely thin. Wearing clothing that was marked with designer brand names and logos, such as those for Calvin Klein and Jordache, became a fashion must. Such labeling subtly indicated that the wearer belonged to the most stylish group —and could afford the clothes.

Advertising continued the trend in ads toward more explicit sexuality. In 1981 Calvin Klein sold expensive jeans with advertisements in which a seminude Brooke Shields, a teenage model and actress, was displayed along with the provocative phrase, "Know what comes between me and my Calvins? Nothing." Jordache, another maker of expensive jeans, kept its competitive edge by showing topless young women astride shirtless young men. Clothing was increasingly scanty in ads in general, and models had sexual, seductive expressions on their faces. Advertisers used sexual "embeds" in their advertisements. These are objects shaped like genitalia or positioned as though being used in sex acts, and viewers are supposed to perceive them subconsciously.

Advertisers continued a long-term trend and reacted to the radical feminism of the 1970s by promoting personal narcissism as liberating and buying glamour and leisure items as the ultimate freedom in their advertisements. The major women's fashion magazines *Vogue, Elle, Cosmopolitan,* and *Glamour*—in the 1980s as today—devoted about two-thirds of each issue to advertising and about one-third to articles. Moreover, they took care in the articles not to criticize the manufacturers that funded them through their payments for running the advertisements.

By the 1980s disco music and dancing declined in popularity. Renamed "dance music," however, it spawned such styles as house, techno, industrial, and trance. It played a role in generating the "rave" movement, which involved dancing and taking drugs at huge events held at secret locations, which were revealed the day of the event. Disco also led the way to rap and hip-hop, which was to a certain extent a masculine reaction to disco, which had female divas and feminized male performers. It also paved the way for Madonna, a complex figure who both drew on the disco divas in creating her persona and satirized them at the same time.

Rap and Hip-hop

Hip-hop, or rap, music began in 1974 in the South Bronx, as an alternative to ghetto violence through a competitive break-dance for young men. The dance involved a controlled, jerking motion, punctuated by acrobatic leaps and glides. The music the young men danced to was syncopated and monotone, and its lyrics, involving clever rhyme schemes, were half spoken and half sung in a fast staccato. Hip-hop allowed young men to channel their aggressiveness into a creative activity. It drew from disco and traditions of African American expression like blues and the call-and-response pattern of slave spirituals, in which a leader sings a musical line and the chorus either repeats it or responds to it. It also appeared among young Hispanic men as well as African American young men. As the music developed, however, it became preoccupied with sex, violence, and the denigration of women, especially in Los Angeles–based "gangsta" rap. Black women, in particular, were called "hos" and "bitches," and violence against them was approved. Rappers often celebrated the sexual prowess of black men and blamed black women for their problems.

Rap music began to reach a large audience with the appearance of music videos in the early 1980s. Young white suburban men were major consumers of such videos, constituting about 60 percent of the market. Some rap historians contend that the only way that black men, alienated from mainstream society and consigned to inferior positions, can have any sense of power is by holding on to patriarchal notions of masculinity, while young white men act out their alienation through following black music and styles. Other historians point out that the music in no way criticizes consumerism or the white power structure. Still others note the campy nature of some hip-hop music, which caricatures black culture as well as the artists singing the music. In addition, some of rap's major stars, such as Ice-T, have been successful in films playing comedy and dramatic roles.

Like most forms of popular music, rap is not static, and female rappers have challenged the misogyny of male rap singers. One of the most important female rappers is Queen Latifah. She was born Dana Elaine Owens, and although her father was largely absent when she was growing up, her mother was a high school teacher in New Jersey who won a state award for excellence in teaching. Owens chose the name Latifah in accord with the Black

Muslim practice of taking a new name; "latifah" is an Arabic word that means sensitive and kind. She called herself Queen after the great queens who once ruled societies in Africa; to her the word meant woman in her full power and glory. Queen Latifah manages her career and writes her own songs. Mostly recently, she has become a Hollywood star, playing in roles in which she uses her large body to convey both humor and sensuality. In 1994 she won a Grammy and an Image Award from the NAACP for her song "U.N.I.T.Y." It ends with the lines: "But don't you be callin' me out my name / I bring wrath to those who disrespect me like a dame."

Madonna

Madonna Louise Ciccone was raised in the suburbs of Detroit, Michigan, part of a large middle-class Italian Catholic family. Her father was an engineer in the automobile industry, and she was named after her mother, who died when Madonna was seven. She was a talented dancer, with a keen understanding of popular culture. In contrast to the disco divas, men did not control her. She choreographed her performances and created her public persona, while she kept financial control over her various enterprises. At the height of her fame, she was called America's most successful businesswoman. She became a celebrity in 1983, singing conventional dance music. Her best-known song from this period, "Like a Virgin," both honored and satirized the belief that girls should remain virgins until marriage. She soared to stardom performing in music videos on the new television channel, MTV, which played music videos exclusively.

In her videos and concerts she performed variations on disco and rock in a new pop modernism. Her numbers were often elaborately staged, and in them she borrowed images from African American and gay culture, and she used back-up singers and dancers from those cultures. She sometimes dressed like Marilyn Monroe as a blonde seductress and sometimes like a dark vixen. Engaging in titillating sensual behavior on stage, she crossed over traditional boundaries, turning herself into a sexual agent, a sexual object, and a parody of both. There were intimations of Mae West, the great sexualized comedienne and parodist of the 1930s, in her self-creation. She changed her clothing style over time from flashy trash to haute couture to lesbian S and M to a pastiche of all of these styles. The muscular body she developed over the course of her career was the product of hours of exercise.

Some critics celebrated her as culturally subversive, while others attacked her as antifeminist or as vulgar. To many, she personified the post-feminism of the younger generation. "To call me an antifeminist is ludicrous," Madonna has stated. "Some people have said that I'm setting

Madonna, 1985. Madonna in her early career as the good-bad girl. She is wearing heavy makeup, a skimpy halter top, white lace gloves, and long strings of pearls. The gloves and the pearls are classic symbols of innocence and elegance.

Madonna, Britney Spears, and Christina Aguilera, 2003. Three pop idols mimic each other on stage. They display a woman as eroticized sex symbol (Christina Aguilera on right); the good-bad girl (Britney Spears, on left); and the powerful, independent older vixen (Madonna, in center). Note that Spears and Aguilera are wearing white lace gloves and pearls, while Madonna is wearing a severe hairstyle and black clothing that resembles exercise garb and is both feminine and masculine. In the photograph, she seems to be instructing Spears.

women back thirty years. Well, I think in the '50s, women weren't ashamed of their bodies. I think they luxuriated in their sexuality and being strong in their femininity. I think that is better than hiding it and saying, 'I'm strong, I'm just like a man.'"[1]

THE ANITA HILL AND CLARENCE THOMAS SCANDAL

Popular culture seemed to embrace men and women of color by the 1990s, but issues of racism and sexism arose in 1991 in the disagreement between Clarence Thomas and Anita Hill. When Thurgood Marshall, the first black appointee to the Supreme Court, retired, President George H. W. Bush appointed Clarence Thomas, a conservative African American from Georgia, to replace him. As the Senate deliberated the appointment, Anita Hill came forward to accuse Thomas of having sexually harassed her when he was her superior at the EEOC through discussions of sexual acts and pornographic films when she refused to date him.

Although the Senate doubted her allegations, they agreed to hold an open hearing on the matter after female members of the House of Representatives marched together to the Senate demanding it. The hearings were televised. For three days the nation watched testimony being given about presumed sexual advances and innuendos on the part of a black man against a black woman in a work situation. If the charges were correct, Thomas's behavior constituted sexual harassment, which was an offense under the law.

Thomas denied Hill's allegations, and he was exonerated by the Senate, thus taking a seat on the Supreme Court. Whether or not the charges were true, they divided the black community on the issue of race versus gender. Maintaining his innocence, Thomas contended that he was akin to the black men who had been lynched in the period from Reconstruction to the 1940s on trumped-up charges involving a sex crime committed against a woman. Most blacks supported Thomas. However, according to black feminists Johnetta Betsch Cole and Beverly Guy-Sheftall, who supported Hill, the attacks on black women involving their sexuality historically had been just as significant as those on black men. In their view, it was regrettable that the black community supported Thomas. They criticized their African American peers for believing that black men's experiences with racism, including lynching and police brutality, were more damaging than black women's experiences with sexism, including rape and lynching.

Hill endured with dignity hours of questioning by the all-male, all-white Senate committee about private and embarrassing experiences. Some of the Senators made light of what they called this "sexual harassment crap" and dwelled on salacious details of her testimony. In addition, there were public innuendos that she was a slut and a liar, trying to capitalize on Thomas's new public prominence. Still, the Hill–Thomas controversy had positive outcomes. Membership in feminist organizations increased, while more women than ever before ran for public office. The numbers of sexual harassment cases that were filed with the EEOC increased and so did judgments in favor of the women who filed the suits. Between 1991 and 1996, according to EEOC records, sexual harassment cases more than doubled, from six thousand to fifteen thousand, while awards to victims under federal law nearly quadrupled, from nearly $8 million to $28 million.

FEMINISM TAKES NEW FORMS

Given the hostility of the federal government to feminism in the 1980s and 1990s, especially during the presidencies of Ronald Reagan and the senior George Bush, much feminist activist energy shifted to the state level, where coalitions were formed to secure government legislation. The Wisconsin Women's Network, for example, was supported by sixty-seven member organizations and over a thousand individuals. Moreover, many single-issue organizations on the local level, such as battered women's shelters, became institutionalized. They secured funding from government agencies and private sources. Now regarded as mainstream groups, with widespread public approval, they no longer seemed striking feminist innovations. On the national level, women's policy institutes were formed that generated sophisticated analysis of data and provided expert testimony on the part of their researchers before congressional committees and the like.

At the same time, the many women entering the professions had little time for activism outside their work. With a shortage of available volunteers, the dynamism of women's organizations decreased. Still, professional women often formed women's organizations within their professions that were implicitly feminist. The history profession, for example, has four such groups: in the West, Midwest, South, and East. The eastern group, the Berkshire Conference of Women Historians, holds a biennial conference in women's history that draws women from throughout the nation. There is also a Central Coordinating committee for Women in the Historical Profession that acts independently from the other organizations and is affiliated with the American Historical Association.

Despite the shortage of volunteers, mainstream feminism still remains strong. NOW and the other national organizations experienced a sizable growth in membership both after the 1989 Supreme Court decision in *Webster v. Reproductive Health Services* and the Anita Hill testimony before the Senate in 1991. Important new organizations also appeared, such as the Feminist Majority, which works for social and economic equality for women in the United States and worldwide through research and education. The Ms. Foundation publishes *Ms.* as a quarterly magazine, and this new version of *Ms.* accepts no advertisements that objectify women. The foundation also supports projects that nurture girls' leadership skills, protect the health and safety of women, and provide low-income women with the tools to lift themselves and their families out of poverty.

"Comparable worth" for women's work became a feminist issue in the 1980s. As the gap in the wages between women and men continued to exist, some feminists concluded that the problem was caused by a national predisposition to place a lower value on women's work than men's work, no

Anita Hill. Anita Hill, a professor in the Oklahoma University School of Law, accused Clarence Thomas, a conservative African American appointee to the Supreme Court, of having sexually harassed her when he was her superior at the Department of Education in the federal government and then at the EEOC. Her charges brought a weekend hearing before the U.S. Senate. Thomas was exonerated and his appointment approved, but Hill continues to maintain that the charges were valid.

Carol Moseley-Braun. Elected to the Senate from Illinois in 1992, Carol Moseley-Braun was the first black woman in the upper house of the U.S. Congress. She reappeared on the national scene in 2003, when she entered the race for the Democratic nomination to the presidency, although she soon dropped out after the polls showed her badly trailing the leading candidates.

matter what the women did. It didn't make sense to these feminists that men employed in selling computers or cars made more money than women selling dresses or cosmetics, or that female nurses made less than male medical personnel, such as laboratory technicians. These feminists came up with the idea of "comparable worth." Under this plan, designed to eliminate any male advantage in compensation, jobs are broken down into skills and point values are assigned to each skill. Then the points are totaled and the totals compared. By 1987 forty states and 1,700 local governments had taken steps toward implementing such policies. From that point on, however, instituting them became difficult due to a growing backlash against giving women special consideration.

The percentages of women in most professions rose throughout the 1980s and 1990s. In 1970 nine percent of all doctors were women; in 1990 the percentage was 19 percent. The numbers of unionized workers decreased, but women held more leadership positions in the labor unions. In 1986 four national unions had female presidents: the National Education Association, the Association of Flight Attendants, Actors' Equity Association, and the Screen Actors' Guild. In 1988 the Congress of Labor Union Women (CLUW) had seventy-five chapters and a membership of eighteen thousand. By 1990 women were 41 percent of the membership of the nation's unions. That percentage would increase as union organization spread among service workers in hotels and restaurants and in domestic labor, fields in which many women are employed, especially women who have been part of the "new immigration." The Service Employees Industrial Organization (SEIU) became the largest union in the nation.

African American women also registered gains in employment, as they moved into employment areas traditionally considered "white." In 1965, 24 percent of all employed black women were white-collar workers, compared with 62 percent of all employed white women. By 1981 these figures were 46 percent for black women and 66 percent for white women. And African American women abandoned the category of domestic service, which they had dominated for nearly a century. In 1965, 30 percent of all employed African American women were domestic workers; by 1977 the figure had dropped to 9 percent. For the most part, immigrants from Mexico and Latin America replaced them.

Politics has been a productive ground for women, and many female politicians have come to support women's rights goals. Emily's List was founded in 1985 to elect more Democratic women to public office. ("Emily" was taken from the first letters in the words of the slogan "Early Money Is Like Yeast—it makes the dough rise." In other words, injecting money into a political campaign at its beginning will bring in more money later.) The nonpartisan National Women's Political Caucus, founded in 1971 and dedicated to electing women of both parties to office, has also been very active in politics. Indicating women's increased importance in politics, in 1984 Democratic presidential candidate Walter Mondale chose New York Congresswoman Geraldine Ferraro as his vice-presidential candidate, establishing another first for women.

In the elections of 1992 many women were inspired to run for office by the failure of Anita Hill's testimony to sway the Senate the year before. That year was dubbed "the year of the woman," as twenty-two women ran for the Senate, where only eight had run two years before. Fifteen women served in the 92nd Congress in 1971; in 2003 in the 107th Congress, there were seventy-two women. In 1969 there were 301 female state legislators nationwide, and in 1981 there were 908. In 2003 there were 1,656. In 1991 almost one out of every five elected public officials in the states was female. By 1991 women were 17 percent of mayors; by 1996 they were 21 percent of state legislators.

With regard to African American women and politics, in 1990 nearly 11 percent of the approximately 1,300 female state legislators were black, as were about 55 percent of female Democratic Party state officials. (In 1990 only seventeen Asian American women, fourteen Hispanic women, and five Native American women were state legislators.) In 1992 Carol Moseley-Braun of Illinois was the first black woman elected to the Senate in the nation's history.

From the 1980s on, experts on voting discerned a "gender gap" in voting behavior, in which women tended to vote in greater numbers than men did for liberal than for conservative candidates. Analysts concluded that women were more sensitive than men to issues involving social welfare and children than men were and that they perceived the Democrats as more attentive to these matters than the Republicans. Experts maintained that these women's votes were the deciding factor in electing Bill Clinton to the presidency in 1992. In could also be said that a male backlash against liberal politics and the women's vote played a role in electing a Republican House and Senate in 1994 and George W. Bush as president in 2000.

"Unobtrusive Mobilization" and the Military

In addition to the obvious indications of the advance of women and feminism in such a areas as law, politics, and the professions, Mary Katzenstein has discerned what she calls an "unobtrusive mobilization" of women in various areas of American life. She uses the military as an example. In 1973, after the end of the Vietnam War, the draft was abandoned and an All Volunteer Force (AVF) was instituted. Increased career opportunities and training in job skills in the military, in addition to wages competitive with those of private-sector jobs brought a large increase in the numbers of women enlisting in the military. Reserve Officer Training Programs (ROTC) on college campuses were opened to women, and so were the service academies that provide officer training—including the army's academy at West Point and the navy's academy at Annapolis. The impressive performance of women in the military campaign in Panama and the one in Kuwait (the Desert Storm campaign) convinced many individuals both in the military and outside of it that they could be effective soldiers.

In 1993 lobbying by women before Congress resulted in the elimination of the existing prohibition on the participation of women in combat, and President Clinton opened 99 percent of military jobs to them. (Women are still not included on submarines, where they would be in especially close contact with men, or in the Special Services, responsible for reconnaissance and small, quick-strike actions that can be very dangerous.) Today, women make up 15 percent of the enlisted ranks and the officer corps in the military. They are 6 percent of the Marines and 19 percent of the Air Force.

Female soldiers have protested discrimination against them in the armed forces, as well as sexual harassment. A series of infamous assaults on the part of sailors against women occurred in 1991 at the Tailhook Convention in Las Vegas. (The Tailhook Association is dedicated to encouraging support for aircraft carriers and their planes as well as the crews that serve both.) The convention was a yearly event at which a tradition had developed that the women present—whether in the navy or not—were forced to run a gauntlet of drunken men in a hotel corridor while being grabbed and groped. In 1991 the gauntlet became a public scandal when several women involved filed charges against the men. Moreover, the issue of women in the military being accused of lesbian behavior and then dishonorably discharged without a fair hearing was brought out in the open and policies against such unfair treatment were instituted. In 2003 date rape at the military academies, especially at the Air Force Academy in Colorado, was publicly aired, especially the lack of punishment of the perpetrators of such sexual crimes. The four top administrators at the Academy were removed and transferred to other positions in the Air Force.

Postmodernism

By the 1980s a new and important strain of feminist theory called post-feminism appeared. It was partly an outgrowth of the appearance of a postmodern philosophy, especially in the universities. Postmodernists were critical of Marxism and of what they called "essentialism," by which they meant theories that posited the existence of biological or social regularities throughout human populations. They argued that the flood of information in mass culture societies had fragmented social reality and individual identity to the point that universalizing truths no longer existed. They urged verbal war against what they saw as the binary nature of Western culture, which divides black against white, nature from culture, men from women. Postmodernism and postfeminism especially resulted from the failure of student movements in the 1970s, both in Europe and the United States, in addition to the rise of "identity" politics, in which racial and ethnic minorities as well as lesbians and gays asserted that their experiences and goals were separate from those of the white majority associated with feminism and radical politics.

Some postmodernists argued that gender was a fluctuating—even a performative—category, by which they meant that individuals performed roles that society had defined for them. Moreover, mass culture, even with its authoritarian elements of control and manipulation, was so large that it offered many spaces for resistance and subversion. Postmodernists played with metaphors and puns, and they described modern culture as "carnivalesque." They rejected the concept of "patriarchy" as out of date. In their view the concept of male control over society was too conditioned by historical change and cultural and individual differences by race, class, ethnicity, and sexual orientation to be useful any longer.

Postmodernism stemmed from the work of male philosophers such as Jacques Derrida, while feminist postmodernism, beginning with the work of philosopher Judith Butler, was linked to younger feminists who formed a "third wave" in the history of feminism. In attacking binary categories, including male and female and black and white, postmodernism was radical in striking at core beliefs of Western culture. Its critics maintained, however, that it de-centered reality to the point that there was no longer any place either for human agency or for identifying power or oppression. Under the postmodern system, they contended, no one had any responsibility for anything.

From this point of view, postmodernism had taken the political sting out of feminism and imprisoned it in a labyrinth from which there was no exit. Critics saw it as linked to the emergence of punk fashions, and to punk's descendants in the 1980s and 1990s—hip-hop and grunge—which had been co-opted by the mainstream by the later decade. In other words, postmodernism's ideas about the fragmentation of reality and about the equal voices of all ethnic and sexual groups had become accepted social stances, while such problems as poverty, homelessness, and unemployment were no closer to being solved. Postmodernism's supporters argued, however, that it allowed individuals to reshape themselves in terms of new, countercultural styles that would ultimately change old ways of behaving. Moreover, they contended that postmodernism addressed the position of marginalized and ethnic groups, who felt at odds with mainstream feminism. Thus it provided feminism with the model for intricate, coalition politics in which all ethnic, racial, and sexual groups could assert a voice. By 2000 "queer" theory was also becoming important, as gays in particular identified the existence of androgyny throughout the history of civilizations and saw a breakdown in stereotyped sex roles as the hope of the future.

THE CLINTON PRESIDENCY

The election of Bill Clinton as president in 1992 promised gains for women, especially since his wife, Hillary, was a successful lawyer and a self-defined feminist. Clinton was prochoice, and he vetoed a bill passed by Congress prohibiting late-term abortions. He also supported the Family and Medical Leave Act, which guaranteed unpaid leave for pregnancy and childbirth, while he appointed many women to office, including Ruth Bader Ginsburg to the Supreme Court.

With the election of a Republican House and Senate in 1994, however, he took over much of the Republican agenda, moving the Democratic Party to the center of the political spectrum. He signed a law that allowed states to ban gay marriage. He called himself "pro-family" and engaged in the rhetoric criticizing mothers on welfare as irresponsible that had been standard among conservatives since the Reagan presidency. He signed the Personal Responsibility Act, which repealed the Aid to Families with Dependent Children prohibition of the Social Security Act, while promoting marriage and paternal support. Under this act, mothers receiving assistance have to perform community service or work for wages, with a maximum of sixty months total of welfare to be given to any single individual. Indeed, this act denied the traditional belief that mothers should remain at home to raise their own children. Rather it decreed that mothers should work and children should be put in day-care centers. Mothers were also encouraged to reunite with their children's father, even if they didn't know who the father was or if the man had beaten them. The act also did not increase spending for day care, which remained inadequate to meet the new demand for day care on the part of mothers entering the workforce.

Clinton survived Republican attacks against both Hillary and himself for improper practices in private land transactions while he was governor of Arkansas. Congress appointed a special prosecutor, Kenneth Starr, to investigate the charges, but he failed to find any wrongdoing on the part of either Hillary or Bill with regard to their real estate dealings. He did, however, catch Clinton in lies regarding an affair he had with a White House intern, Monica Lewinsky. This impropriety led to the attempt to impeach him, which was ultimately unsuccessful.

Clinton was not the first president to engage in an extramarital affair. John Kennedy, for one, has become legendary for such involvements. The Lewinsky affair, however, was particularly tawdry, since Monica Lewinsky, twenty-two years old when the affair took place, was the same age as Clinton's daughter, and the encounters between Clinton and Lewinsky took place in the halls and bathrooms adjacent to the Oval Office, the president's primary workspace. Critics had charged Clinton with having initiated such escapades throughout his career, although the proof of these involvements wasn't entirely conclusive. He had initially lied about his involvement with Lewinsky until Starr, deeply anti-Clinton, forced him to admit it. An impeachment indictment was subsequently passed by the House, but the Senate voted it down, and Clinton served out his term.

The affair was of special interest to feminists because it raised the issue of sexual harassment. Was Lewinsky, a powerless office worker, taken advantage of sexually by a powerful man? Had Clinton violated the laws against sexual harassment, since the encounters took place in work-related space? For many feminists the answer was no. Lewinsky herself was adamant both in testimony before Starr and in subsequent statements that the sex was consensual and that she had initiated it by flirting outrageously with Clinton whenever she was in his presence. In her public appearances, she came across as a liberated young women, sexually experienced, who was bold and brassy and enjoyed having seduced a powerful man. If anything she seemed, like Madonna, to personify the new postfeminist "power" feminism that perceived women as similar to men in their sexual appetites and their eagerness to initiate sexual encounters whenever and with whomever they wanted.

GENERATIONAL CONFLICT

As it had in the American past, generational conflict emerged in the feminist movement in the 1980s. Younger women, who had not lived through the militant years of second-wave feminism, were often ambivalent about—and even hostile to—the stands of their elders. The media dubbed these younger women the "postfeminist" generation. They also called them members of "Generation X" or, referring to the baby boom generation that had preceded them, "post-boomers." Some of these younger women launched an attack on feminism. They contended that, with its emphasis on oppression, feminism had made women into "victims." To the contrary, they argued, women should embrace their power and become more like

men. In 1991, in *The Beauty Myth,* Naomi Wolf castigated fashion design-
ers and the media, as well as the culture in general, for perversely controlling women's bodies through constant changes in styles of dress and appearance. In 1993, however, in *Fire with Fire,* she did an about-face. She
now called for women to give up "victim" feminism to adopt "power" feminism. She wanted women to acknowledge their electoral, financial, and
professional authority and to use it boldly to get what they wanted.

Katie Roiphe, the daughter of the successful second-wave author, Anne
Roiphe, took a similar stance in *The Morning After* in 1993. In this book,
which Roiphe wrote when she was a graduate student at Princeton University, she argued that the incidence of date rape on college campuses was
greatly exaggerated, that women should take responsibility for themselves,
and that, by focusing so strongly on violence against women, feminism had
become a sisterhood of victims. Other authors accused feminists of being
insensitive to the special issues facing married women and children. Or they
attacked women's studies programs as women-only ghettos that preached a
party line. Camille Paglia became a media favorite when she asserted that
women secretly wanted to be dominated sexually and that they, not men,
had the real power in relationships and in society. In her view all men were
controlled by their desire to possess female bodies. Because of their obsession with sex, men, not women, she argued, were the weaker sex. Paglia
contended that Madonna was the true feminist because she "has taught
young women to be fully female and sexual while retaining control over
their lives."[2]

In *Backlash,* Susan Faludi had written about the male reaction against
second-wave feminism, which she presented as overblown and dangerous.
In *Stiffed: The Betrayal of the American Man* she did an about-face to explore
what she saw as the plight of men who were victimized by structural
changes in employment and felt threatened by the women's movement. She
concluded that both women in particular and society in general must treat
them gently and understand their insecurities.

THIRD-WAVE FEMINISM

Younger women involved in the feminist movement accepted many of
these ideas. They coined the term "third-wave feminism" to describe their
stance. Their realignment was similar to that of the second generation of gay
activists, who in the 1980s separated themselves from preceding generations
by adopting the formerly pejorative word "queer" as their label. Moreover,
younger blacks established an independent voice by calling themselves "niggers." Third-wave feminists refer to themselves as "girls" and call for "girl

power," using a term that second-wave feminists rejected as sexist. Third-wave feminists view using makeup as sexy and camp, and they embrace re-vealing clothing as liberating. They also undergo body piercing as a mark of cultural rebellion, learn martial arts for self-defense and power, and revel in their sexuality. They look on their childhood play with Barbie as liberating, not confining.

"It is as though the sexual revolution never died," wrote Paula Kamen in *Her Way,* one of the books written by members of this generation to describe their attitudes. Rather, Kamen contended, the sexual revolution of the 1960s "slowly evolved from a male movement into one in which women call the shots." To Kamen, Monica Lewinsky was the model for the new movement because she knew what she wanted and she got it. In her relationship with Clinton, she was, according to Kamen, "relentless and brazen and self-centered in her quest for sex and power."[3] Kamen con-cluded that all women should follow Lewinsky's example.

Popular music and art directed to teenagers and young women reflected these ideas. New female bands in the early 1990s strutted on stage and sang songs encouraging personal independence, while they praised aggressive behavior. The Spice Girls were the most prominent of these bands. Some bands grouped themselves together in what they called the Riot Grrrl movement. By this term they meant the preadolescent, tomboy period in girls, when they are independent and act like boys, before adolescence brings an obsession with their appearance and with attracting males. Lilith Fair was a festival held by prominent female musicians, such as Melissa Etheridge and k.d. lang. Several artists on the tour were lesbian, and they expressed their pride in being gay through their songs. The Guerilla Girls, a group of New York artists, designed posters in which they drew guerilla heads on reproductions of famous paintings of women that they found sex-ist. They also wore leather jackets and put on guerilla heads that they con-structed, to engage in "guerilla" theater at major museums—and gain in-stant media attention—as they protested the lack of paintings by women in the nation's museums.

Young women who were "third-wave feminists" focused on issues that interested their own generation. These especially included sexual abuse, in-cest, and the fact that teenagers are denied complete sexual education when the United States has the highest rate of teenage pregnancy and STDs in the industrialized world. The Riot Grrrls often sang about harrowing personal experiences of abuse, and band members started Web sites and 'zines (self-published, small circulation magazines). Through these magazines teenagers who had been abused could communicate with one another.

Young women formed action groups. The Women's Health Action Mobilization (WHAM), composed of women in their twenties and thirties,

© Catherine Karnow/Corbis

Muslim American Women. The dress of these women is an example of hijab, or the practice of covering the body, that many Muslim women follow for a variety of reasons: as an act of obedience to their religion and their god (Allah); to avoid sexual objectification; to denote chastity and express their self-esteem as Muslim women; as a sign of resistance to what they view as Western imperialism against Muslim countries. The covering varies from region to region; the dress shown in this picture is typical of sub-Saharan Africa. The immigration of increasing numbers of Muslims to the United States, at a time when the nation is involved in military actions against Muslim extremists in both Afghanistan and Iraq, has brought new social issues. How, for instance, will Muslim women, who seem increasingly drawn to the more extreme versions of hijab as a symbol of resistance to the West, and Western women, who are wearing increasingly sexualized dress in public, coexist?

was formed in 1989. Inspired by the radical AIDS protest group, ACT UP, it used guerilla theater tactics to agitate for health issues such as the value of herbal medicine and abortion rights. The Women's Action Coalition (WAC) was founded in 1992 in New York, and similar groups appeared in Minneapolis, Houston, Toronto, Los Angeles, and other cities. Composed of younger women, the organizations used street theater and demonstrations to protest against a variety of practices, including nonpayment of child support and the rape of women in Bosnia, a Balkan state in which civil war raged. According to Myra Ferree and Beth Hess, "the Third Wave has attempted to bridge the gap between spontaneous local protest actions, ongoing direct action groups, and more conventional forms of political action."[4]

Prom, 2001. A new age of sexual tolerance is emerging, as an interracial lesbian couple prepare for the high school prom. The masculine garb is a parody of the traditional tuxedo, with the classic ponytail of the 1950s adding an additional spoof. The female dress draws directly from the revealing fashions of the recent era.

Younger lesbians, disliking the seriousness of the lesbian politics of the 1970s, reintroduced makeup and sexy clothing, calling themselves "lipstick lesbians." Yet by the late 1980s, some young lesbians demanded greater intensity in personal style and in political activism. Joining with gays to protest the government's slow response to the AIDS epidemic, they participated in forming groups like ACT UP and Queer Nation. These groups used direct protest and "guerilla theater" tactics to make the case for gay and lesbian rights.

THE RECENT SITUATION

Indications of increasing equality for women are strong. Growing numbers of women, for example, are entering the professions. Forty-three percent of medical graduates are now women, and comparable figures exist for law schools. Even some business and accounting schools are approaching the halfway mark. Women continue to win political office, and two female senators are mentioned as possible presidential candidates: Democrat Hillary Clinton of New York, elected to the Senate in 2000, and Republican Elizabeth Dole of Virginia, who is the wife of former senator and vice-presidential candidate Robert Dole.

Yet discrimination against women still remains. The workforce is still, for the most part, segregated by sex. Such segregation continues to underlie wage discrimination. In 1982 women made about 57 cents for every dollar men made, and although this figure has increased, the advance is partly due to a drop in men's wages. What is called a "glass ceiling" to the advancement of women into high executive positions still exists. Twelve percent of police officers in the United States are women, but women are police chiefs in only 123 of the 17,000 police forces in the nation. Of the top 2,500 wage earners in the Fortune 500 companies, 63 are women. Women are 7 percent of officers in high-tech companies. Five percent of partners in the major law firms are women. Forty-three percent of medical school graduates are women, but they are only 7 percent of deans in medical schools and 11 percent of full professors. Forty percent of doctorates are awarded to women, but men still comprise the vast majority of full professors and administrators in colleges.

THE GEORGE W. BUSH PRESIDENCY

The election of George W. Bush to the presidency and the election of a Republican-controlled House and Senate in 2000 signaled the renewed ascendancy of the New Right in politics. Bush surprised many when he appointed women, blacks, and Hispanics to high-level administrative offices. These positions included members of his cabinet and African American Condoleezza Rice as his National Security Advisor.

But Bush has also overturned many feminist gains. Many of his appointees to the federal judiciary have been conservative and antifeminist, and he signed the law Congress passed forbidding late-term abortions and cutting funds for family planning assistance both in the United States and overseas. Opponents of late-term abortion laws argue that they are so loosely written that they could easily be applied to abortions in the first and second terms (three and six months). They also contend that late-term abortions are rarely performed, except to save a mother's life, and that the laws making them illegal usually contain no provisions about the mother's health. Up to this point, the Supreme Court has consistently overturned such laws passed by the states because of the lack of this provision.

Like most of his predecessors since Reagan, Bush castigated welfare mothers and reduced the funds for both food stamps and whatever was left of the "safety net" against poverty. Arguing that the economic recession that began after he assumed the presidency was a short-term readjustment in the economic cycle, Bush moved to create jobs by giving vast tax cuts to the wealthy, arguing that businessmen would use the funds to hire more workers.

Supporting neither side too strongly on the contentious issues of affirmative action and gay rights, Bush distanced himself from Supreme Court decisions in 2003 that upheld affirmative action and struck down the sodomy laws, which had been used to arrest and prosecute gays. But in his State of the Union speech before Congress in January 2004, he came out strongly in favor of a constitutional amendment restricting marriage to a man and a woman. On abortion, potentially the most volatile matter in politics, his public statements have straddled the issue, sometimes seeming to support one side and sometimes the other, although he signed the bill prohibiting late-term abortions. In the spring of 2003, however, he appointed a commission of individuals hostile to Title IX to "analyze" it. Title IX of the Education Act of 1972 is the federal law that bans gender discrimination in federally funded schools and colleges and that has been widely implemented in athletic programs. The real purpose of the commission, it appears, is to dismantle Title IX on the grounds that it has undermined the funding of male sports and has been used to create women's sports teams in colleges and universities where there was neither interest nor available female athletes.

On September 11, 2001, terrorists hijacked two commercial airplanes and flew them into the twin towers of the World Trade Center, destroying the towers and killing several thousand individuals. Two other commercial airplanes were hijacked and flown by terrorists. One crashed into the Pentagon and the other in a field in rural Pennsylvania. The latter was most likely bound for the capital, but it was brought down by passengers who attacked the hijackers in an act of heroism that cost them their own lives. After these events, national security against the threat from Islamic extremists absorbed much of the administration's energy. In 2002 Bush sent forces into Afghanistan to overthrow the Taliban government there, since it was openly hostile to the United States and contained terrorist training camps. In the spring of 2003 Bush sent armed forces into Iraq to "liberate" the country from a despotic Saddam Hussein and to end his presumed threat to American security. These actions resulted in an outpouring of patriotism and a willingness to support Bush's schemes, even as he moved toward the New Right agenda.

WOMEN AND AGING
IN CONTEMPORARY TIMES

One of the major trends in the recent history of women in America has been the aging of the population. In 1982 individuals under twenty years of age constituted 31 percent of the population, while 12 percent were over sixty-five. If the current low levels of fertility and mortality are maintained, it is estimated that in the year 2050 individuals under twenty will comprise 18 percent of the population and those over sixty-five will comprise 29 percent.

These figures represent both possibilities and problems for women. As among the general population, there has been a "feminization of poverty" among the elderly. Women constitute about 59 percent of the elderly and about 72 percent of the elderly poor. Women generally live longer than men—about seven years longer—and this disparity has created demographic imbalances that dictate that many heterosexual aging women will not be able to find a man as their partner. Caring for aging unwell parents has created problems for middle-aged daughters, since women invariably are the caretakers of elderly relatives. Analysts now refer to a "sandwich generation" of women who care not only for their own children but also for aging parents and, given increased life expectancy, sometimes even grandparents.

Still, aging itself is undergoing changes in definition, as gerontologists conclude that proper diet and exercise can eliminate many of the physical problems associated with growing old. And the expected behavior of the elderly has become increasingly flexible. From the 1950s on, women moved lockstep through the life cycle. They spent their early years in school before marrying in their late teens or early twenties and raising their children before entering the workforce in their late thirties and working until retiring in their early sixties. Today, however, both men and women marry later. They move in and out of the workforce and educational institutions, bearing their children at older ages. Moreover, divorce at any point during the life span can propel individuals into unexpected behavior, in which women of fifty or sixty or even older may find themselves dating and entering into short-term or long-term affairs.

THE PRESENT:
REVOLUTIONARY OR NOT?

The broad social changes affecting women's lives throughout America's modern age have recently followed a revolutionary direction, prompting some analysts to predict that the traditional ways in which Americans have lived will cease to exist. Census data reveal that the birthrate is producing near-zero population growth, the age of first marriage is rising, more and more individuals are living alone, the divorce rate is rising, and women, especially married women and women with preschool children, are increasingly in the workforce. In 1965 about 39 percent of adult American women were employed for remuneration outside the home, and the rate of women at work rose to 53 percent in 1982 and 60 percent in 1996. In the latter year, women constituted 46 percent of the labor force. Surveys reveal that only 19 percent of Americans continue to live in the legendary American family, in which the husband works and the wife stays at home with the children.

As the nation moves further into a postindustrial economy and technology radically changes American lives, women may be eliminated from sectors of the workforce, especially as clerical labor is taken over by computers. Alternatively, work may move to the home, thus increasing the privatization of the family. Some analysts, however, speak of a "feminization" of the workforce, as cheaper female workers are hired to replace more expensive male workers.

Social indicators are never easy to interpret. Young women's interest in traditional marriages and the rise in sales of diamond engagement rings may indicate the resurgence of a new conservatism among the younger generation—or these trends may reflect a psychological need to adjust to new forces by reaffirming traditional rituals. Unmarried women in their thirties have recently been buying diamond "engagement" rings and wearing them on their right ring finger to celebrate their independence. At present body image is bifurcated. The vogue of extreme thinness continues (and rates of anorexia and bulimia remain high), while obesity has become a national problem. Stomach stapling and other surgical procedures to reduce appetite and overeating are very popular. Big breasts, now shaped like melons, have come into vogue, and the fashion has resulted in a steady growth in the numbers of surgical breast implants among women.

At the same time a muscular look is also popular among women. Pop singer Britney Spears has promoted the exposure of the naval, pierced with a diamond or a ring, in addition to the lowering of pants to the line of the pubic hair. The vogue of these looks has spread like wildfire among young women. Such revealing fashions have never before been seen in Western culture. Men also resort to body shaping and cosmetic surgery, particularly in the form of penile enlargement, pectoral implants, and facial reconstruction. Men constitute 20 percent of cosmetic surgery clients, and they are the fastest growing market for this specialty.

Popular singers and videos promote free love. Female performers on MTV regularly perform what amounts to a strip tease. The vast majority of sites on the Internet are pornographic. Manufacturers promote nail polish, makeup, high heels, and "slut" clothing to girls as young as five. Is this liberation, commodification, oppression, or a self-indulgent culture gone too far? The definition of acceptable sex practices continues to expand, with petting and oral sex expected in sexual encounters.

The attitudes of the major characters of the hit television show, *Sex and the City*, seem to constitute a new mantra for liberated women. The series revolves around the lives of four New York women in their early thirties, who spend most of their time shopping, drinking cocktails, or engaging in one-night stands. They discuss with each other the details of their sexual encounters with as much gusto as men do in locker rooms; their careers seem secondary to their search for the "right man"; they continually worry about winding up as spinsters. They wear tight dresses with plunging necklines, skirts to the crotch, and shoes with high, stiletto heels. Their openness about sex may be a breakthrough and their close friendship admirable. Should their values be a model for young women? Do they represent liberation for women or a new stereotyping, masked as freedom?

The numbers of teenage pregnancies are decreasing, partly due to a new emphasis on virginity and partly due to the growing popularity of sexual techniques other than intercourse. And in the spring of 2004, after Janet Jackson bared her breast while performing at halftime of the Superbowl football game, Victoria's Secret withdrew its sexualized underwear fashion show from television. Moreover, Clear Channel Communications was fined nearly $500,000 for allowing Howard Stern to use explicit sexual material on his show. Do these events indicate that a new sexual conservatism is appearing in the nation? Are they the results of the pressure of right-wing conservatives who support an end to abortion and to gay marriage? Or are they simply episodic, with no connection to a general trend?

Poverty rates continue to expand, while the "feminization of poverty" escalates, with women now constituting 80 percent of the poor. Food stamps have been cut, but more than thirty-six million Americans suffer from uncertain access to food. Between 2000 and 2003, 2.7 million private-sector jobs were lost, while few families are capable of living on the $5.15 to $7.15 an hour minimum wage, especially since most of these jobs carry neither medical benefits nor maternity leave. With the recent escalation in housing costs, there is no state in the nation where a low-income worker can afford a modest one- or two-bedroom rental unit.

Capitalism goes through cycles of inflation and depression, and employment rates have generally been cyclical as well. Thus this problem with poverty may right itself, although long-term trends in income distribution show growing discrepancies in wealth. The wealthiest 1 percent of individuals in the nation own more than 50 percent of the nation's wealth. In 1981 the ratio of CEO compensation to worker compensation was 42 to 1; in 2001 it was 500 to 1. The United States, in fact, has the greatest income disparities of any nation in the industrialized world, and women, often with children, are at the bottom of the income hierarchy.

But rates of upward social mobility remain steady, and there has been a sizable movement of blacks and Hispanics into the middle class. The rate of poverty has decreased from 23 percent of the population in the 1980s to 13 percent today. (Given the fact that expenses such as child care and medical care are not included in determining the poverty rate, however, some experts contend that the percentage is actually considerably higher.) The President's Economic Report for 2003 pointed out that between 50 to 80 percent of those in the bottom one-fifth of the income scale will push themselves into at least the next one-fifth over a period of ten years. A recent opinion poll found that 19 percent of American taxpayers believed themselves to be in the top 1 percent of earners. A further 20 percent thought they would end up there within their lifetimes. These figures seem to indicate that the American dream of upward social mobility remains alive and well.

By 2003 owning a huge sport utility vehicle (SUV) had become a national vogue, while eating at fast-food restaurants and consuming products full of carbohydrates and sugar was producing ever-larger bodies among the American population. Buying and building "monster mansions" has become popular among the well-to-do. Americans seem intent on asserting their identities through size or displaying their pretensions to wealth in every way possible. Yet the nation has had to deal with emotional challenges beyond even 9/11. Periodic economic downturns and the continuing restructuring of the economy produce insecurity, while the new immigration is producing a multicultural society, with stresses for the Anglo-American majority and tensions between ethnicities themselves.

The movement of women into work outside the home and into positions of public authority is undermining patriarchal arrangements. Children rebel against parents, while new generations arise to contest the authority and mores of older generations. Rapidly changing technology destabilizes the workforce and renders older ways of living obsolete. Meanwhile the United States seems to be involved in a long and complex war against terrorism, with the atom bomb still a threat.

Americans seem overwhelmed by the new social trends, by the high incidence of divorce and the breakdown of the traditional family, by the danger of nuclear attack and the seeming inability of government administrators to solve the nation's economic difficulties, by women's new threat to traditional definitions of masculinity. With increasing rates of violence on television and in films and videos and with "macho," muscular looks and behavior an increasing ideal for men, they seem to be reacting against women's new freedom and authority. In a similar manner, men at the turn into the twentieth century indulged in a "hypermasculinity" in reaction to the advent of the "New Woman."

But many Americans seem willing to explore new sexual and social roles with intelligence and sensitivity and to applaud the extension of equality to women. In spite of the turn to idealizing aggressive male behavior, the sensitive man has not been lost. Indeed, although studies show that married men are reluctant to participate in cooking or housework, their participation in childrearing has significantly increased over the last decades, while the profeminist men's movement exists to point the way to a gentler image for men. Indeed, the "metrosexual" man has recently emerged to prominence as a model for men. This person combines a masculine style with attention to clothes, cosmetics, and fashions. *Queer Eye for the Straight Guy,* currently a popular television show, features gay men showing straight men how to decorate their apartments in the latest mod fashions, what clothes to wear, and how to style their hair and care for their skin.

As to the future of feminism, that is hard to predict. Once before in the history of modern America, with the attainment of suffrage and the movement of women into the workforce, equality for women seemed in sight. Yet the momentum slowed down in the hedonistic 1920s and the economically troubled 1930s. But the feminist revolution of the last fifty years has so permeated the national consciousness and changed behavior that it is difficult to visualize its demise. The dissension of feminists of different points of view and of differing generations over the last several decades may be a sign of strength. Although individuals may disagree over what direction to take, feminist organizational vitality remains strong. With its emphasis on flexibility in gender definitions and its sensitivity to race and class, feminism holds out a humane way of life for men as well as for women.

NOTES

1. Allan Metz and Carol Benson, eds., *Madonna: Two Decades of Commentary* (New York: Schirmer Books, 1999), 42.

2. Metz and Benson, *Madonna,* 216.

3. Paula Kamen, *Her Way: Young Women Remake the Sexual Revolution* (New York: Broadway Books, 2000), 4, 7.

4. Myra Marx Ferree and Beth B. Hess, *Controversy and Coalition: The New Feminist Movement Across Four Decades of Change* (New York: Routledge, 2000), 192.

Bibliography

CHAPTER 1

On the Gibson Girl and dress in general, see Lois W. Banner, *American Beauty* (New York: Knopf, 1983). On gender and the law, see Joan Hoff, *Law, Gender, and Injustice: A Legal History of United States Women* (New York: New York University Press, 1991), and Linda K. Kerber's study of five important Supreme Court cases, *No Constitutional Right to be Ladies: Women and the Obligations of Citizenship* (New York: Hill and Wang, 1998).

On primary and secondary education see Redding Sugg, *Motherteacher: The Feminization of American Education* (Charlottesville: University Press of Virginia, 1978). The major work on women and higher education is Barbara Miller Solomon, *In the Company of Educated Women: A History of Women and Higher Education in America* (New Haven, Conn.: Yale University Press, 1985). See also Lynn D. Gordon, *Gender and Higher Education in the Progressive Era* (New Haven, Conn.: Yale University Press, 1990), and Helen Lefkowitz Horowitz, *Alma Mater: Design and Experience in Women's Colleges from Their Nineteenth Century Beginnings to the 1930s* (New York: Knopf, 1984). Julie Roy Jeffrey has written about western education in *Frontier Women: The Trans-Mississippi West, 1840–1880* (New York: Hill & Wang, 1979).

On women, medicine, and sexuality, see John D'Emilio and Estelle B. Freedman, *Intimate Matters: A History of Sexuality in America* (New York: Harper & Row, 1988), and John S. Haller Jr. and Robin M. Haller, *The Physician and Sexuality in*

Victorian America (Urbana: University of Illinois Press, 1974). In *Searching the Heart: Women, Men, and Romantic Love in Victorian America* (New York: Oxford University Press, 1990), Karen Lystra contends that married couples in the nineteenth century had exuberant sex. She is challenged by Carol Z. Stearns and Peter N. Stearns, "Victorian Sexuality: Can Historians Do It Better?" *Journal of Social History* 18 (1984–85): 626–33, and Steven Seidman, "The Power of Desire and the Pleasure of Danger: Victorian Sexuality Reconsidered," *Journal of Social History* 24 (fall 1990): 47–60. For an attack on the treatment of women by nineteenth-century doctors, see C. J. Barker-Benfield, *The Horrors of the Half-Known Life: Male Attitudes Toward Women and Sexuality in Nineteenth-Century America* (New York: Harper & Row, 1976).

On abortion, see James C. Mohr, *Abortion in America: The Origins and Evolution of National Policy* (New York: Oxford University Press, 1978). On birth control in general, see Linda Gordon, *The Moral Property of Women: A History of Birth Control in America* (Urbana: University of Illinois Press, 1990). On more specific issues, see Andrea Tone, *Devices and Desires: A History of Contraceptives in America* (New York: Hill and Wang, 2001), and Leslie J. Reagan, *When Abortion Was a Crime: Women, Medicine, and Law in the United States, 1867–1973* (Berkeley: University of California Press, 1997). The most recent study of the Victorian antivice reformers remains David J. Pivar, *Purity Crusade: Sexual Morality and Social Control, 1868–1900* (Westport, Conn.: Greenwood Press, 1973). Sarah J. Stage, *Female Complaints: Lydia Pinkham and the Business of Women's Medicine* (New York: Norton, 1981), studies both women's health in the nineteenth century and the life of Lydia Pinkham, a successful businesswoman, who marketed her "soothing syrup" for women's complaints to a phenomenal success.

Carroll Smith-Rosenberg explores the "separate culture of women" in "The Female World of Love and Ritual: Relations Between Women in Nineteenth-Century America," *Signs: Journal of Women in Culture and Society* 1 (autumn 1975): 125. On lesbianism and the sexologists in this era, see Lois W. Banner, *Intertwined Lives: Margaret Mead, Ruth Benedict, and Their Circle* (New York: Alfred A. Knopf, 2003); Jennifer Terry, *An American Obsession: Science, Medicine, and Homosexuality in Modern America* (Chicago: University of Chicago Press, 1999); and Lillian Faderman, *Surpassing the Love of Men: Romantic Friendship and Love Between Women, From the Renaissance to the Present* (New York: Morrow, 1981). On women and aging, see Lois W. Banner, *In Full Flower: Aging Women, Power, and Sexuality* (New York: Alfred A. Knopf, 1992).

The middle-class family is covered in Steven Mintz and Susan Kellogg, *Domestic Revolutions: A Social History of American Family Life* (New York: Free Press, 1988), and in Carl N. Degler, *At Odds: Women and the Family in America from the Revolution to the Present* (New York: Oxford University Press, 1980). Glenna Mathews explores domestic technology in *"Just a Housewife": The Rise and Fall of Domesticity in America* (New York: Oxford University Press, 1987), as does Susan Strasser in *Never Done: A History of American Housework* (New York: Pantheon Books, 1982). For divorce, see Glenda Riley, *Divorce: An American Tradition* (New York: Oxford University Press, 1991), and Elaine Tyler May, *Great Expectations: Marriage and Divorce in Post-Victorian America* (Chicago: University of Chicago Press, 1980). Margaret S. Marsh's book on the "companionate family" in the 1890s is *Surburban Lives* (New Brunswick, N.J.: Rutgers University Press, 1990).

On women in vaudeville and on the stage, see Susan A. Glenn, *Female Spec-*

tacle: The Theatrical Roots of Modern Feminism (Cambridge, Mass.: Harvard University Press, 2001), and M. Alison Kibler, *Rank Ladies: Gender and Cultural Hierarchy in American Vaudeville* (Chapel Hill: University of North Carolina Press, 1999). William Leach, *Land of Desire: Merchants, Power, and the Rise of a New American Culture* (New York: Pantheon, 1993), examines the new institutions of consumer culture. Elaine S. Abelson explores "kleptomania" in *When Ladies Go A-thieving: Middle-Class Shoplifters in the Victorian Department Store* (New York: Oxford University Press, 1989). Information about Helen Mary Butler and Annie Taylor is in Dorothy Schneider and Carl J. Schneider, *American Women in the Progressive Era, 1900–1920* (New York: Doubleday, 1993). An excellent study of women as inventors and entrepreneurs is Virginia G. Drachman, *Enterprising Women: 250 Years of American Business* (Chapel Hill: University of North Carolina Press, 2002). The latest biography of Madame C. J. Walker is A'Leila Perry Bundles, *On Her Own Ground: The Life and Times of Madame C. J. Walker* (New York: Scribner's, 2001).

For scientific views of women, see Cynthia Eagle Russett, *Sexual Science: The Victorian Construction of Womanhood* (Cambridge, Mass.: Harvard University Press, 1989). For the feminist response to male academic research on women, see Rosalind Rosenberg, *Beyond Separate Spheres: The Intellectual Roots of Modern Feminism* (New Haven, Conn.: Yale University Press, 1982). Childbirth and midwifery are covered in Judy Barrett Litoff, *American Midwives: 1860 to the Present* (Westport, Conn.: Greenwood Press, 1978), and Richard W. Wertz and Dorothy C. Wertz, *Lying-In: A History of Childbirth in America* (New York: Free Press, 1977). On childrearing, see Rima D. Apple, *Mothers and Medicine: A Social History of Infant Feeding, 1890–1950* (Madison: University of Wisconsin Press, 1987). For demographic analysis, consult Robert V. Wells, "Women's Lives Transformed: Demographic and Family Patterns in America, 1600–1970," in Carol Ruth Berkin and Mary Beth Norton (eds.), *Women of America: A History* (Boston: Houghton Mifflin, 1979), pp. 17–33.

On the entry of women into the professions, see Pernina Migdal Glazer and Miriam Slater, *Unusual Colleagues: The Entrance of Women into the Professions, 1890–1940* (New Brunswick, N.J.: Rutgers University Press, 1987). Studies of women in specific professions and occupations have appeared. On law, see Virginia G. Drachman, *Sisters in Law: Women Lawyers in Modern American History* (Cambridge, Mass.: Harvard University Press, 1998). On medicine, see Ellen S. More, *Restoring the Balance: Women Physicians and the Profession of Medicine, 1850–1955* (Cambridge, Mass.: Harvard University Press, 1999), and Regina Markell Morantz-Sanchez, *Sympathy and Science: Women Physicians in American Medicine* (New York: Oxford University Press, 1985). For women in business, see Angel Kwolek-Folland, *Engendering Business: Men and Women in the Corporate Office, 1870–1930* (Baltimore: Johns Hopkins University Press, 1994). On women scientists, see Margaret S. Rossiter's *Women Scientists in America: Before Affirmative Action, 1940–1972* (Baltimore: Johns Hopkins University Press, 1995), and the same author's *Women Scientists in America: Struggles and Strategies to 1940* (Baltimore: Johns Hopkins University Press, 1982). For other professions, see Susan Reverby, *Ordered to Care: The Dilemma of American Nursing, 1850–1945* (New York: Cambridge University Press, 1987); L. Dee Garrison, *Apostles of Culture: The Public Librarian and American Society, 1876–1920* (New York: The Free Press, 1979); and Marion Marzolf, *Up From the Footnote: A History of Women Journalists*

(New York: Hastings House, 1977). On clerical workers, see Cindy Slonik Aron, *Ladies and Gentlemen of the Civil Service: Middle-Class Workers in Victorian America* (New York: Oxford University Press, 1987), and Margery W. Davies, *Woman's Place Is at the Typewriter: Office Work and Office Workers, 1870–1930* (Philadelphia: Temple University Press, 1982).

The remasculinization thesis for the 1890s and 1900s is explored in Gail Bederman, *Manliness and Civilization: A Cultural History of Gender and Race in the United States, 1880–1917* (Chicago: University of Chicago Press, 1995). Sharon Hartman Strom discusses the phenomenon as it appeared in office work in *Beyond the Typewriter: Gender, Class, and the Origins of Modern American Office Work* (Urbana: University of Illinois Press, 1992). Helena Silverberg (ed.), *Gender and American Social Science: The Formative Years* (Princeton, N.J.: Princeton University Press, 1998) addresses the issue of masculinization in the social sciences.

For rural women, see Katherine Jellison, *Entitled to Power: Farm Women and Technology, 1913–63* (Chapel Hill: University of North Carolina Press, 1993); Deborah Fink, *Agrarian Women: Wives and Mothers in Rural Nebraska* (Chapel Hill: University of North Carolina Press, 1992); Joan Jensen, *Promise to the Land: Essays on Rural Women* (Albuquerque: University of New Mexico Press, 1990); and Arlene Scadron (ed.), *On Their Own: Widows and Widowhood in the American Southwest, 1848–1939* (Urbana: University of Illinois Press, 1988).

Women's work in service occupations and factories has received much attention. See Ava Baron, *Work Engendered: Toward a New History of American Labor* (Ithaca, N.Y.: Cornell University Press, 1990); Alice Kessler-Harris, *Out to Work: A History of Wage-Earning Women in the United States* (New York: Oxford University Press, 1982); and Barbara Mayer Wertheimer, *We Were There: The Story of Working Women in America* (New York: Pantheon Books, 1977).

For individual occupations and industries, see Nancy L. Green, *Ready-to-Wear and Ready-to-Work: A Century of Industry and Immigrants in Paris and New York* (Durham, N.C.: Duke University Press, 1997); Eileen Boris, *Home to Work: Motherhood and the Politics of Industrial Homework in the U.S.* (New York: Cambridge University Press, 1994); Susan J. Kleinberg, *In the Shadow of the Mills: Working-Class Families in Pittsburgh, 1870–1907* (Pittsburgh: University of Pittsburgh Press, 1989); Mary H. Blewett, *Men, Women, and Work: Class, Gender, and Protest in the New England Shoe Industry, 1780–1910* (Urbana: University of Illinois Press, 1988); Patricia A. Cooper, *Once a Cigar Maker: Men, Women, and Work Culture in American Cigar Factories, 1900–1919* (Urbana: University of Illinois Press, 1987); Susan Porter Benson, *Countercultures: Saleswomen, Managers, and Customers in American Department Stores, 1890–1940* (Urbana: University of Illinois Press, 1986); and David Katzman, *Seven Days a Week: Women and Domestic Service in Industrializing America* (New York: Oxford University Press, 1978). See also Jacqueline Jones, *The Dispossessed: America's Underclasses from the Civil War to the Present* (New York: Basic Books, 1992).

Women and immigration is covered in Donna R. Gabaccia, *From the Other Side: Women, Gender, and Immigrant Life in the United States, 1820–1990* (Bloomington: University of Indiana Press, 1994), and in Elizabeth Ewen, *Immigrant Women in the Land of Dollars* (New York: Monthly Review Press, 1985). For specific groups, see Paula Hyman and Deborah Dash Moore, *Jewish Women in America: An Historical Encyclopedia* (New York: Routledge, 1998); Susan A. Glenn, *Daughters of the Shtetl: Life and Labor in the Immigrant Generation* (Ithaca, N.Y.:

Cornell University Press, 1990); Judith Smith, *Family Connections: A History of Italian and Jewish Immigrant Lives in Providence, Rhode Island, 1909–1914* (Albany: State University of New York Press, 1985); and Virginia Yans-McLaughlin, *Family and Community: Italian Immigrants in Buffalo, 1880–1930* (Ithaca, N.Y.: Cornell University Press, 1977). Two powerful novels by participants are Anzia Yezierska, *Bread Givers* (1925), and Agnes Smedley, *Daughter of Earth* (1929).

On Asian, Hispanic, and Native American women, see Karen Anderson, *A History of Racial Ethnic Women in Modern America* (New York: Oxford University Press, 1996), and Ellen Carol DuBois and Vicki L. Ruiz (eds.), *Unequal Sisters: A Multicultural Reader in U.S. Women's History* (New York: Routledge, 1990, 1994, 2000). For Chinese immigration and work patterns, see Judy Yung, *Unbound Feet: A Social History of Chinese Women in San Francisco* (Berkeley: University of California Press, 1995). Interesting autobiographies include Jade Snow Wong, *Fifth Chinese Daughter* (1950; Seattle: University of Washington Press, 1989); Akemi Kikumura, *Through Harsh Winters: The Life of a Japanese Immigrant Woman* (Novato, Calif.: Chandler & Sharp, 1981); and Mary Paik Lee, *Quiet Odyssey: A Pioneer Korean Woman in America* (Seattle: University of Washington Press, 1990).

The most recent history of Hispanic women is Vicki L. Ruiz, *From Out of the Shadows: Mexican-American Women in Twentieth-Century America* (New York: Oxford University Press, 1998). See also Sarah Deutsch, *No Separate Refuge: Culture, Class, and Gender on an Anglo-Hispanic Frontier in the American Southwest, 1880–1940* (New York: Oxford University Press, 1987).

For recent histories of black women, see Deborah Gray White, *Too Heavy a Load: Black Women in Defense of Themselves, 1894–1994* (New York: Norton, 1999); Darline Clark Hine and Kathleen Thompson, *A Shining Thread of Hope: The History of Black Women in America* (New York: Broadway Books, 1998); and Jacqueline Jones, *Labor of Love, Labor of Sorrow: Black Women, Work and the Family, from Slavery to the Present* (New York: Vintage, 1986). Insightful books on women in the South in the pre-1900 period include: Tera W. Hunter, *To 'Joy my Freedom: Southern Black Women's Lives and Labors after the Civil War* (Cambridge, Mass.: Harvard, 1997), and Glenda Elizabeth Gilmore, *Gender and Jim Crow: Women and the Politics of White Supremacy in North Carolina, 1896–1920* (Chapel Hill: University of North Carolina, 1996). In *Eradicating the Evil: Women in the American Anti-lynching Movement, 1892–1940* (New York: Garland, 2000), Mary Jane Brown provides a compelling picture of the horrors of lynching.

Paula Gunn Allen, *The Sacred Hoop: Recovering the Feminine in American Indian Traditions* (Boston: Beacon Press, 1986), writes about Indian spirituality. Studies of women in Native American tribal societies include Patricia Albers and Beatrice Medicine, *The Hidden Half: Studies of Plains Indian Women* (New York: Lanham, 1983); Clara Sue Kidwell, "The Power of Women in Three American Indian Societies," *Journal of Ethnic Studies* 6 (fall 1978): 113–21; and Diane Lebow, "Rethinking Matriliny among the Hopis," in Ruby Rohrlich and Elaine Hoffman Baruch (eds.), *Women in Search of Utopia: Mavericks and Mythmakers* (New York: Schocken Books, 1984). On the more recent period, see James Olson and Raymond Wilson, *Native Americans in the Twentieth Century* (Provo, Utah: Brigham Young University Press, 1984). On the berdache, see Sabine Lang, *Men as Women, Women as Men, Changing Gender in Native Culture*, trans. John L. Vantine (Austin:

University of Texas Press, 1998). In *The Spirit and the Flesh: Sexual Diversity in American Indian Culture* (Boston: Beacon, 1992), Walter L. Williams analyzes those societies in which men-women were spiritual leaders.

Jeanne Madeline Weimann, *The Fair Women: The Story of the Woman's Building, World's Columbian Exposition, Chicago, 1893* (Chicago: Academy Chicago, 1981), provides a comprehensive view of women's participation in the 1893 exposition. On the mammy image, see Cheryl Thurber, "The Development of the Mammy Image," in Virginia Bernhard, Betty Brandon, Elizabeth Fox-Genovese, and Theda Perdue (eds.), *Southern Women: Histories and Identities* (Columbia: University of Missouri Press, 1992).

For every period of the history of American women, biographies and autobiographies are available. Useful for the late nineteenth and early twentieth centuries are Mary Austin, *Earth Horizon: Autobiography* (New York: Literary Guild, 1932); Lois W. Banner, *Elizabeth Cady Stanton: A Radical for Woman's Rights* (Boston: Little, Brown, 1979); Elizabeth Blackwell, *Pioneer in Opening Up the Medical Profession to Women* (London and New York: Longmans, Gree, 1895); Edna Ferber, *A Peculiar Treasure* (Garden City, N.Y.: Doubleday, 1938); Helen Thomas Flexner, *A Quaker Girlhood* (New Haven, Conn.: Yale University Press, 1940); Margaret Mead, *Blackberry Winter: My Earlier Years* (New York: William Morrow, 1972); Maude Nathan, *Once upon a Time and Today* (New York: Putnam's, 1933); Kathryn Kish Sklar, *Catharine Beecher: A Study in American Domesticity* (New Haven, Conn.: Yale University Press, 1973); Jean Strouse, *Alice James: A Biography* (Boston: Houghton Mifflin, 1980); and the revealing autobiography of Agnes de Mille, *Where the Wings Grow* (Garden City, N.Y.: Doubleday, 1978). See also Rheta Childe Dorr, *A Woman of Fifty* (New York: Funk & Wagnalls, 1924), and Frances Parkinson Keyes, *All Flags Flying: Reminiscences of Frances Parkinson Keyes* (New York: McGraw-Hill Book Co., 1972).

Acclaimed contemporary novels about gender include Willa Cather, *My Antonia* (1918); Kate Chopin, *The Awakening* (1890); Theodore Dreiser, *Sister Carrie* (1900); Charlotte Perkins Gilman, *The Yellow Wallpaper* (1892); and Edith Wharton, *The House of Mirth* (1905).

Indispensable to research in women's history is Edward T. James, Janet Wilson James, and Paul S. Boyer (eds.), *Notable American Women, 1607–1950,* 3 vols. (Cambridge, Mass.: Harvard University Press, 1970), a collection of brief biographies, and an additional volume: Barbara Sicherman and Carol Hurd Green (eds.), *Notable American Women: The Modern Period* (Cambridge, Mass.: Harvard University Press, 1980). More biographies have recently been published in another volume in the series: Susan Ward (ed.), *Notable American Women: A Biographical Dictionary: Completing the Twentieth Century* (Cambridge, Mass.: Harvard University Press, 2004). Valuable also is Andrea Hinding, Ames Sheldon Bowers, and Clarke A. Chambers (eds.), *Women's History Sources: A Guide to Archives and Manuscript Collections in the United States* (New York: Bowker, 1979).

CHAPTER 2

On women's organizations in general, see Glenna Matthews, *Rise of Public Woman: Woman's Power and Woman's Place in the United States, 1630–1970* (New York: Oxford University Press, 1992), and Ann Firor Scott, *Natural Allies: Women's*

Associations in American History (Urbana: University of Illinois Press, 1991). On the Women's Christian Temperance Union (WCTU), see Catherine Gilbert Murdock, *Domesticating Drink: Women, Men, and Alcohol in America, 1870–1940* (Baltimore: Johns Hopkins University Press, 1999), and Ruth Bordin, *Woman and Temperance: The Quest for Power and Liberty, 1873–1900* (Philadelphia: Temple University Press, 1981). On the women's clubs, see Anne Ruggles Gere, *Intimate Practices: Literacy and Cultural Work in U.S. Women's Clubs, 1880–1920* (Urbana: University of Illinois Press, 1997), and Karen J. Blair, *The Clubwoman as Feminist: True Womanhood Redefined, 1868–1914* (New York: Holmes & Meier, 1980).

On the Daughters of the American Revolution (DAR), see Margaret Gibbs, *The Daughters of the American Revolution* (New York: Holt, Rinehart & Winston, 1969). Susan Levine has written on the American Association of University Women (AAUW) and feminism more generally in *Degrees of Equality: The American Association of University Women and the Challenges of Twentieth-Century Feminism* (Philadelphia: Temple University Press, 1995). The YWCA awaits its historian.

On racism in the women's movement, see Nancie Caraway, *Segregated Sisterhood: Racism and the Politics of American Feminism* (Knoxville: University of Tennessee, 1991). Two insightful works criticize reformers' paternalism: Peggy Pascoe, *Relations of Rescue: The Search for Female Moral Authority in the American West, 1874–1939* (New York: Oxford University Press, 1990), which highlights four western reform agencies, and Linda Gordon, *Heroes of Their Own Lives: The Politics and History of Family Violence: Boston, 1880–1960* (New York: Viking Penguin, 1988), which focuses on family agencies in Boston.

Much writing has appeared on women's involvement in Progressive reform. The major works include Daphne Spain, *How Women Saved the City* (Minneapolis: University of Minnesota, 2001); Elizabeth J. Clapp, *Mothers of All Children: Women Reformers and the Rise of Juvenile Courts in Progressive Era America* (University Park: Pennsylvania State University Press, 1998); Molly Ladd-Taylor, *Mother-Work: Women, Child Welfare, and the State, 1890–1930* (Urbana: University of Illinois Press, 1994); Sonya Michel and Seth Koven, *Mothers of a New World: Maternalist Politics and the Origins of Welfare States* (New York: Routledge, 1993); Theda Skocpol, *Protecting Soldiers and Mothers: The Political Origins of Social Policy in the United States* (Cambridge, Mass.: Harvard University Press, 1992); Noralee Frankel and Nancy S. Dye (eds.), *Gender, Class, Race, and Reform in the Progressive Era* (Lexington: University Press of Kentucky, 1991); Robyn Muncy, *Creating a Female Dominion in American Reform* (New York: Oxford University Press, 1991); Estelle B. Freedman, *Their Sisters' Keepers: Women's Prison Reform in America, 1830–1930* (Ann Arbor: University of Michigan Press, 1981); and Linda Gordon, "Black and White Visions of Welfare: Women's Welfare Activism, 1890–1945," in DuBois and Ruiz.

On women's involvement in Progressive reform in specific locales, see Maureen A. Flanagan, *Seeing with Their Hearts: Chicago Women and the Vision of the Good Life, 1877–1933* (Princeton, N.J.: Princeton University Press, 2002); Sarah Deutsch, *Women and the City: Gender, Power, and Space in Boston, 1870–1940* (New York: Oxford University Press, 2000); Elizabeth York Enstam, *Women and the Creation of Urban Life: Dallas, Texas, 1843–1920* (College Station: Texas A&M University Press, 1998); Judith N. McArthur, *Creating the New Women: The Rise of Southern Women's Progressive Culture in Texas, 1893–1918* (Urbana: University of Illinois Press, 1998); and Elizabeth Hayes Turner, *Women, Culture, and Community: Religion and Reform in Galveston, 1880–1923* (New York: Oxford University Press, 1993).

See also Elizabeth H. Pleck, *Domestic Tyranny: The Making of Social Policy Against Family Violence from Colonial Times to the Present* (New York: Oxford University Press, 1987), and Delores Hayden, *The Grand Domestic Revolution: A History of Feminist Designs for American Homes, Neighborhoods, and Cities* (Cambridge: Massachusetts Institute of Technology, 1981). For the details of the debate over protective legislation, see Susan Lehrer, *Origins of Protective Legislation for Women, 1905–1925* (Albany: State University of New York, 1987).

The only general history of the settlement-house movement is Allen F. Davis, *Spearheads for Reform: The Social Settlements and the Progressive Movement, 1890–1914* (New York: Oxford University Press, 1967). It can be supplemented by Camilla Stivers, *Bureau Men, Settlement Women: Constructing Public Administration in the Progressive Era* (Lawrence: University of Kansas Press, 2000); Ruth Crocker, *Social Work and Social Order: The Settlement House Movement in Two Industrial Cities* (Urbana: University of Illinois Press, 1992); and Mary Jo Deegan, *Jane Addams and the Men of the Chicago School, 1890–1918* (New Brunswick, N.J.: Transaction Books, 1990). The most recent biography of Addams is Jean Bethke Elshtain, *Jane Addams and the Dream of American Democracy: A Life* (New York: Basic Books, 2002). Both Addams and Lillian Wald wrote autobiographies: Jane Addams, *Twenty Years at Hull House with Autobiographical Notes* (Urbana: University of Illinois Press, 1990), and Lillian Wald, *The House on Henry Street* (1915; New York: Dover, 1971).

The story of women in art in this period is told by Laura R. Prieto, *At Home in the Studio: The Professionalization of Women Artists in America* (Cambridge, Mass.: Harvard University Press, 2001), and by Kathleen D. McCarthy, *Women's Culture: American Philanthropy and Art, 1830–1930* (Chicago: University of Chicago Press, 1991). Kathleen Waters Sander, *The Business of Charity: The Women's Exchange Movement, 1832–1900* (Urbana: University of Illinois Press, 1998), covers the women's exchange movement.

On the pre–World War I Greenwich Village radicals, see Christine Stansell, *American Moderns: Bohemian New York and the Creation of a New Century* (New York: Metropolitan Books, 2000). The most recent biography of Charlotte Perkins Gilman is Ann J. Lane, *To Herland and Beyond: The Life and Work of Charlotte Perkins Gilman* (New York: Pantheon Books, 1990). See also Gilman's autobiography, *The Living of Charlotte Perkins Gilman: An Autobiography* (1935; Madison: University of Wisconsin Press, 1991). On Emma Goldman, see Candace Serena Falk, *Love, Anarchy, and Emma Goldman* (New Brunswick, N.J.: Rutgers University Press, 1990); Alice Wexler, *Emma Goldman: An Intimate Life* (New York: Pantheon Books, 1984); and Goldman's autobiography, *Living My Life* (1934; New York: New American Library, 1977). On Margaret Sanger, the definitive biography is Ellen Chesler, *Woman of Valor: Margaret Sanger and the Birth Control Movement in America* (New York: Simon & Schuster, 1992). Margaret Sanger's autobiography is *Margaret Sanger: An Autobiography* (New York: Norton, 1938).

Nancy F. Cott discusses the origins of feminism in *The Grounding of Modern Feminism* (New Haven, Conn.: Yale University Press, 1987). On women and labor unions, consult the bibliography in chapter 1 of *Women in Modern America* and also Annelise Orleck, *Common Sense & a Little Fire: Women and Working-Class*

Politics in the United States, 1900–1965 (Chapel Hill: University of North Carolina Press, 1995); Meredith Tax, *The Rising of the Women* (New York: Monthly Review Press, 1980); and Philip S. Foner, *Women and the American Labor Movement: From Colonial Times to the Eve of World War One* (New York: Free Press, 1979). On the telephone operators' union, see Stephen H. Norwood, *Labor's Flaming Youth: Telephone Operators and Worker Militancy, 1878–1923* (Urbana: University of Illinois, 1990).

Kathryn Kish Sklar has analyzed the Consumers' League in *Florence Kelley & the Nation's Work: The Rise of Women's Political Culture, 1830–1900* (New Haven, Conn.: Yale University Press, 1995). Nancy Schrom Dye covers the Women's Trade Union League in *As Equals and as Sisters: Feminism, the Labor Movement and the Women's Trade Union League of New York* (Columbia: University of Missouri Press, 1980), as does Elizabeth Anne Payne, in *Reform, Labor, and Feminism: Margaret Dreier Robins and the Women's Trade Union League* (Urbana: University of Illinois Press, 1988).

On black women's organizations, see the bibliography for chapter 1 in the current edition of *Women in Modern America,* as well as Floris Barnett Cash, *African American Women and Social Action: The Clubwoman and Volunteerism from Jim Crow to the New Deal, 1896–1936* (Old Westport, Conn.: Greenwood Press, 2001), and Evelyn Brooks Higginbotham, *Righteous Discontent: The Women's Movement in the Black Baptist Church, 1880–1920* (Cambridge, Mass.: Harvard University Press, 1994). The most recent biography of Ida Wells-Barnett is Patricia A. Schechter, *Ida B. Wells and American Reform* (Chapel Hill: University of North Carolina Press, 2001).

Elizabeth Enstam has written about working-class women and leisure in *Ladies of Labor, Girls of Adventure: Working Women, Popular Culture, and Labor Politics at the Turn of the Century* (New York: Columbia University Press, 1999). Also consult Kathy Peiss, *Cheap Amusements: Working Women and Leisure in Turn-of-the-Century New York* (Philadelphia: Temple University Press, 1986). For single women in the cities, see Joanne J. Meyerowitz, *Women Adrift: Independent Wage Earners in Chicago, 1880–1930* (Chicago: University of Chicago Press, 1988).

For the concerns about "wayward girls," see Mary E. Odem, *Delinquent Daughters: Protecting and Policing Adolescent Female Sexuality in the United States, 1885–1920* (Chapel Hill: University of North Carolina Press, 1995), mostly about Los Angeles, and Ruth M. Alexander, *The "Girl Problem": Female Sexual Delinquency in New York, 1900–1930* (Ithaca, N.Y.: Cornell University Press, 1995). Prostitution and the vice commissions are discussed in David J. Pivar, *Purity and Hygiene: Women, Prostitution, and the "American Plan," 1900–1930* (Westport, Conn.: Greenwood Press, 2002); Timothy J. Gilfoyle, *City of Eros: New York City, Prostitution, and the Commercialization of Sex, 1790–1920* (New York: Norton, 1992); and Ruth Rosen, *The Lost Sisterhood: Prostitution in America, 1900–1918* (Baltimore: Johns Hopkins University Press, 1982). On the dance craze, see Lewis A. Erenberg, *New York Nightlife and the Transformation of American Culture, 1890–1930* (Westport, Conn.: Greenwood Press, 1981).

The most recent study of the women's suffrage movement is Suzanne M. Marilley, *Woman Suffrage and the Origins of Liberal Feminism in the United States, 1868–1920* (Ann Arbor: University of Wisconsin Press, 1997). Eleanor Flexner, *Century of Struggle: The Woman's Rights Movement in the United States* (Cambridge, Mass.: Harvard University Press, 1959), is still useful. Ellen Carol DuBois, *Harriot*

Stanton Blatch and the Winning of Women's Suffrage (New Haven, Conn.: Yale University Press, 1997) is insightful. David Morgan discusses the final years of the suffrage movement in *Suffragists and Democrats: The Politics of Woman Suffrage in America* (East Lansing: Michigan State University Press, 1972).

For moving statements by participants, see Sherna Gluck (ed.), *From Parlor to Prison: Five American Suffragists Talk About Their Lives: An Oral History* (New York: Random House, 1976), and Mary Jo Buhle and Paul Buhle (eds.), *The Concise History of Woman Suffrage: Selections from the Classic Work of Stanton, Anthony, Gage, and Harper* (Urbana: University of Illinois Press, 1978). On the anti-suffragists, see Susan E. Marshall, *Splintered Sisterhood: Gender and Class in the Campaign Against Woman Suffrage* (Madison: University of Wisconsin Press, 1997). On women in World War I, see Carrie Brown, *Rosie's Mom: Forgotten Women Workers of the First World War* (Boston: Northeastern University Press, 2002).

CHAPTER 3

Gary S. Cross has written about consumerism in the 1920s and later in *An All-Consuming Century: Why Commercialism Won in Modern America* (New York: Columbia University Press, 2000). Roland Marchand addresses the history of advertising in this decade and later in *Advertising the American Dream: Making Way for Modernity, 1920–1940* (Berkeley: University of California Press, 1985), as does Juliann Sivulka in *Stronger than Dirt: A Cultural History of Advertising Personal Hygiene in America, 1875–1940* (Amherst, N.Y.: Humanity Books, 2001), and in "Historical and Psychological Perspectives of the Erotic in Advertising," in Tom Reichert and Jacqueline Lambiase (eds.), *Sex in Advertising: Perspectives on the Erotic Appeal* (Mahwah, N.J.: Lawrence Erlbaum, 2003). See also Simone Weil Davis, *Living Up to the Ads: Gender Fictions of the 1920s* (Durham, N.C.: Duke University Press, 2000). On cosmetics, see Kathy Peiss, *Hope in a Jar: The Making of America's Beauty Culture* (New York: Holt, 1998). On dieting see Peter N. Stearns, *Fat History: Bodies and Beauty in the Modern West* (New York: New York University, 1997).

Frederick Lewis Allen, *Only Yesterday: An Informal History of the 1920s* (New York: Harper & Row, 1931), remains a key text on the decade. Paula S. Fass explores the culture of college students in *The Damned and the Beautiful: American Youth in the 1920s* (New York: Oxford University Press, 1977). Specific cultural practices are traced by Virginia Scharff, *Taking the Wheel: Women and the Coming of the Motor Age* (New York: Free Press, 1991); Beth L. Bailey, *From Front Porch to Back Seat: Courtship in Twentieth-Century America* (Baltimore: Johns Hopkins University Press, 1988); and Ellen K. Rothman, *Hands and Hearts: A History of Courtship in America* (New York: Basic Books, 1984). To understand 1920s culture, Helen Merrell Lynd and Robert S. Lynd, *Middletown: A Study in Contemporary American Culture* (New York: Harcourt Brace Jovanovich, 1929), is indispensable.

On "compulsory heterosexuality" in the 1920s, see Reyna Rapp and Ellen Ross, "The Twenties' Backlash: Compulsory Heterosexuality, the Consumer Family and the Waning of Feminism," in Amy Swerdlow and Hanna Lessinger (eds.), *Class, Race, and Sex: The Dynamics of Control* (Boston: G. K. Hall, 1983). On homosexuality, see George Chauncey, *Gay New York: Gender, Urban Culture, and the Making of the Gay Male World, 1890–1940* (New York: Basic Books,

1994); Elizabeth Lapovsky Kennedy and Madeline D. Davis, *Boots of Leather, Slippers of Gold: The History of a Lesbian Community* (New York: Routledge, 1992); and Lillian Faderman, *Odd Girls and Twilight Lovers: A History of Lesbian Life in Twentieth-Century America* (New York: Columbia University Press, 1991).

The Katharine Bement Davis study is *Factors in the Sex Life of Twenty-two Hundred Women* (New York: Harper & Bros., 1929). On Butte, see Mary Murphy, *Mining Cultures: Men, Women, and Leisure in Butte, 1914–1941* (Urbana: University of Illinois Press, 1997). Vicki L. Ruiz discusses Mexican American women and the movies in "'Star Struck': Acculturation, Adolescence, and Mexican American Women, 1920–1950," in DuBois and Ruiz (2000). The autobiographies collected by Elaine Showalter, *These Modern Women: Autobiographical Essays from the Twenties* (Old Westbury, N.Y.: Feminist Press, 1978) reveal the discontent of professional women.

Mary McCarthy's autobiography is *Memoirs of a Catholic Girlhood* (New York: Harcourt Brace Jovanovich, 1957). On conservatism and women in the 1920s, see Kathleen M. Blee, *Women of the Klan: Racism in the 1920s* (Berkeley: University of California Press, 1990). An excellent source on the eugenics movement and forced sterilization is Elaine Tyler May, *Barren in the Promised Land: Childless Americans and the Pursuit of Happiness* (New York: Basic Books, 1995).

The subject of women and work is addressed in Winifred D. Wandersee, *Women's Work and Family Values, 1920–1940* (Cambridge, Mass.: Harvard University Press, 1981); Philip S. Foner, *Women and the American Labor Movement: From World War One to the Present* (New York: Free Press, 1980); and Irving Bernstein, *The Lean Years: A History of the American Worker, 1920–1933* (Boston: Houghton Mifflin, 1960). On individual industries and unions, see Dana Frank, *Purchasing Power: Consumer Organizing, Gender, and the Seattle Labor Movement, 1919–1929* (New York: Cambridge University Press, 1994), and Dorothy Sue Cobble, *Dishing It Out: Waitresses and Their Unions in the Twentieth Century* (Urbana: University of Illinois Press, 1991). Susan Levine has written on the participation of wives of workers in the consumerism of the 1920s, in "Workers' Wives: Gender, Class, and Consumerism in the 1920s United States," *Gender & History* 3 (spring 1991): 45–64.

Patricia M. Hummer, *The Decade of Elusive Promise: Professional Women in the United States, 1920–1930* (Ann Arbor: University of Michigan Research Press, 1979) remains the best source on women and the professions in this era.

Several works by literary critics provide an introduction to the subject of female writers. These include Nina Baym, *Feminism and American Literary History: Essays* (New Brunswick, N.J.: Rutgers University Press, 1992), and Elaine Showalter, *Sister's Choice: Tradition and Change in American Women's Writing* (New York: Oxford University Press, 1991). Nina Miller, *Making Love Modern* (New York: Oxford University Press, 1998), makes a case that the milieu for female writers in Greenwich Village in the 1920s was sexist. Studies of individual writers include Sharon O'Brien, *Willa Cather: The Emerging Voice* (New York: Oxford University Press, 1987); Nancy Milford, *Savage Beauty: The Life of Edna St. Vincent Millay* (New York: Random House, 2001); and her biography of Zelda Fitzgerald, the wife of F. Scott Fitzgerald and an icon for the 1920s, *Zelda: A Biography* (New York: Harper & Row, 1970). On female writers in the Harlem Renaissance, see Cheryl A. Wall, *Women of the Harlem Renaissance* (Bloomington: Indiana University Press, 1995). The most recent biography of Zora Neale Hurston is Valerie

Boyd, *Wrapped in Rainbows: The Life of Zora Neale Hurston* (New York: Scribner, 2003). Also consult Carla Kaplan (ed.), *Zora Neale Hurston: A Life In Letters* (New York: Doubleday, 2002).

On Georgia O'Keeffe, see Laurie Lisle, *Portrait of an Artist: A Biography of Georgia O'Keeffe* (New York: Harper & Row, 1980). In *The "New Woman" Revised: Painting and Gender Politics on Fourteenth Street* (Berkeley: University of California Press, 1993), Ellen Wiley Todd links a group of painters known as the Fourteenth Street School with significant gender trends of the 1920s and 1930s.

For interesting studies of women and modern dance, see Suzanne Shelton, *Divine Dancer: A Biography of Ruth St. Denis* (Garden City, N.Y.: Doubleday, 1981), and Elizabeth Kendall, *Where She Danced: American Dancing, 1880–1930* (New York: Knopf, 1979).

On Mexican women, work, and immigration, see Ruiz, *Out of the Shadows;* Rosalinda M. Gonzales, "Chicanos and Mexican Immigrant Families, 1920–1940: Women's Subordination and Family Exploitation," in Lois Scharf and Joan J. Jensen (eds.), *Decades of Discontent: The Women's Movement, 1920–1940* (Westport, Conn.: Greenwood Press, 1983), and George J. Sánchez, *Becoming Mexican American: Ethnicity, Culture and Identity in Chicano Los Angeles, 1900–1950* (New York: Oxford University Press, 1993). On Puerto Rican women, see Virginia Sánchez Korrol, *From Colona to Community: The History of Puerto Ricans in New York City, 1917–1948* (Berkeley: University of California Press, 1994).

Historians disagree over the unity of organized women in the 1920s. J. Stanley Lemons, *The Woman Citizen: Social Feminism in the 1920s* (Urbana: University of Illinois Press, 1973), and Cott, *Grounding of Modern Feminism,* stress the positive aspects, while an opposite position is taken by Dorothy M. Brown in *Setting a Course: American Women in the 1920s* (Boston: Twayne, 1987) and Judith Sealander, *As Minority Becomes Majority: Federal Reaction to the Phenomenon of Women in the Workforce, 1920–1963* (Westport, Conn.: Greenwood Press, 1983). Kristi Anderson, *After Suffrage: Women in Partisan and Electoral Politics Before the New Deal* (Chicago: University of Chicago Press, 1996) is more positive, and Estelle B. Freedman, *Maternal Justice: Miriam Van Waters and the Female Reform Tradition* (Chicago: University of Chicago Press, 1996) is more negative. Also consult Flanagan, *Seeing with Their Hearts;* Sandra Schackel, *Social Housekeepers: Women Shaping Public Policy in New Mexico, 1920–1940* (Albuquerque: University of New Mexico Press, 1991); Carole Nichols, "Votes and More for Women: Suffrage and After in Connecticut," *Women & History* (spring 1983); and Susan Becker, *The Origins of the Equal Rights Amendment: American Feminism Between the Wars* (Westport, Conn.: Greenwood Press, 1981).

Several biographies address the issue of organized women in the 1920s. Cf. Kristie Miller, *Ruth Hanna McCormick: A Life in Politics, 1880–1944* (Albuquerque: University of New Mexico Press, 1991); Elizabeth Israels Perry, *Belle Moskowitz: Feminine Politics and the Exercise of Power in the Age of Alfred E. Smith* (New York: Oxford University Press, 1987); and Susan Ware, *Partner and I: Molly Dewson, Feminism, and New Deal Politics* (New Haven, Conn.: Yale University Press, 1987). Ware's book covers both the 1920s and the 1930s.

On the social work profession, the settlement houses, and social reform in general in the 1920s, see Daniel J. Walkowitz, *Working with Class: Social Workers and the Politics of Middle-Class Identity* (Chapel Hill: University of North Carolina Press, 1999); Kathleen W. Jones, "'Mother Made Me Do It': Mother-Blaming and the Women of Child Guidance," in Molly Ladd-Taylor and Lauri Umansky (eds.), *"Bad" Mothers: The Politics of Blame in Twentieth-Century America* (New York: New York University Press, 1998); Clarke A. Chambers, *Seedtime of Reform: American Social Service and Social Action, 1918–1933* (Minneapolis: University of Minnesota Press, 1963); and Jane Addams, *The Second Twenty Years at Hull House* (New York: Macmillan, 1930).

The most recent biography of Margaret Mead is Lois W. Banner, *Intertwined Lives.* On Amelia Earhart, see Susan Ware, *Still Missing: Amelia Earhart and the Search for Modern Feminism* (New York: Norton, 1993). On women in sports, see Allen Guttmann, *Women's Sports: A History* (New York: Columbia University Press, 1991), and Susan K. Cahn, *Coming on Strong: Gender and Sexuality in 20th Century Women's Sport* (New York: Free Press, 1993). For general histories of women in Hollywood films, see Molly Haskell, *From Reverence to Rape: The Treatment of Women in the Movies* (New York: Holt, Rinehart & Winston, 1973), and Marjorie Rosen, *Popcorn Venus: Women, Movies, & the American Dream* (New York: Coward, McCann & Geoghegan, 1973). On women and film in the 1920s, see Jennifer M. Beam and Diane Negra (eds.), *A Feminist Reader in Early Cinema* (Durham, N.C.: Duke University Press, 2002), and Lary May, *Screening out the Past: The Birth of Mass Culture and the Motion Picture Industry* (New York: Oxford University Press, 1980). See also Gaylyn Studlar's *This Mad Masquerade: Stardom and Masculinity in the Jazz Age* (New York: Columbia University Press, 1996). Karen Ward Mahar documents the "masculinization" of the film industry in her "Women, Filmmaking, and the Gendering of the American Film Industry, 1896–1928," Ph.D. diss., University of Southern California, 1995.

On the history of beauty contests, see Banner, *American Beauty.* For an interesting exploration of the cultural meaning of the Miss America Pageant, see Sarah Banet-Weiser, *The Most Beautiful Girl in the World: Beauty Pageants and National Identity* (Berkeley: University of California Press, 1999).

CHAPTER 4

For the history of women in the 1930s, see Susan Ware, *Holding Their Own* (Boston: Twayne, 1982), and Lois Scharf, *To Work and to Wed: Female Employment, Feminism, and the Great Depression* (Westport, Conn.: Greenwood Press, 1980). Also interesting are Richard Lowitt and Maurine Beasley (eds.), *One-Third of a Nation: Lorena Hickok Reports on the Great Depression* (Urbana: University of Illinois Press, 1981); Jeane Westin, *Making Do: How Women Survived the '30s* (Chicago: Follett, 1976); Helen Merrell Lynd and Robert S. Lynd, *Middletown in Transition: A Study in Cultural Conflicts* (New York: Harcourt Brace Jovanovich, 1937); and Studs Terkel, *Hard Times: An Oral History of the Great Depression* (New York: Pantheon Books, 1970).

Landon R. Y. Storrs has written on the National Consumers' League in his *Civilizing Capitalism: The National Consumers' League, Women's Activism, and Labor Standards in the New Deal Era* (Chapel Hill: University of North Carolina Press, 2000). On political actions by impoverished women, see Annelise Orleck, "We Are that Mythical Thing Called the Public," *Feminist Studies* 19 (spring 1993): 147–72.

Jacquelyn Dowd Hall has written about Jessie Daniel Ames and the anti-lynching movement in *Revolt Against Chivalry: Jessie Daniel Ames and the Women's*

Crusade Against Lynching (New York: Columbia University Press, 1979). For a moving account of the situation in the South written by a contemporary, see Lillian Smith, *Killers of the Dream* (Garden City, N.Y.: Anchor Books, 1963).

Among the best biographies of Eleanor Roosevelt are Joseph P. Lash, *Eleanor and Franklin: The Story of Their Relationship* (New York: Norton, 1971), and *Eleanor: The Years Alone* (New York: Norton, 1972). On Eleanor's relationships with women and involvement with women's groups, see Blanche Wiesen Cook, *Eleanor Roosevelt,* vol. 1: 1884–1933 (New York: Viking, 1992). For a sample of her ideas, see *It's Up to the Women* (New York: Frederick A. Stokes, 1933). J. William T. Youngs has written a good brief biography in *Eleanor Roosevelt: A Personal and Public Life* (New York: Longman, 2000).

On women's role in New Deal administrations, see Susan Ware, *Beyond Suffrage: Women and the New Deal* (Cambridge, Mass.: Harvard University Press, 1981). The standard biography of Frances Perkins is George Martin, *Madame Secretary: Frances Perkins* (Boston: Houghton Mifflin, 1976). Mary Anderson's autobiography, *Women at Work: The Autobiography of Mary Anderson, as Told to Mary N. Winslow* (Minneapolis: University of Minnesota Press, 1951), is useful on New Deal female administrators.

Insightful studies of gender and New Deal programs include Grace Abbott, *From Relief to Social Security: The Development of the New Public Welfare Services and Their Administration* (Chicago: University of Chicago Press, 1941) and Josephine Chapin Brown, *Public Relief, 1929–1939* (New York: Henry Holt, 1940). For an interesting discussion of gender in New Deal art, see Barbara Melosh, *Engendering Culture: Manhood and Womanhood in New Deal Public Art and Theater* (Washington, D.C.: Smithsonian Institution Press, 1991).

On women at work and on the labor movement in the 1930s, see Irving Bernstein, *Turbulent Years: A History of the American Worker, 1933–1941* (Boston: Houghton Mifflin, 1970); Grace Hutchins, *Women Who Work* (New York: International, 1934); and Alice Kessler-Harris, *Out to Work.* On farm women in the South, see Margaret Jarman Hagood, *Mothers of the South: Portraiture of the White Tenant Farm Woman* (Chapel Hill: University of North Carolina Press, 1939).

On ethnicity and race in the 1930s, see the works cited in the bibliographies for chapters 2 and 3 in the current edition of *Women in Modern America* and also Louise Año Nuevo Kerr, "Chicanas in the Great Depression," in Adelaida Del Castillo (ed.), *Between Borders: Essays on Mexicana/Chicana History* (Encino, Calif.: Floricanto Press, 1990), pp. 257–68; Julia Kirk Blackwelder, *Women of the Depression: Caste and Culture in San Antonio, 1929–39* (College Station: Texas A&M University Press, 1984); and Vicki L. Ruiz, *Cannery Women, Cannery Lives: Mexican Women, Unionization, and the California Food Processing Industry, 1939–1950* (Albuquerque: University of New Mexico Press, 1987). African American writer Maya Angelou has written an outstanding autobiography set in this period in *I Know Why the Caged Bird Sings* (New York: Random House, 1969).

Philip S. Foner has written on women and labor unions in the 1930s in *Women and the American Labor Movement: From World War One to the Present* (New York: Free Press, 1980). Studies of individual industries, unions, and workers include Lizabeth Cohen, *Making a New Deal: Industrial Workers in Detroit* (Cambridge: Cambridge University Press, 1990); Elizabeth Faue, *Community of Suffering and Struggle: Women, Men and the Labor Movement in Minneapolis, 1915–1945* (Chapel Hill: University of North Carolina Press, 1990); Jacquelyn Dowd Hall, *Like A*

Family: The Making of a Southern Cotton Mill World (Chapel Hill: University of North Carolina Press, 1987); and Dolores Janiewski, *Sisterhood Denied: Race, Gender, and Class in a New South Community* (Philadelphia: Temple University Press, 1986) on textile workers in Durham, North Carolina. On women and the Communist Party in the 1930s, see Kate Weigard, *Red Feminism: American Communism and the Making of Women's Liberation* (Baltimore: Johns Hopkins University Press, 2001).

On the oppression of lesbians and gays in the 1930s, see Jennifer Terry, *An American Obsession;* George Chauncey, *Gay New York;* and Lillian Faderman, *Odd Girls and Twilight Lovers.* Estelle B. Freedman has written about the "sex crime" panic in "'Uncontrolled Desires': The Response to the Sexual Psychopath, 1920–1960," in Kathy Peiss and Christina Simmons (eds.), *Passion and Power: Sexuality and History* (Philadelphia: Temple University Press, 1989).

Studies by contemporary sociologists remain the best source on the family during the Depression. See Mirra Komarovsky, *The Unemployed Man and His Family: The Effect of Unemployment upon the Status of the Man in Fifty-Nine Families* (New York: Institute of Social Research, 1940); Winona L. Morgan, *The Family Meets the Depression: A Study of a Group of Highly Selected Families* (Minnesota: University of Minnesota Press, 1939); Samuel A. Stouffer and Paul F. Lazarsfeld, *Research Memorandum on the Family in the Depression* (New York: Social Science Research Council, 1937); and Robert Cooley Angell, *The Family Encounters the Depression* (New York: Scribner's, 1936). Also consult Winifred D. Wandersee, *Women's Work and Family Values, 1920–1940* (Cambridge, Mass.: Harvard University Press, 1981). Ricki Solinger, *The Abortionist: A Woman Against the Law* (New York: Free Press, 1994) contains much information about abortion in the 1930s.

On youth during the Depression, see Dorothy Dunbar Bromley and Florence Britten, *Youth and Sex: A Study of Thirteen-Hundred College Students* (New York: Harper & Row, 1938); Maxine Davis, *The Lost Generation: A Portrait of American Youth Today* (New York: Macmillan, 1936); and Thomas Minehan, *Boy and Girl Tramps of America* (New York: Farrar, Straus & Giroux, 1934).

On fashions in the 1930s, see Banner, *American Beauty.* On brassieres, see Jane Farrell-Beck and Colleen Gau, *Uplift: The Bra in America* (Philadelphia: University of Pennsylvania Press, 2002). For a history of cosmetic surgery see Elizabeth Haiken, *Venus Envy: A History of Cosmetic Surgery* (Baltimore: Johns Hopkins University Press, 1997). Tania Modleski has written about soap operas in *Loving with a Vengeance: Mass-Produced Fantasies for Women* (Hamden, Conn.: Archon Books, 1982).

For women in film in the 1930s and later, see Rosen, *Popcorn Venus;* Lucy Fischer, *Designing Women: Cinema, Art Deco, and the Female Form* (New York: Columbia University Press, 2003); Diane Negra, *Off White Hollywood: American Culture and Ethnic Female Stardom* (New York: Routledge, 2001); Sarah Berry, *Screen Style: Fashion and Femininity in 1930s Hollywood* (Minneapolis: University of Minnesota Press, 2000); and Jeanine Basinger, *A Woman's View: How Hollywood Spoke to Women, 1930–1960* (New York: Knopf, 1993). Thomas Doherty has written about the production code in *Pre-Code Hollywood: Sex, Immorality, and Insurrection in American Cinema, 1930–34* (New York: Columbia University Press, 1998). Mae West has recently interested a number of scholars: see Marybeth Hamilton, "'When I'm Bad, I'm Better': Mae West, Sex, and American Entertainment* (Berkeley: University of California Press, 1997) and Jill Watts, *Mae West: An Icon in Black and White* (New York: Oxford University Press, 2001).

On women and screwball comedy, see Elizabeth Kendall, *The Runaway Bride: Hollywood Romantic Comedy of the 1930s* (New York: Knopf, 1990). On blues singers and black women in film, see Angela Y. Davis, *Blues Legacies and Black Feminism: Gertrude "Ma" Rainey, Bessie Smith, and Billie Holiday* (New York: Pantheon, 1998), and Donald Bogle, *Brown Sugar: Eighty Years of America's Black Female Superstars* (New York: Harmond, 1980).

On women in World War II, see Beth Bailey and David Farber, *The First Strange Place: The Alchemy of Sex and Race in World War II Hawaii* (New York: Free Press, 1992); Ruth Milkman, *Gender at Work: The Dynamics of Job Segregation by Sex During World War Two* (Urbana: University of Illinois Press, 1987); Susan M. Hartmann, *The Home Front and Beyond: American Women in the 1940s* (Boston: G. K. Hall, 1982); and Karen Anderson, *Wartime Women: Sex Roles, Family Relations, and the Status of Women During World War Two* (Westport, Conn.: Greenwood Press, 1981).

Leisa D. Meyer has written on women in the military in *Creating G.I. Jane: Sexuality and Power in the Women's Army Corps During World War II* (New York: Columbia University Press, 1996), and John D'Emilio has written about the situation for lesbians and gays in *Sexual Politics, Sexual Communities: The Making of a Homosexual Minority in the United States, 1940–1970* (Chicago: University of Chicago Press, 1983). An interesting study of the all-girl bands is found in Sherrie Tucker, *"Swing Shift": All-Girl Bands of the 1940s* (Durham, N.C.: Duke University Press, 2000). On gender in film noir, see Megan E. Abbott, *The Street Was Mine: White Masculinity in Hardboiled Fiction and Film Noir* (New York: Palgrave Macmillan, 2002), and E. Ann Kaplan (ed.), *Women in Film Noir* (London: British Film Institute, 1998).

A fascinating study of the history of teenagers in the twentieth century is found in Grace Palladino, *Teenagers: An American History* (New York: Basic Books, 1996). For the history of cheerleading, see Natalie Grace Adams and Pamela J. Bettis, *Cheerleaders! An American Icon* (New York: Palgrave, 2003).

CHAPTER 5

The most insightful studies of post–World War II anticommunism include David Caute, *The Great Fear: The Anti-Communist Purge under Truman and Eisenhower* (New York: Simon & Schuster, 1978), and Ellen Schrecker, *Many Are the Crimes: McCarthyism in America* (Boston: Little Brown, 1998). Lillian Hellman's *Scoundrel Time* is a moving depiction of those years, as well as of the anticommunist committees. In *Fireweed: A Political Autobiography* (Philadelphia: Temple University Press, 2002), Gerda Lerner, the dean of historians of American women, describes her experiences as a member of the Communist Party in New York and Hollywood. In his autobiography *Time Bends: A Life* (New York: Grove Press, 1987), Arthur Miller depicts the anticommunism of those years, as well as his relationship with Marilyn Monroe. Simone de Beauvoir comments on the mood of the nation in *America Day by Day*, trans. Carol Gosman (Berkeley: University of California Press, 1999). Ilene J. Philipson investigates the life of accused Communist spy Ethel Rosenberg, in *Ethel Rosenberg: Beyond the Myths* (New Brunswick, N.J.: Rutgers University Press, 1993). Rosenberg was the second woman in the history of the United States to be executed by the federal government.

Lizabeth Cohen analyzes the consumerism and suburbanization of the 1950s in *A Consumers' Republic: The Politics of Mass Consumption in Postwar America* (New York: Knopf, 2003).

On anticommunism as directed against homosexuals, see D'Emilio, *Making of a Homosexual Minority,* and David K. Johnson, *The Lavender Scare: The Cold War Persecution of Gays and Lesbians in the Federal Government* (Chicago: University of Chicago Press, 2003). On masculinity in this era, see Michael Davidson, *Guys Like Us: Citing Masculinity in Cold War Poetics* (Chicago: University of Chicago Press, 2003), and K. A. Cuordileone, "'Politics in an Age of Anxiety': Cold War Political Culture and the Crisis in American Masculinity, 1949–1960," *Journal of American History* 87 (2000): 1–31. Barbara Ehrenreich contends that men are the key to understanding the gender issues of the era, for men developed an ethic of pleasure, based on the exploitation of women, evidenced by the popularity of *Playboy.* See her *The Hearts of Men: American Dreams and the Flight From Commitment* (New York: Doubleday, 1983). Other historians maintain that men's real fear in the 1950s was that the corporate culture was feminizing them. See Wini Breines, *Young, White, and Miserable: Growing Up Female in the Fifties* (Boston: Beacon, 1992).

Rickie Solinger has written about policies toward unwed mothers in *Wake Up Little Susie: Single Pregnancy and Race Before Roe v. Wade* (New York: Routledge, 1992). For a general background to the subject, see Marian J. Morton, *And Sin No More: Social Policy and Unwed Mothers in Cleveland, 1885–1900* (Columbus: Ohio State University Press, 1993). On abortion, see Solinger, *The Woman Abortionist,* and Patricia G. Miller, *The Worst of Times* (New York: HarperCollins, 1993).

Betty Friedan's *The Feminine Mystique* (New York: Norton, 1963) remains an excellent introduction to the domesticity of the 1950s, although some younger historians are critical of her negative portrayal of the decade. (Later editions of the book contain forwards and afterwards by Friedan updating her analysis.) The major reinterpretations include Joanne J. Meyerowitz (ed.), *Not June Cleaver: Women and Gender in Postwar America, 1945–1960* (Philadelphia: Temple University Press, 1994); Elaine Tyler May, *Homeward Bound: American Families in the Cold War Era* (New York: Basic Books, 1988); and Eugenia Kaledin, *Mothers and More: American Women in the 1950s* (Boston: Twayne, 1984). Jessica Weiss has written about marital satisfaction in the 1950s in *To Have and to Hold: Marriage, the Baby Boom, and Social Change* (Chicago: University of Chicago Press, 2000). See also Brett Harvey, *The Fifties: A Woman's Oral History* (New York: HarperCollins, 1993). Wini Breines, *Young, White, and Miserable,* makes a case for both oppression and resistance in the high school culture of the decade. For differing views, see Sherry B. Ortner, *New Jersey Dreaming: Capital, Culture, and the Class of '58* (Durham, N.C.: Duke University Press, 2003), and Lois W. Banner, *Finding Fran: History and Memory in the Lives of Two Women* (New York: Columbia University Press, 1989).

On childrearing, see Peter N. Stearns, *Anxious Parents: A History of Childrearing in Modern America* (New York: New York University Press, 2003), and Bernice L. Hausman, *Mother's Milk: Breastfeeding Controversies in American Culture* (New York: Routledge, 2003). On the family, see May, *Homeward Bound;* Stephanie Coontz, *The Way We Never Were: American Families and the Nostalgia Trap* (New York: Basic Books, 1992), and Arlene Skolnick, *Embattled Paradise: The American Family in an Age of Uncertainty* (New York: Basic Books, 1991). On the new suburbanization see Cohen, *A Consumers' Republic* and Rosalyn Baxendall and Elizabeth Ewen, *Picture Windows: How the Suburbs Happened* (New York: Basic Books, 2000). Amy Swerdlow discusses suburban women's organizing in *Women Strike for Peace: Traditional Motherhood and Radical Politics in the 1960s* (Chicago: University of Chicago Press, 1993). See also Sylvie Murray, *The Progressive Housewife: Community Activism in Suburban Queens, 1945–1965* (Philadelphia: University of Pennsylvania Press, 2003).

I describe the fashions in dress and hair in the 1950s from my own experience as a teenager during that decade. See also Diana Crane, *Fashion and Its Social Agendas: Class, Gender, and Identity in Clothing* (Chicago: University of Chicago Press, 2000), and Valerie Steele, *Fifty Years of Fashion: New Look to Now* (New Haven, Conn.: Yale University Press, 1997). Shirley Polykoff describes her life as an advertising executive in *Does She . . . Or Doesn't She? Or How She Does It* (New York: Doubleday, 1975).

In *Mirror, Mirror: Images of Women Reflected in Popular Culture* (Garden City, N.Y.: Anchor Books, 1977), Kathryn Weibel provides a useful introduction to women and popular culture, as does Susan Douglass in *Where the Girls Are: Growing Up Female with the Mass Media* (New York: Times Books, 1994). On movies in the 1940s and 1950s, see Lary May, *The Big Tomorrow: Hollywood and the Politics of the American Way* (Chicago: University of Chicago Press, 2000); Jackie Byars, *All That Hollywood Allows: Re-Reading Gender in 1950s Melodrama* (Chapel Hill: University of North Carolina Press, 1991); Nora Sayre, *Running Scared: Films of the Cold War* (New York: Dial Press, 1982); Andrea S. Walsh, *Women's Film and Female Experience, 1940–1950* (New York: Praeger, 1984); and Brandon French, *On the Verge of Revolt* (New York: Frederick Ungar, 1968). Interesting studies of Marilyn Monroe are provided by Yona Zeldis McDonough, *All the Available Light: A Marilyn Monroe Reader* (New York: Simon & Schuster, 2002), and Graham McCann, *Marilyn Monroe* (New Brunswick, N.J.: Rutgers University Press 1988). On Audrey Hepburn, see Gaylyn Studlar, "'Chi-Chi Cinderella': Audrey Hepburn as Couture Countermodel," in David Desser and Garth S. Jowett (eds.), *Hollywood Goes Shopping* (Minneapolis: University of Minnesota Press, 2000): 159–78.

For an excellent study of masculinity in general in Hollywood films, see Joan Mellen, *Big Bad Wolves: Masculinity in the American Film* (New York: Pantheon Books, 1977). On Brando and Dean, see Graham McCann, *Rebel Males: Clift, Brando and Dean* (New Brunswick, N.J.: Rutgers University Press, 1994). On masculinity in 1950s films, see Steven Cohan, *Masked Men: Masculinity and Movies in the 1950s* (Bloomington: Indiana University Press, 1997). On television in this era, see Lynn Spigel, *Make Room for TV: Television and the American Family* (Chicago: University of Chicago Press, 1992); Ella Taylor, *Prime Time: TV Culture in Postwar America* (Berkeley: University of California Press, 1987); and Diana M. Meehan, *Ladies of the Evening: Women Characters of Prime-Time Television* (Metuchen, N.J.: Scarecrow Press, 1983).

Paul Robinson, *The Modernization of Sex* (New York: Harper & Row, 1977) analyzes the changing ideas of sex experts, and Vance Packard, *The Sexual Wilderness: The Contemporary Upheaval in Male-Female Relations* (New York: David McKay, 1968) explores the sexual revolution of the 1960s, as do Barbara Ehrenreich,

Elizabeth Hess, and Gloria Jacobs, in *Re-Making Love: The Feminization of Sex* (Garden City, N.Y.: Doubleday, 1986). A recent discussion is Beth L. Bailey, *Sex in the Heartland* (Cambridge, Mass.: Harvard University Press, 2000). In *Madwives: Schizophrenic Women in the 1950s* (New Brunswick, N.J.: Rutgers University Press, 1987), Carol A. B. Warren analyzes how roles in the traditional family structure of the 1950s, together with psychiatry, could cause a woman's emotional difficulties to be diagnosed by psychiatrists as schizophrenia. For an introduction to the Barbie doll, see M. G. Lord, *Forever Barbie: The Unauthorized Biography of a Real Doll* (New York: Morrow, 1994).

An insightful contemporary evaluation of feminism is found in Arnold W. Green and Eleanor Melnick, "What Has Happened to the Feminist Movement," in Alvin W. Gouldner (ed.), *Studies in Leadership: Leadership and Democratic Action* (New York: Russell & Russell, 1950), pp. 277–302. More recent assessments include Susan Lynn, *Progressive Women in Conservative Times: Racial Justice, Peace, and Feminism, 1945 to the 1960s* (New Brunswick, N.J.: Rutgers University Press, 1992); Cynthia Harrison, *On Account of Sex: The Politics of Women's Issues, 1945–1968* (Berkeley: University of California Press, 1988); and Leila J. Rupp and Verta Taylor, *Survival in the Doldrums: The American Women's Rights Movement, 1945 to the 1960s* (New York: Oxford University Press, 1987). See also Beverly Cassara (ed.), *American Women: The Changing Image* (Boston: Beacon Press, 1962), and Elizabeth Bragdon (ed.), *Women Today: Their Conflicts, Their Frustrations, and Their Fulfillments* (New York: Bobbs-Merrill, 1953). Joanne Meyerowitz's survey of articles in women's magazines is found in Meyerowitz, "Beyond the Feminine Mystique: A Reassessment of Postwar Mass Culture, 1946–1958," in Meyerowitz, *Not June Cleaver.*

A good source for the beat poets is Dennis McNulty, *Desolate Angel: Jack Kerouac, the Beat Generation, and America* (Cambridge, Mass.: Da Capo, 2003). General information is provided by Dornelius A. Van Minnen, Jaap van der Bent, and Mel van Elteren (eds.), *Beat Culture: The 1950's and Beyond* (Amsterdam: VU University Press, 1999). On Elvis Presley, see Erika Doss, *Elvis Culture: Fans, Faith, & Image* (Lawrence: University Press of Kansas, 1999), and Connie Kirchberg and Marc Hendricks, *Elvis Presley, Richard Nixon, and the American Dream* (Jefferson, N.C.: McFarland, 1999).

Much writing has appeared on African American women in the civil rights movement. General works include Belinda Robnett, *How Long? How Long? African American Women in the Struggle for Civil Rights* (New York: Oxford University Press, 1997), and Jo Ann Robinson, *The Montgomery Bus Boycott and the Women Who Started It* (Knoxville: University of Tennessee Press, 1987). Biographies include Barbara Ransby, *Ella Baker and the Black Freedom Movement* (Chapel Hill: University of North Carolina Press, 2003); Chana Kai Lee, *For Freedom's Sake: The Life of Fannie Lou Hamer* (Bloomington: University of Indiana Press, 1999); and Cynthia Griggs Fleming, *Soon We Will Not Cry: The Liberation of Ruby Doris Smith Robinson* (Lanham, Md.: Rowman & Littlefield, 1998). Autobiographies include Pauli Murray, *Song in a Weary Throat: An American Pilgrimage* (New York: Harper & Row, 1987); Anne Moody, *Coming of Age in Mississippi* (New York: Dial Press, 1968); and Daisy Bates, *The Long Shadow of Little Rock: A Memoir* (New York: David McKay, 1962). Also consult Ruth Feldman, *Motherhood in Black and White: Race and Sex in American Liberalism* (Ithaca, N.Y.: Cornell University Press, 2000).

A large literature exists on the emergence of second-wave feminism. See the bibliographies for chapters 6 and 7 of *Women in Modern America;* Sara Evans, *Personal Politics: The Roots of Women's Liberation in the Civil Rights Movement & the New Left* (New York: Alfred A. Knopf, 1979); and Mary Aickin Rothschild, *A Case of Black and White: Northern Volunteers and the Southern Freedom Summers, 1964–65* (Westport, Conn.: Greenwood Press, 1982). On the radical Students for a Democratic Society (SDS) and the conservative Young Americans for Freedom (YAF), see Rebecca E. Klatch, *A Generation Divided: The New Left, the New Right, and the 1960s* (Berkeley: University of California Press, 1999).

Contemporary documents and surveys are useful. The 1963 report of the President's Commission on the Status of Women was published as Margaret Mead and Frances Bagley Kaplan (eds.), *American Women: Report of the President's Commission on the Status of Women and Other Publications of the Commission* (New York: Scribner's, 1965). Another useful compilation is Kate Stimpson (ed.), *Women and the "Equal Rights" Amendment: Senate Subcommittee Hearings of the Constitutional Amendment, 91st Congress* (New York: R. R. Bowker, 1972).

Nancy F. Gabin, *Feminism in the Labor Movement: Women and the United Auto Workers, 1935–1975* (Ithaca, N.Y.: Cornell University Press, 1990), is an interesting study of a union with feminist inclinations. The UAW's Women's Department was the first of its kind, and two UAW leaders were among the founders of NOW.

In 1953, despite McCarthyite anticommunism, a group of filmmakers braved repression to make the movie *Salt of the Earth,* about a strike in 1950 on the part of New Mexico copper miners. The film documents women's daily lives and their growing power through sisterhood. See Michael Wilson, *Salt of the Earth,* with commentary by Deborah Silverton Resenfelt (Old Westbury, N.Y.: Feminist Press, 1978).

CHAPTER 6

On developments in the 1960s and 1970s, see Davis, *Moving the Mountain;* Winifred Wandersee, *On the Move: American Women in the 1970s* (Boston: Twayne, 1988); and Sara Evans, "American Women in a New Millennium," in Cynthia B. Costello, Shari Miles, and Anne J. Stone (eds.), *The American Woman, 1999–2000: A Century of Change: What's Next* (New York: Norton, 2000), pp. 45–101. On the union movement in this period, see Dennis A. Deslippe, *'Rights, Not Roses': Unions and the Rise of Working-Class Feminism, 1945–1980* (Urbana: University of Illinois Press, 2000). For case studies of women and labor activism in recent eras see Cynthia G. Costello, *We're Worth It! Women and Collective Action in the Insurance Workplace* (Urbana: University of Illinois Press, 1991), an analysis of four strikes in Wisconsin in the 1970s and 1980s; Karen Brodkin Sacks, *Caring by the Hour: Women, Work, and Organizing at Duke Medical Center* (Urbana: University of Illinois Press, 1988); and Laurie Coyle, Gail Hershatter, and Emily Honig, "Women at Farah: An Unfinished Story," in *Mexican Women in the United States: Struggles Past and Present* (Los Angeles: University of California, Chicano Studies Research Center, 1980), on a garment workers' strike in El Paso, Texas.

For studies done in the 1960s and 1970s documenting discrimination, see Kirsten Amundsen, *The Silenced Majority: Women and American Democracy* (Englewood Cliffs, N.J.: Prentice-Hall, 1971); Cynthia Fuchs Epstein, *Woman's Place: Options and Limits in Professional Careers* (Berkeley: University of California Press, 1970); and Caroline Bird, *Born Female: The High Cost of Keeping Women Down* (New York: David McKay, 1968).

Interesting autobiographies by feminists include the brief memoirs collected by Rachel DuPlessis and Ann Snitow, in *Feminist Memoir Project* (New York: Three Rivers Press, 1998), and Susan Brownmiller, *In Our Time: Memoir of a Revolutionary* (New York: Dial, 1999). Betty Friedan's autobiography is *Life So Far* (New York: Simon & Schuster, 2000). Daniel Horowitz, *Betty Friedan and the Making of the Feminist Movement: The American Left, the Cold War, and Modern Feminism* (Amherst: University of Massachusetts Press, 1998), locates the origins of Friedan's ideas in radical politics. Carolyn Heilbrun has written a memoir of Gloria Steinem, the founder of *Ms.*, in *The Education of a Woman: The Life of Gloria Steinem* (New York: Dial, 1994).

Susan Schechter writes about the early years of the battered women's movement in *Women and Male Violence: The Visions and Struggles of the Battered Women's Movement* (Boston: South End Press, 1982). On rape, see Emilie Buchwald, Pamela R. Fletcher, and Martha Roth (eds.), *Transforming a Rape Culture* (Minneapolis: Milkweed, 1993), and Susan Estrich, *Real Rape* (Cambridge, Mass.: Harvard University Press, 1987).

On films in the 1960s, see Peter Biskind, *How the Sex-Drugs-and-Rock 'n' Roll Generation Saved Hollywood* (New York: Simon & Schuster, 1998). Judy Chicago's "Dinner Party" (at the Brooklyn Museum) is discussed in Amelia Jones, *Sexual Politics: Judy Chicago's Dinner Party in Feminist Art History* (Berkeley: University of California Press, 1996)

Introductions to the subject of feminist spirituality include Monica Sjoo and Barbara Mor, *The Great Cosmic Mother: Rediscovering the Religions of the Earth* (San Francisco: Harper & Row, 1987), and Charlene Spretnak (ed.), *The Politics of Women's Spirituality: Essays on the Rise of Spiritual Power Within the Feminist Movement* (Garden City, N.Y.: Doubleday, 1982). On communes and the Lama Foundation, see Banner, *Finding Fran*.

On protest movements among people of color, see the bibliography to chapter 1 of the current edition of *Women in Modern America* and the articles in Costello, *A Century of Change*. See also Margaret Eleanor Rose, "Women in the United Farm Workers: A Study of Chicana and Mexicana Participation in a Labor Union, 1950–1980," Ph.D. diss., UCLA, 1988; Rose, "Gender and Civic Activism in Mexican American Barrios in California: The Community Service Organization, 1947–1962," in Meyerowitz, *Not June Cleaver;* and the insightful memoir by Native American Mary Crow Dog, *Lakota Woman* (New York: Grove, Weidenfeld, 1990). For women in the Black Panthers, see Elaine Brown's autobiography, *A Taste of Power: A Black Woman's Story* (New York: Pantheon, 1992). On Stonewell, see D'Emilio, *Sexual Politics,* and Martin Duberman, *Stonewall* (New York: Dutton, 1993). Donna Penn discusses lesbian politics in "The Meanings of Lesbianism in Postwar America," *Gender & History* 3 (summer 1991): 190–203.

Two works review feminist theory from 1970 on: Alison M. Jaggar and Paula S. Rothenberg, *Feminist Frameworks,* 3rd ed. (New York: McGraw-Hill, 1993), and Rosemarie Tong, *Feminist Thought: A Comprehensive Introduction* (Boulder, Colo.: Westview Press, 1989). The major work in the "difference" versus "similarity" debate is Carol Gilligan, *In A Different Voice: Psychological Theory and Women's Development* (Cambridge, Mass.: Harvard University Press, 1982). Differing points of view are provided by Marianne Hirsh and Evelyn Fox Keller (eds.), *Conflicts in Feminism* (New York: Routledge, 1990), and Juliet Mitchell and Ann Oakley, *What is Feminism? A Re-Examination* (New York: Pantheon, 1986). Mari Jo Buhle, in *Feminism and Its Discontents: A Century of Struggle with Psychoanalysis* (Cambridge, Mass.: Harvard University Press, 1998), discusses the relationship between feminism and psychoanalysis.

Discussions of the "sex war" debates can be found in Lynn S. Chancer, *Reconcilable Differences: Confronting Beauty, Pornography, and the Future of Feminism* (Berkeley: University of California Press, 1998), and Jane M. Ussher, *Fantasies of Femininity: Reframing the Boundaries of Sex* (New Brunswick, N.J.: Rutgers University Press, 1997). Catharine MacKinnon presented her position in *Feminism Unmodified: Discourses on Life and Law* (Cambridge, Mass.: Harvard University Press, 1987).

For feminist theory written by women of color, see Patricia Hill Collins, *Black Feminist Thought: Knowledge, Consciousness, and the Politics of Empowerment* (New York: Routledge, 1990); Asian Women United of California, *Making Waves: An Anthology of Writings By and About Asian Women* (Boston: Beacon, 1989); bell hooks, *Thinking Feminist, Thinking Black* (Boston: South End Press, 1988); and Patricia Spelman, *Inessential Woman: Problems of Exclusion in Feminist Thought* (Boston: Beacon Press, 1988).

Among the autobiographies and novels by women of color are Maya Angelou, *I Know Why the Caged Bird Sings* (1969); Sandra Cisneros, *The House on Mango Street* (1985); Maxine Hong Kingston, *The Woman Warrior: Memoirs of a Girlhood Among Ghosts* (1976); Audre Lorde, *Zami* (1982); Toni Morrison, *Song of Solomon* (1977) and *Tar Baby* (1991); Alice Walker, *The Color Purple* (1982) and *Possessing the Secret of Joy* (1992). An interesting lesbian "coming-of-age" novel is Rita Mae Brown, *Rubyfruit Jungle* (1973).

The struggle for the ERA is examined in Donald G. Mathews and Jane S. DeHart, *Sex, Gender and the Politics of the ERA* (Chapel Hill: University of North Carolina Press, 1990), and Mary Frances Berry, *Why the ERA Failed: Politics, Women's Rights, and the Amending Process of the Constitution* (Bloomington: Indiana University Press, 1986). On the New Right, see Andrea Dworkin, *Right-Wing Women* (New York: Putnam's 1968), and Judith Stacey, *Brave New Families: Stories of Domestic Upheaval in Late Twentieth-Century America* (New York: Basic Books, 1990). On Phyllis Schlafly, see Carol Felsenthal, *The Sweetheart of the Silent Majority: The Biography of Phyllis Schlafly* (Garden City, N.Y.: Doubleday, 1981). Sonia Johnson has documented her difficulties as a feminist in the Mormon Church in *From Housewife to Heretic* (Garden City, N.Y.: Doubleday, 1981).

On the abortion debate, see Lawrence Tribe, *Abortion: The Clash of Absolutes* (New York: Norton, 1990); Rosalind P. Petchesky, *Abortion and Women's Rights: The State, Sexuality, and Reproductive Freedom* (Boston: Northeastern University Press, 1985); and Kristin Luker, *Abortion and the Politics of Motherhood* (Berkeley: University of California Press, 1984). Two major works on "backlash" are Susan Faludi, *Backlash: The Undeclared War Against American Women* (New York: Crown, 1991), and Naomi Wolf, *The Beauty Myth: How Beauty Images are Used Against Women* (New York: William Morrow, 1991). See also Susan Jeffords, *The Remasculinization of America: Gender and the Vietnam War* (Bloomington: Indiana University Press, 1989). Patricia Bradley discusses the media's negative response to women in *Mass Media and the Shaping of American Feminism, 1963–1975* (Jackson: University Press of Mississippi, 2003). On anorexia nervosa and the cult of thinness, see Susan Bordo, *Unbearable Weight: Feminism, Western Culture, and the Body* (Berkeley: University of California Press, 1993), and Joan Jacobs Brumberg, *The Body Project: An Intimate History of American Girls* (New York: Random House, 1997).

On cosmetic surgery, see Haiken, *Venus Envy,* and Virginia L. Blum, *Flesh Wounds: The Culture of Cosmetic Surgery* (Berkeley: University of California Press, 2003). On breast implants, consult Nora Jacobson, *Cleavage: Technology, Controversy, and the Ironies of the Man-Made Breast* (New Brunswick, N.J.: Rutgers University Press, 2000). Lynne Luciano discusses the history of male body image in *Looking Good: Male Body Image in Modern America* (New York: Hill and Wang, 2001). On advertising in the 1970s, see Steve Craig, "Madison Avenue Versus The Feminine Mystique: The Advertising Industry's Response to the Women's Movement," in Sherrie A. Inness (ed.), *Disco Divas, Women and Popular Culture in the 1970s* (Philadelphia: University of Pennsylvania Press, 2003), pp. 13–23.

The "disco divas" and music in the 1970s more generally are covered in "'You Probably Think This Song Is About You': 1970s Women's Music from Carole King to the Disco Divas," in Inness (ed.), *Disco Divas.* In "'Shaky Ground': Popular Music in the Disco Years," in *Shaky Ground: The Sixties and Its Aftershocks* (New York: Columbia University Press, 2002), pp. 159–92, Alice Echols adds useful information. Rebecca Arnold discusses punk fashions in *Fashion, Desire, and Anxiety: Image and Morality in the 20th Century* (New Brunswick, N.J.: Rutgers University Press, 2001).

On the complexities of immigration, Americanization, and work for women in ethnic communities, see Pierrette Hondagneu-Sotelo (ed.), *Gender and Immigration: Contemporary Trends* (Berkeley: University of California Press, 2003); Nazli Kibria, *Family Tightrope: The Changing Lives of Vietnamese Americans* (Princeton, N.J.: Princeton University Press, 1993); Louise Lamphere, Alex Stepick, and Guillermo Grenier (eds.), *Newcomers in the Workplace: Immigrants and the Restructuring of the American Economy* (Philadelphia: Temple University Press, 1994); Louise Lamphere, Patricia Zavella, and Felipe Gonzales (eds.), *Sunbelt Mothers: Reconciling Home and Work* (Ithaca, N.Y.: Cornell University Press, 1993); and Patricia Zavella, *Women's Work and Chicano Families: Cannery Workers of the Santa Clara Valley* (Ithaca, N.Y.: Cornell University Press, 1987).

CHAPTER 7

On feminism in the 1990s, see the bibliography in chapter 6 of the current edition of *Women in Modern America.* See also Myra Marx Free and Beth H. Hess, *Controversy and Coalition: The New Feminist Movement Across Three Decades of Change* (New York: Routledge, 2000); Sheila Tobias, *The Faces of Feminism: An Activists's Reflection on the Women's Movement* (Boulder, Colo.: Westview Press, 1997); and Paula Ries and Anne J. Stone (eds.), *The American Woman, 1992–93: A Status Report,* (New York: Norton, 1993). Tanya Melich discusses women and New Right politics in *The Republican War Against Women: An Insider's Report from Behind the Lines* (New York: Bantam Books, 1996). Material about women and poverty is in Loretta Schwartz-Nobel, *Getting Up Empty: The Hunger Epidemic in America* (New York: HarperCollins, 2003); Barbara Ehrenreich and Frances Fox Piven, "Without a Safety Net," *Mother Jones,* May–June, 2002; Lynn Hancock, *Hands to Work: The Stories of Three Families Racing Against the Welfare Clock* (New York: Morrow, 2002); Barbara Ehrenreich, *Nickel and Dimed: On (Not) Getting By in America* (New York: Metropolitan Books, 2001); and Gwendolyn Mink, *Welfare's End* (Ithaca, N.Y.: Cornell University Press, 1998).

Emilie Stoltzfus writes about child care in *Citizen, Mother, Worker: Debating Public Responsibility for Child Care after World War II* (Chapel Hill: University of North Carolina Press, 2003). Elaine Bell Kaplan debunks the myth of the existence of large numbers of black teenage mothers in *Not Our Kind of Girl: Unravelling the Myths of Black Teenage Motherhood* (Berkeley: University of California Press, 1997). On mythologies of African American motherhood, see Mary Frances Berry, *Politics, Childcare, and the Myth of the Good Mother* (New York: Viking, 1993).

Susan Estrich writes about women in the professions and in the economy more generally in *Sex and Power* (New York: Riverhead Books, 2000). For an interesting discussion of women's recent advance to power in the Hollywood film industry, see Mollie Gregory, *Women Who Run the Show* (New York: St. Martin's Griffin, 2003). Joan Williams, *Unbending Gender: Why Family and Work Conflict and What to do About It* (New York: Oxford University Press, 2002), gives pragmatic advice on how to handle the conflict between home and work. The subject of women and politics is discussed by Jo Freeman, *A Room at a Time: How Women Entered Party Politics* (New York: Rowman & Littlefield, 2000), and Linda Witt, Karen M. Paget, and Glenna Matthews, *Running as a Woman: Gender and Power in American Politics* (New York: Free Press, 1993).

William Saletan contends that the New Right has won the abortion debate in *Bearing Right: How Conservatives Won the Abortion Wars* (Berkeley: University of California Press, 2003).

On fashions in the 1990s, see Crane, *Fashion and its Social Agendas,* Steele, *Fifty Years of Fashion;* and Arnold, *Fashion, Desire, and Anxiety.* See also Juliet Ash and Elizabeth Wilson (eds.), *Chic Thrills: A Fashion Reader* (Berkeley: University of California Press, 1993). On movies, see in particular Susan Jeffords, *Hard Bodies: Hollywood Masculinity in the Reagan Era* (New Brunswick, N.J.: Rutgers University Press, 1994). On advertising see Sivulka, "Historical and Psychological Perspectives of the Erotic in Advertising," in Reichert and Lambiase, *Sex in Advertising.* There is a large literature on hip-hop and rap. See in particular George Nelson, *Hip Hop America* (New York: Viking, 1998); Craig Werner, *A Change Is Going to Come: Music, Race, and the Soul of America* (New York: Penguin, 1998); and Tricia Rose, *Black Noise: Rap Music and Black Culture in Contemporary America* (Hanover, N.H.: Wesleyan University Press, 1994). Beverly Guy-Sheftall and Johnnetta Betsch Cole criticize the misogyny of hip-hop and rap as undermining the black community in *Gender Talk: The Struggle for Women's Equality in African-American Communities* (New York: Ballentine, 2003). For autobiographies of rap artists, see Queen Latifah, with Karen Hunter, *Ladies First: Revelations of a Strong Woman* (New York: William Morrow, 1999); Joan Moran, *When Chickenheads Come Home to Roost* (New York: Simon & Schuster, 1999); and Ice-T, *The Ice Opinion* (New York: St. Martin's Press, 1994).

Cathy Schwichtenberg has edited an interesting collection of articles on Madonna in *The Madonna Collection: Representational Politics, Subcultural Identities, and Cultural Theory* (Boulder, Colo.: Westview Press, 1993). Also interesting are Allan Metz and Carol Benson (eds.), *Madonna: Two Decades of Commentary* (New York: Schrimer Books, 1999), and Douglas Kellner, "Madonna, Fashion, and Identity," in Shari Benstock and Suzanne Ferris (eds.), *On Fashion* (New Brunswick, N.J.: Rutgers University Press, 1994). On the Clarence Thomas/Anita Hill controversy, see *Race, Gender, and Power in America: The Legacy of the Hill-Thomas Hearings* (New York: Oxford University Press, 1995); and Toni Morrison (ed.), *Race-ing Justice, En-Gendering Power: Essays on Anita Hill, Clarence Thomas, and the Construction of Social Reality* (New York: Pantheon, 1992). Anita Hill has told her story in *Telling Truth to Power* (New York: Doubleday, 1997).

Recent information on women in the military is in Jodi Wilgoren, "A Nation at War: Women in the Military: A New War Brings New Role for Women," *New York Times*, March 28, 2003. Mary Fainsod Katzenstein discussed her concept of "unobtrusive mobilization" in "American Institutions and Feminism: Unobtrusive Mobilization in the 1980s," *Signs: Journal of Women in Culture and Society* 16 (autumn 1990): 27–54. See also Judith Hicks Stiehm, *Arms and the Enlisted Woman* (Philadelphia: Temple University Press, 1989).

On postmodernism, see Imelda Whelehan, *Modern Feminist Thought from the Second Wave to Post-Feminism* (New York: New York University Press, 1995). The major texts of postmodernism include Teresa de Lauretis, *The Practice of Love: Lesbian Sexuality and Perverse Desire* (Bloomington: Indiana University Press, 1994), and Judith Butler, *Bodies That Matter: On the Discursive Limits of 'Sex'* (New York: Routledge, 1993). For a discussion of postmodern feminist cultural theory, see Suzanne Danuta Walters, *Material Girls: Making Sense of Feminist Cultural Theories* (Berkeley: University of California Press, 1995).

Monica Lewinsky has told her side of the story of her affair with Bill Clinton in Andrew Morton, *Monica's Story* (New York: St. Martin's Press, 1999). Lauren Berlant and Lisa Duggan have discussed the affair's cultural impacts in *Our Monica, Our Selves: The Clinton Affair and the National Interest* (New York: New York University Press, 2001). Hillary Clinton's autobiography is Hillary Rodham Clinton, *Living History* (New York: Simon & Schuster, 2003). Camille Paglia's major work is *Sexual Personae: Art and Decadence from Nefertiti to Emily Dickinson* (New Haven, Conn.: Yale University Press, 1990). Naomi Wolf's most recent work is *Fire with Fire: The New Female Power and How It Will Change the 21st Century* (New York: Random House, 1993).

Major works on the third wave include Jennifer Baumgardner and Amy Richards, *Manifesta: Young Women, Feminism and the Future* (New York: Farrar, Straus, and Giroux, 2000), and Paula Kamen, *Her Way: Young Women Remake the Sexual Revolution* (New York: Broadway Books, 2000). Even as young women celebrate postfeminism, hip-hop, and Britney Spears, analysts write of the difficulty of adolescence for them in the modern consumer, sexualized culture. Interesting works in this vein include Cynthia B. Costello, Vanessa R. Wight, and Anne J. Stone (eds.), *The American Woman, 2003–2004: Daughters of a Revolution: Young Women Today* (New York: Macmillan/Palgrove, 2003), and Mary Pipher, *Reviving Ophelia: Saving the Selves of Adolescent Girls* (New York: Ballentine, 1994). In "Feminism: It's All About Me!" *Time*, June 29, 1998, Ginia Bellafante accuses feminism of having degenerated among the younger generation into a narcissism concerned mainly with the body.

Positive forecasts about the economy and about George W. Bush's financial policies can be found in the *Economist,* Sept. 6, 2003. On aging women, see Margaret Morganroth Gullette, *Aged by Culture* (Chicago: University of Chicago Press, 2004), and Banner, *In Full Flower.*

Sylvia Ann Hewlett maintains that women who put off having children while they establish a career run the risk of never having any in *Creating a Life: Professional Women and the Search for Children* (New York: Miramax, 2002), and David Shumway is concerned about the future of the modern family in *Modern Love: Romance, Intimacy, and the Marriage Crisis* (New York: New York University Press, 2003). Cele C. Otnes and Elizabeth H. Pleck discuss the fixation on large weddings in *Cinderella Dreams: The Allure of the Lavish Wedding* (Berkeley: University of California Press, 2003). For interesting recent demographic information, see Lisa Belkin, "The Opt-Out Revolution," *New York Times Magazine,* Oct. 26, 2003, and *Business Week,* Oct. 2003.

Photo Credits

Chapter 1: xx, Library of Congress; 4, Culver Pictures; 5, Corbis; 14, Harcourt Brace Library; 15, Bettmann/Corbis; 22, Brown Brothers; 23, Corbis; 30, Bettmann/Corbis; 31, Brown Brothers.

Chapter 2: 38, Library of Congress; 54 Bettmann/Corbis; 55, Sophia Smith Collection, Smith College; 56, Hulton-Deutsch/Corbis; 67, Bettmann/Corbis.

Chapter 3: 70, Culver Pictures; 80, Bettmann/Corbis; 81, Underwood and Underwood/Corbis; 84, Photographs and Prints Division, Schomburg Center for Research in Black Culture, The New York Public Library, Astor, Lenox and Tilden Foundations; 85, Corbis; 96, Institute for Intercultural Studies, Inc., New York; 97, Bettmann/Corbis.

Chapter 4: 100, Library of Congress; 106, Culver Pictures; 107, Photographs and Prints Division, Schomburg Center for Research in Black Culture, The New York Public Library, Astor, Lenox and Tilden Foundations; 116, Library of Congress; 117, Bettmann/Corbis; 124, UPI/Bettmann/

Corbis; 125, Underwood and Underwood/Corbis; 130, Library of Congress; 131, UPI/ Bettmann/Corbis.

Chapter 5: 136, National Organization of Women; 144, H. Armstrong Roberts/Corbis; 145, UPI/Bettmann/Corbis; 150, Bettmann/Corbis; 151, Bettmann/Corbis.

Chapter 6: 162 (top), UPI/Bettmann/Corbis; 162 (bottom), Reuters/ Bettmann/Corbis; 166, UPI/Bettman/Corbis; 167, FDR Library;178, Nancy Clover, Schlesinger Library, Radcliffe College; 179, UPI/Bettmann/Corbis;188, Reuters/ Bettmann/Corbis; 189, Bettmann/Corbis.

Chapter 7: 194, Leland Bobbe/Corbis; 202, Neal Preston/Corbis; 203, Neal Preston/Corbis; 206, AP/Wide World Photos; 207, Reuters/ Bettmann/Corbis; 216, Catherine Karnow/Corbis; 217, Mark Peterson/ Corbis.

Index

A

Abortion, 7, 116, 118, 140–41, 187, 212, 218–19
ACT-UP, 179, 216, 217
Addams, Jane, 41, 45–46, 51, 67, 78, 93, 95, 102, 105
Adkins v. Children's Hospital, 90
Adler, Alfred, 120
Advertising, and women,
  1900s, 13, 15
  1920s, 74–76, 82
  1930s, 120
  1950s, 143–46, 147
  1970s, 190
  1980s, 199
Affirmative action, 219
African American women
  beauty, 13–15, 182
  and civil rights movement, 159–61, 170
  education, 4, 5
  employment, 11, 19, 32, 88, 112, 208
  as farmers and sharecroppers, 19
  family, 32–33
  and feminism, 1970s
  in films, 1930s
  and Harlem Renaissance, 85–86
  in military, World War II, 126
  movement North, 29, 87, 94
  and new middle class, 223
  organizations, 49, 154, 180
  and politics, 209
  and poverty, recent, 171
  reaction to Anita Hill, 204
  and work, 1940s, 132
Age of Innocence, The (Wharton), 56
Aging, and women, 9, 220
Aid to Families with Dependent Children, 108, 110, 196, 212
AIDS, 195
Aiguilera, Christina, 203
Airline hostesses, 89, 97
Alcatraz, occupation of, 177
Alice Doesn't Live Here Anymore (1976), 176
All-American Girls' Baseball League, 127
All-girl bands (1940s), 127
Allen, Florence, 92, 105
Alliance Against Sexual Coercion, 173
All That Heaven Allows (1956), 146
Alvarez, Julia, 184
American Association of University Women (AAUW) 43, 154, 169. *See also* Association of Collegiate Alumnae

American Birth Control League, 55, 78
American Civil Liberties Union (ACLU), 58, 72
American Federation of Labor (AFL), 59, 60–61, 90, 113
American Home Economics Association, 43, 93, 102
Americanization, 47, 73
American Legion, 78
American Medical Association, 78, 94
American Psychiatric Association, 139
Americans for Indian Opportunity (AIO), 178
Ames, Jessie Daniel, 103
Anarchism, 39, 53, 57. See also Industrial Workers of the World (IWW)
Anderson, Karen, 35
Anderson, Margaret, 102
Anderson, Marian, 105, 107
Anderson, Mary, 62, 92
Anorexia nervosa, 152, 188, 221
Anthony, Susan B., 4, 52, 64
Antiabortion movement, 197
Anticommunism, 115, 138–40, 149, 154
Antifeminism, 74, 164, 218
Anti-Lynching Crusaders, 103
Antilynching movement, 103–104
Antioch College, 4, 5
Antisuffragists, 65
Arts and crafts movement, 51
Asians, 25–28, 88, 192. See also Chinese; Filipinos; Japanese; Koreans
Association of Collegiate Alumnae, 43. See also American Association of University Women (AAUW)
Association of Southern Women for the Prevention of Lynching, 103
Athletics, and women. See Sports
Aunt Jemima, as symbol, 31, 37
Austin, Mary, 8
Automobile Strike, Flint, Michigan (1937), 113
Aviation, and women, 97

B

Baby boom generation, 141
Bacall, Lauren, 128
"Backlash," 186–87, 188–90, 197–98, 208
Backlash (Faludi), 186, 219
Back-to-the Home Movement, 142
Bacon, Albion Fellows, 44
Baez, Joan, 191
Baker, Ella, 160
Baker, Josephine, 83
Ball, Lucile, 148
Bands, all-women, 13, 86, 127
Baptist Women's Home Mission, 5
Bara, Theda, 98
Barbie (doll), 138, 150, 152, 188
Battered women's shelters, 205
Beatas, 51
Beatles, 165
Beatniks, 159

Beat poets, 138
Beauty, 13–15, 73, 152, 190. See also Cosmetics; Fashion; Undergarments
Beauty contests, 98–99
Beauty Myth, The (Wolf), 214
Beauvoir, Simone de, 153
Bedford Hills Reformatory, 63
Bell Jar, The (Plath), 170
Benedict, Ruth, 86
Berdache, 34. See also Men-women
Berkshire Conference of Women Historians, 205
Bethune, Mary McCleod, 107–08
Bethune-Cookman College, 108
Bewitched, 176
Big Sleep, The (1946), 128
Bikini bathing suit, 149
Bild Lili (doll), 152
Birth control
    Comstock Law and, 7
    and early feminists, 58
    late 1800s, 8
    legalization of, 57
    and Margaret Sanger, 57
    in 1930s, 116, 118
    and "the pill," 155
Bisexuality, 75, 119, 139
Biskind, Peter, 176
"Black Is Beautiful," 180
Black Muslims, 180
Black Panthers, 180
"Black Power," 180
Blackwell, Elizabeth, 12, 15
Black women. See African American women
Blair, Emily Newall, 91
"Blaxploitation" films, 176
Blee, Susan, 79
Blondie and Dagwood (cartoon and film characters), 121, 148
Blues, and African American women, 125
Bluestockings, 3
Bly, Nellie (Elizabeth Seaman), 13, 22
Bly, Robert, 198
Bostonians, The (James), 9
"Boston marriage," 9, 46, 47, 75–76
Boston Women's Health Collective, 173
Bow, Clara, 98
Boy Scouts, 17–18
BPW. See National Federation of Business and Professional Women's Clubs
Bracero program, 87
Brando, Marlon, 147, 158
Brassieres. See Undergarments
Breadwinner ethic, 24–25, 118
Breast fixation, 1950s, 146
Breckinridge, Sophonisba, 46
Brico, Antonia, 86
Brides, picture. See Mail-order brides
Bridge Called My Back, This (Moraga), 184
Brinkley, Nell, 52

Bronson, Charles, 176
Brown, Helen Gurley, 166
Brown v. Board of Education of Topeka, Kansas, 159
Bryn Mawr College, 4
Bulimia, 188, 221
Burroughs, Edgar Rice, 17–18
Bush, George H. W., 187, 203, 204
Bush, George W., 209, 218–220
Business, women as executives and entrepreneurs, 13, 15, 82–83, 111, 218
Butler, Helen Mary, 13
Butler, Judith, 211

C

Cassatt, Mary, 52
Catalyst, 169
Cather, Willa, 83
Catholic Church against ERA, 186
   and Mexican American women, 29, 51, 179
   and orphan asylums, 29
   and racial controversy, Clifton, Arizona, 29
   against woman suffrage, 65
Catt, Carrie Chapman, 4, 65–66, 67, 93
Censorship, movies, 98, 122, 123, 129, 149
Charlie's Angels, 177
Chavéz, César, 178
Chavéz, Helen, 178–79
Cheerleading, girls' entry into, 127
Cherokee Female Seminary, 35
Chicago, Judy, 174
Chicago Columbia Exposition (1893), 35–37
   racism at, 36–37
Childcare, 89, 126, 129, 148, 182
Child labor, 117–18
Child Labor Amendment, 91
Childrearing, 11–12
Children's Bureau, Federal Department of Labor, 47, 91, 94, 108, 177
Chinese women
   family, 25–27
   immigration, 25–27, 191
   prostitution, 25
   work patterns, 25–27
Chinese Women's Jeleab (Self-Reliance Association), 50
Chisholm, Shirley, 180
Cisneros, Sandra, 184
Civilian Conservation Corps (CCC), 105, 108, 110
Civil Rights Act (1964), 160, 163, 173
Civil rights movement, 104, 138, 154, 159–61, 163, 164, 170, 171, 181
Civil Works Administration (CWA), 105
Clarke, Edward H., 6
Claytor, Helen Wilkins, 154
Clerical labor
   and BPW, 93
   entry of women, 12
   male dominance in, 17
   and 1930s, 110–111

and 1950s, 156
and 1960s, 171
in recent period, 221
and unionization, 1970s, 169
World War II and, 129
Clinton, Bill, 209, 210, 212–13
Clinton, Hillary, 212, 218
Clothing styles. *See* Fashion
Clubs. *See* Women's clubs
Coca, Imogene, 148
Cofradias, 51
Cold War, 138, 146, 149
Cole, Johnetta Betsch, 204
Combahee River Collective, 180
Coming of Age in Samoa (Mead), 95, 96
Commission on Interracial Cooperation, 103
Commission on the Status of Women, 164, 167
Committee for Industrial Organization, 113–14, 133. *See also* Congress of Industrial Organizations; Union activities
Committee to Defeat the Unequal Rights Amendment, 153
Communes (1970s), 179
Communism
   charges against gays and lesbians in 1950s, 138–40
   charges against women in 1920s, 78
   charges against women's organizations in 1950s, 154
   definition, 89
   and film noir, 128
   in 1920s, 89
   in 1930s, 114–15
   in 1950s, 139
Community chests, 1920s, 94
Comparable worth, 205, 208
"Compulsory heterosexuality" (1920s), 95
Compulsory sterilization. *See* Sterilization abuse
Comstock, Anthony, 7
Comstock laws, 7, 8, 141
Congress, U.S., women elected to, 171, 209
Congress of Industrial Organizations (CIO), 113–14. *See also* Committee for Industrial Organization; Union activities
Congress of Labor Union Women (CLUW), 169, 208
Congress of Racial Equality (CORE), 160
"Consciousness-raising," 56, 170
Consumer goods industry, 110–111
Consumerism
   and teenagers, 157
   and women, 11, 72, 117, 138
Consumers' League, 62, 90, 104, 153
Consumers' movement, 1930s, 102
Contraception. *See* Birth control
Cooper, Anna Julia, 36
Cooperative housing, and Progressive women reformers, 52, 56
Coppola, Francis Ford, 176
Cornell University, 4

Cosmetics, 73, 74, 75, 83, 190, 224
Cosmetic surgery, 120, 189–90, 221, 222
Corsets. *See* Fashion; Undergarments
Cott, Nancy, 91
Counterculture
  in 1960s, 165–66
  in 1970s, 190
Coward, Noel, 117
Crawford, Joan, 122, 123, 143
Croly, Jane (Jennie June), 42
Crumpler, Rebecca Lee, 12

D
Dame schools, 3
Dancing
  Charleston, 71, 80
  dance craze, 1912, 63–64
  and dance halls, 40, 63–64
  swing, 133
  See also Hip-hop; Raves
Dark Victory (1939), 123
Date rape, 214
Daughters of Bilitis, 140
Daughters of the American Revolution (DAR),
  43–44, 78, 105, 107
Davis, Bette, 123
Davis, Katharine Bement, 44, 63, 76
Dawes Severalty Act (1887), 34, 177
Day, Doris, 146
Day-care centers, 111, 126, 182, 212
Dean, James, 147, 158
Deloria, Ella, 35
Delta Sigma Theta, 43
Demographic transition, 8
Depression, 1930s
  family response to, 117–18
  marriage as security in, 117–18
  and popular culture, 120–26
  unemployment in, 110–112
  unions in, 113
Derrida, Jacques, 211
Design for Living (Coward), 117
Deutsch, Helene, 140
Dewson, Mary, 108
Dialectic of Sex, The, 170
Dietrich, Marlene, 127
"Dinner Party, The" (Chicago), 174
Dior, Christian, 143
Disco, 164, 189, 190, 199
Disco divas, 191
Divorce, 18–19, 77, 141, 220, 221, 223
Doctors, women as
  admission to medical schools, 12, 15, 16
  opportunities, during World War II, 129
  1970–90, 208
  recent, 218
Dole, Elizabeth, 218
Doll's House, A (Ibsen), 56
Domesticity, and 1950s, 141–43, 148, 153
Domestic science, 11, 93
Domestic service, 11, 15, 88, 132, 142, 171, 208

Donna Reed Show, The, 148
Don't Bother to Knock (1952), 132
Double Indemnity (1944), 128
Drag balls, New York City, 1920s, 75
Dress styles. *See* Fashion
Duncan, Isadora, 83
Dylan, Bob, 165

E
Earhart, Amelia, 95, 97
Eastwood, Clint, 176, 198
Easy Rider (1969), 176
Economic Opportunity Act, 1964, 165
Ederle, Gertrude, 73
Education, women's entry into
  in 1950s, 141–42
  in 1960s, 172
Emily's List, 208
Employment
  in 1890s, 15–16, 32
  in 1920s, 80–81, 88
  in 1930s, 110–13
  1945–60, 132, 141, 155–56
  1960s and 1970s, 169, 171
  recent period, 208
  in World War I, 67–68
  in World War II, 126, 129
  See also Factory workers; Professions
Equal Employment Opportunity Commission,
  federal (EEOC), 169, 196, 204, 206
Equal Pay Act (1963), 193
Equal Rights Amendment (ERA), 91, 92–93,
  102, 110, 153–54, 181, 185, 196, 197
Escuelitas, 6
Esquire, 121, 131, 150
Etheridge, Melissa, 215
Eugenics, 78–80

F
Factory workers, 12, 20, 24, 33, 59, 88–89,
  112–114, 126, 129, 132, 199
Fair Labor Standards Act (1938), 109–10, 154
Faludi, Susan, 186, 214
Family
  African American, 32–33
  in 1890s and 1900s, 11–12
  feminist views on, 182
  Mexican American, 20, 51
  in 1930s, 117–19
  in 1940s, 1141–42
  in recent period, 223
Family and Medical Leave Act (1993), 212
Family Protection Act, 197
Farm women, 15, 18–20, 72, 108, 118. *See also*
  Rural women
Fashion
  and New Woman, 2
  in 1920s, 89
  in 1930s, 120
  in 1950s, 149–50
  in 1970s, 188

in 1980s and 1990s, 195, 199
in recent period, 221–22, 224
versus uniform clothing, radicals, 1900s, 53
Victorian, 2
and World War II, 127, 143–44
zoot suits, 134
See also Undergarments
Fatal Attraction (1987), 198
Father Knows Best, 148
Faue, Elizabeth, 114
Fauset, Jessie Redman, 85, 86
Fear of Flying (Jong), 170
Federal Art Project, 109
Federal Council on Negro Affairs, 108
Federal Emergency Relief Act (FERA), 105, 108
Federal Music Project, 105
Federal Theatre Project, 105
Federal Writers' Project, 105
Federation for Child Study, 12
Female Eunuch (Greer), 170
Feminine Mystique, The (Friedan), 156
Feminism, 58, 82, 153–54, 163–75, 182, 195–96, 205, 209, 224
Feminist Alliance, 56
Feminist Majority, 205
Feminization
of poverty, 220, 222
of professions, 16–17, 93
of work force, 221
Femmes fatales, 128
Ferraro, Geraldine, 209
Ferree, Myra, 216
Filipinos
as domestic servants, 88
immigration, 28, 88
mail-order brides, 28, 88, 192
as single males, 28, 88
See also Asians
Film industry
and Communist Party, in 1950s, 115
in 1920s, 98
in 1930s, 122
in 1940s, 127–28
in 1950s, 146–47
in 1970s, 176–77
Film noir, 127–28
Firestone, Shulamith, 170
Fire with Fire (Wolf), 214
Fitzgerald, Ella, 125
Flanagan, Maureen, 92
Flappers, 52, 63, 64, 71–73, 80, 89, 98, 117
Flynn, Elizabeth Gurley, 58, 59
Flynt, Larry, 183
Fontaine, Lynn, 117
Fool There Was, A, 98
Freed, Alan, 158
Freedom Summer, 164
Freud, Anna, 76

Freud, Sigmund, 10, 76, 139, 148
Friedan, Betty, 156, 166, 183
Friendly visitors, 44. *See also* Social workers

G
"Gag rule," 197
"Gangsta" rap, 200
Gangster films, 1930s, 122
Garbo, Greta, 122
Gardner, Ava, 123
Garment industry, 20–21, 24, 89
Gay pride movement, 180
Gays, 119, 126–27, 180, 211, 212, 216
Gender gap, in voting, 209
General Federation of Women's Clubs, 48, 94.
See also Women's clubs
Generation of Vipers (Philip Wylie), 140
Generation X, 195, 213–214
Gibson, Charles Dana, 2
Gibson Girl, 2, 15, 38, 63, 70, 71
Gilman, Charlotte Perkins, 52, 55, 56
Gilmore, Glenda, 50
Ginsburg, Allen, 158
Ginsburg, Ruth Bader, 212
Girl groups (vocalists, 1950s), 159
Girl Scouts, 18, 185
Glamour, 199
Glass ceiling, 218
Glasspell, Susan, 56
Going steady, as courtship ritual, 149
Goldman, Emma, 53, 57, 72
Gone with the Wind (Mitchell), 121–23
Good Housekeeping, 11
Gordon, Linda, 46, 51
Grable, Betty, 31, 131
Graham, Martha, 83
Grant, Jane, 73
Grapes of Wrath (Steinbeck), 118
Green, Hetty, 13
Greenwich Village, 53, 56, 75, 83, 86, 170, 180
Greer, Germaine, 170
Grier, Pam, 176
Guerilla Girls, 215
Guest, Amy Phipps, 95
Guy-Sheftall, Beverly, 2–4

H
Hadassah, 50
Haines Normal and Industrial Institute, 5
Hale, Ruth, 73
Hamilton, Alice, 41
Hamilton, Cicely, 53
Hamilton, Edith, 52
Hamilton, Norah, 52
Handler, Ruth, 152
Harlem Renaissance, 75, 85, 86
Harlow, Jean, 122
Harriman, Florence Jaffray, 105
Harris, La Donna, 177
Havemeyer, Louisine, 52

Hayden, Sophia, 36
Hayworth, Rita (Margarita Carmen Cansino)
     123, 128, 149
Hefner, Hugh, 138, 150, 151
Held, John, Jr., 71
Hellman, Lillian, 74, 139
Henry Street Settlement, 45–46, 54, 59
Hepburn, Audrey, 146
Hepburn, Katharine, 123
Herland (Gilman), 55
Her Way (Kamen), 215
Hess, Beth, 216
Heterodoxy, 56–57, 58, 75–76, 170
Hickok, Lorena, 105
High Noon (1952), 147
Hill, Anita, 195–96, 203–204, 205, 206, 209
Hip-hop, 199–200, 211
Hispanic Americans, 29, 112, 178, 223. *See also*
     Latino/as; Mexican Americans
Hitchcock, Alfred, 147
Hobby, Oveta Culp, 171
Hoffman, Dustin, 198
Holiday, Billie, 125
Hollywood Production Code, 122, 123, 124.
     See also Film censorship
Home economics, 43, 93
Homestead Act (1865), and women, 19
Homophobia, 10, 101
Homosexuality, 10, 80, 139–40, 164 *See also*
     Lesbians and gays
House of Mirth (Wharton), 56
House Un-American Activities Committee
     (HUAC), 138–39
Houston National Women's Conference, 185
"How It Feels to Be Colored Me" (Hurston),
     86
"Howl" (Ginsburg), 158
Huerta, Dolores, 178–79
Hughes, Howard, 146–47
Hull House, 41, 45, 94
Hunter, Jane, 46
Hurston, Zora Neale, 84, 86, 109
Hustler, 183
Hyde Amendment, 187

I

Ibsen, Henrik, 56
Identity politics, 211
I Dream of Jeannie, 176
Illegitimacy, 1950s, 140
I Love Lucy, 148
Immigrants
     Mexican Americans, 19, 87–88
     1890s, 2, 21, 24–28
     1920s, 72
     recent, 191
Immigration Act of 1965, 191–92
Immigration Restriction Act, 1924, 79
Incest, 140
Indian Reorganization Act, 35
Indians. *See* Native Americans
Industrial Workers of the World (IWW), 58, 61

Institute for Women's Policy Research, 185
International Council of Women, 4
International Ladies' Garment Workers Union
     (ILGWU), 59, 89–90, 113, 115, 119
International Woman Suffrage Association, 66
Iron John (Bly), 198
Islam. *See* Muslims
Italian women, 24
It's Up to the Women (Roosevelt), 104

J

Jackson, Janet, 222
Jackson, May Howard, 52
James Bond (film character), 176
Japanese Americans
     immigration, 27, 191
     and picture brides, 27
     and protest, 28
     work patterns, 27
     See also Asians
Jazz
     and African American women singers, 125
     in general, 71, 83
     and Josephine Baker, 83
Jewish women
     bat mitzvahs, 1960s, 175
     and factory work, 24–25
     and immigration, 24–25
     and organizations, 49–50
     as radicals, 63, 61
     and sexual revolution of 1920s, 77
     as street vendors, New York City, 1900s, 25
Johnson, Adelaide, 52
Johnson, Lyndon, 154, 160, 165, 171, 184
Jones, Mary "Mother," 58
Jong, Erica, 170
Joplin, Janis, 158, 173
Journalism, women in, 13, 22

K

Kamanamoku, Duke, 97
Kamen, Paula, 215
Keene, Carolyn, 121
Kelley, Florence, 46, 78
Kennedy, John F., 160, 167, 171, 213
Kerouac, Jack, 158
Kertbeny, Karl (Karoly Maria Benkert), 10
Key, Ellen, 53, 58
Keyes, Frances Parkinson, 7
Kindergartens, 42, 67
King, Martin Luther, Jr., 160
Kingston, Maxine Hong, 184
Kinsey, Alfred, 139, 149
Kinsey studies of male and female sexuality,
     139, 149
Klein, Viola, 140
Kleptomania, 11
Knights of Labor, 60, 61
Komarovsky, Mirra, 153
Koreans
     employment, 27–28
     family and culture, 27–28

immigration, 27–28
See also Asians
Ku Klux Klan, 78–79, 186

L

Labor movement. *See* Union activities
Ladies' Home Journal, 11, 170
Lady Chatterly's Lover (Lawrence), 149
Lady from Shanghai (1948), 128
Lady in the Dark (1944), 123
LaFollette, Suzanne, 74
La Leche League, 141
Lama Foundation, 175
Lamaze natural childbirth method, 141
Lamour, Dorothy, 123
Laney, Lucy C., 5
Lange, Dorothea, 108
Lap dancing, 195
Larsen, Nella, 86
Lasch-Quinn, Elizabeth, 46
Lathrop, Julia, 46, 94
Latino/as, 88, 192, 208. *See also* Hispanic
    Americans; Mexican Americans
Lawrence, D. H., 149
Lawrence, Mass., textile mills, 59
Lawyers, women as, 12, 16, 129, 218
League of Women Voters, 91–93, 94, 104, 108,
    143, 153, 154, 169, 185
Lee, Dorothy McCulloch, 156
Legal codes, women's rights, 2–3, 172
Lesbians, 10, 126–27, 164, 180, 183–84, 211,
    215, 216
LeSueur, Meridel, 109
Levittown, 142
Lewinsky, Monica, 195–96, 213, 215
Librarians, women as, 16, 93, 111
Life, 2
Lilith Fair, 215
Limbaugh, Rush, 197
Lindbergh, Charles, 95, 97
Lindsey, Ben W., 145
Little Egypt. *See* Mazhur, Farida
Little Orphan Annie (cartoon character), 121
Log Cabin Settlement (Lyman), 51–52
Low, Juliet, 18
Lucy Stone League, 153
Lunt, Alfred, 117
Lyman, Susan Chester, 51–52
Lynching, 103, 204

M

MacKinnon, Catharine, 182–83
Madonna (Madonna Louise Ciccone), 200–
    203, 214
Magnificent Obsession (1954), 146
Magnin, Mary Ann, 13
Mail-order brides, 28, 191
Male and Female (Mead), 143
"Man in the gray flannel suit," 157
Mansfield, Arabella, 12
Marine Corps Women's Reserve, 126
Marnie (1964), 147

Marriage
    companionate, 12
    middle class, in 1890s, 11–12
    in 1920s, 77–78
    in 1930s, 117–119
    in 1950s, 141–42
    recent, 212, 220
Marriage manuals, 75, 148
Married women
    increase in numbers working, 117, 126, 141,
        155
    work prohibitions during New Deal, 117–
        18
Marsh, Margaret, 12
Marshall, Thurgood, 203
Martineau, Harriet, 12
Masculinity,
    1890s, 224
    1930s, 118
    1950s, 157
Masculinization, 17–18
Masturbation, 6–7
Maternal feminists, 48, 49
Mattachine Society, 140
Maximum hour laws. *See* Protective legislation
May, Elaine, 149
Mazhur, Farida, 36, 98
McCarthy, Joseph, 139, 149
McCarthy, Mary, 77
McCormick, Ruth Hanna, 92
McDaniel, Hattic, 123
Mead, Margaret, 95, 96, 119, 139, 143
Medicine
    female sexuality and, 6–8
    See also Doctors, women as
Mellen, Joan, 147
Memorial Day Massacre, 113
Menopause, 8, 34
Menstruation, among Indian women, 34
Men-women, 45. *See also* Berdache
"Meterosexual," 224
Methodist Board of Foreign Missions, 41
Mexican American National Association
    (MAMA), 179
Mexican Americans
    and Catholic Church, 29
    employment, 19–20, 87–88, 112–13
    family, 20, 51
    immigration, 19, 87, 88
    movement into middle-class, 223
    organizations, 51, 179
    and racial controversy, Clifton, Arizona, 29
    radicalized by Mexican Revolution of 1910,
        51
    and sexual revolution, 1920s, 77
    unions, 178–79
    and zoot suits, 134
Meyer, Agnes, 153
Meyerowitz, Joanne, 156
Military, and women
    World War I, 67

Military, and women (*continued*)
World War II, 126–27, 129
recent period, 209–210
Millay, Edna St. Vincent, 83
Millett, Kate, 128, 170
Mills, Tarpe, 127
Minimum-wage laws. *See* Protective legislation
for women
Minor v. Happersett, 3
Miscegenation laws, 29, 88
Miss America Pageant, 170
Mitchell, Margaret, 121
Mondale, Walter, 209
Monroe, Marilyn, 131–32, 140, 145, 150–51,
152, 201
Moraga, Cherrie, 184
Morgan, Robin, 170
Morning After, The (Roiphe), 214
Morrison, Toni, 184
Moseley-Braun, Carol, 207, 209
Motherhood
and feminist beliefs about, 58, 182
and Freudianism, 148
glorifying of, 141
illegitimacy and, 140
and pacifist rhetoric, 93, 104, 143
Mother's pensions, 48–49, 91
Movies. *See* Film industry
Moynihan, Daniel Patrick, 184
Ms. Foundation, 205
Ms. Magazine, 174, 205
Muller v. Oregon, 48
Muncy, Robyn, 47
Muslims, 191, 216
Myrdal, Alva, 140

N

Nancy Drew (fictional character), 121
National Abortion Rights Action League
(NARAL), 169, 181, 188
National American Woman Suffrage Associa-
tion (NAWSA), 4, 64–65, 66–67, 91
National Association for the Advancement of
Colored People (NAACP), 85, 86, 93,
103, 159–60
National Association of Black Professional
Women, 180
National Association of Colored Women, 90,
103, 107, 108, 180
National Black Feminist Organization, 180
National Coalition of 100 Black Women, 180
National Committee of Endorsers Against the
ERA, 186
National Conference of Puerto Rican Women,
179
National Congress of Mothers, 48
National Congress of Parent and Teacher Asso-
ciations, 91, 94
National Consumers' League, 108. *See also*
Consumers' League

National Council of Jewish Women, 50, 94, 185
National Council of Negro Women, 108, 154,
180
National Federation of Business and Profes-
sional Women's Clubs (BPW), 90–91, 93,
94
National Federation of Women's Clubs, 153
National Industrial Recovery Act (NRA), 105,
109–10, 112, 113
National Labor Relations Board, 113
National Organization for Women (NOW),
163, 169, 180, 182, 183, 185, 205
National Organization of Business and Profes-
sional Women, 169
National Women's Political Caucus, 208–209
National Youth Administration (NYA), 105,
107, 108, 119
Native American women, 23, 33–35, 177, 209
Near, Holly, 173
Negro Family: The Case for National Action, The
(Moynihan), 184
Nevelson, Louise, 109
New Deal, 102, 107–110
"New Look," 143
New Right, 164, 185–87, 195, 196–97, 218
"New Woman," 15, 18, 39, 71, 224
New York City Foundling Home, 29
Niagara (1953), 132
Nineteenth Amendment, passage of, 68
Nixon, Richard, 143, 187
Nobel Peace Prize, awarded to Jane Addams,
102
Now, Voyager (1942), 123
Nurses, women as, 12, 15, 32, 93, 140, 192

O

Oberlin College, 4, 5
O'Connor, Sandra Day, 197
O'Keeffe, Georgia, 86
On the Road (Kerouac), 158
Opinion, La, 77
Organization of Pan Asian Women, 182
Our Bodies/Our Selves (Boston Women's Health
Collective), 173
Outlaw, The (1948), 187
Owen, Ruth Bryan, 105

P

Pacifism, and women, 93, 94, 104, 143
Paglia, Camille, 214
Parker, Dorothy, 83, 119
Parks, Rosa, 159
Pascoe, Peggy, 25
Passing (Larsen), 86
Patriarchy, in feminist theory, 172, 184, 211
Paul, Alice, 65–66, 92
Perils of Pauline, 98
Perkins, Frances, 105, 108, 171, 260
Personal Responsibility Act (1996), 212
Petty, George, 121
Petty girl, 121

Philippines. *See* Filipinos
Phillips, Irma, 121
Pickford, Mary, 95, 97–98
Picnic (1956), 146
Picture brides
    Filipino, 28, 192
    Japanese, 27
    Korean, 28
Pinkham, Lydia, 13
"Pin money" theory, 20
"Pinup" photos, 129, 150
Plath, Sylvia, 170
Playboy, 138, 150–52, 183
Playboy bunnies, 151
Playboy clubs, 151
Polish women, 24, 77
Polykoff, Shirley, 145
Pornography, 7, 150–52, 182–85, 195, 222
Postfeminism, 195, 210–12
Postfeminist generation, 213–214
Postmodernism, 210–212
Poverty, and women, 171–72, 196–97, 219, 223
Presley, Elvis, 133, 138, 158, 165
Pretty Woman (1990), 198
Pro-choice (abortion), 187–188, 212. *See also* Abortion
Profeminist men's movement, 197
Professions
    and marriage, 155
    in 1890s, 12, 15, 16
    in 1920s, 82–83
    in 1930s, 111
    in 1950s, 156
    in recent period, 208, 218
    World War II
    See also Doctors; Lawyers
Professors, women as, 16, 111
Progressive movement
    1890s, 39–49
    1920s, 90–95
    1930s, 102, 104, 108–109
Prohibition amendment, 68
Pro-life, 187–88. *See also* Abortion
Prostitution
    and African American blues singers, 125
    in Butte, Montana, 77
    and Chinese women, 25–27
    1890–1920, 63
    in Hawaii during World War II, 134
    1960s feminist attitude toward, 172
    in 1930s films, 122
    and tramps, 111
    in World War II, 135
Protective legislation, 48, 58, 61, 109, 126, 132, 153
Protestant Churches and Progressive reform, 41
Pruette, Lorine, 81
Psycho (1960), 147
Psychology of Women (Deutsch), 140

Public Works Administration (PWA), 105
Puerperal fever, 6
Puerto Ricans, 88
Punk, 164, 211
Pure Food and Drug Act (1906), 43

Q
Queen Latifah (Dana Elaine Owens), 200–201
Queer, 212, 214, 219
Queer Eye for the Straight Guy, 224
Queer Nation, 217
Quicksand (Larsen), 86

R
Radicalism
    1900s, 52–53, 57, 61
    1920s, 89
    1930s, 114–15
    1960s and 1970s, 164–71
    radical feminism, 1960s and 1970s, 164–71
Radio, 116, 197
Raging Bull (1960), 176
Rainey, Ma, 129
Ramirez, Sara Estela, 51
Rape, 172, 182, 181, 184, 204
    and military, 210
Rave clubs, 199
Ray, Charlotte, 12
Reagan, Ronald, 187, 196, 205, 212
Rear Window (1954), 147
Rebel Without a Cause (1954), 147
"Red diaper babies," 164
Reddy, Helen, 173
Red Scare, 72
Reisman, David, 157
Reserve Officer Training Program (ROTC), 210
Resor, Helen, 13
Reynolds, Debbie, 146
Rice, Condoleezza, 218
Richards, Ellen, 43, 93
Ride, Sally, 179
Riot Grrrls, 215
Robins, Margaret Dreier, 62
Robinson, JoAnn, 159
Rockefeller, Laura Spelman, 5
Rock'n'roll, 158–59
Roe v. Wade, 181, 187, 188
Rogers, Ginger, 123
Roiphe, Katie, 214
Rolling Stones, 165
Roosevelt, Eleanor, 102–104–107, 108, 153
Roosevelt, Franklin, 101–102, 104, 106
Roosevelt, Theodore, 27
"Rosie the Riveter," 126, 129, 130, 131, 143
Rubenstein, Helena, 83
Rural women, 18–19, 72, 108, 118. *See also* Farm women
Russell, Jane, 147
Russell, Lillian, 9, 13
Russell, Rosalind, 123

S

Sandwich generation, 220
Sanger, Margaret, 55, 59, 78, 79, 97
Saturday Night Fever (1977), 190
Scarlett O'Hara (*Gone with the Wind*), 121
Schlafly, Phyllis, 186
Schreiner, Olive, 53
Schwarzenegger, Arnold, 198
Scott, Anne Firor, 41
Screwball comedy, film, 123
Seaman, Elizabeth (Nellie Bly), 13, 22
Sears, Roebuck, and Company, 73
Second Sex, The (de Beauvoir), 227
Second wave feminism, 74, 163, 215
Servants, women. *See* Domestic service
Service Employees Industrial Organization
    (SEIU), 208
Settlement houses, 45–47, 91, 94
Seventeen, 133
Seven Year Itch (1955), 145
Sex and Temperament in Three Primitive Societies
    (Mead), 119
Sex and the City, 222
Sex and the Single Girl (Brown), 166
Sex crime panic, 119, 139
Sex in Education (Clarke), 6
Sexology, 10
Sexual harassment, 182, 195, 203–204, 206,
    213
Sexuality
    1920s, 75–78
    1930s, 116–17
    1950s, 148–49
    1960s, 165
    recent, 221–24
    World War II, 134
Sexual Politics (Millett), 128, 170
Shane (1953), 147
Shaw, Anna Howard, 4, 64–65, 67, 91
Sheppard-Towner Act (1921), 94–95, 108
Sheppard-Towner Clinics, 94–95
Shields, Brooke, 199
Shirelles, 159
Shirtwaist workers, 59
Simon, Carly, 190–91
Sinatra, Frank, 133
Sirk, Douglas, 146
Sisterhood Is Powerful (Morgan), 170
Slavic women, 24, 29, 77
Sleepy Lagoon incident, 134
Smith, Bessie, 125
Smith College, 4
Soap operas, on radio, 1930s, 120, 121
Social Darwinism, 2, 34
Socialism
    definition, 39
    1900s, 56, 58, 61
    and unions, 61
    and Women's Trade Union League, 62
Social purity campaigns, 44, 149

Social Security Act (1935), 108, 110
Social workers, 45–47, 89, 91, 94, 111. *See also*
    Friendly visitors
Sodomy laws, 10, 119, 219
Sororities (1890–1920), 43
Sorosis, 42
Spain, Daphne, 43
Spears, Britney, 203, 221
Special legislation for women. *See* Protective
    legislation for women
Spelman College, 5
Spice Girls, 215
Spirituality, feminist, 175
Spock, Benjamin, 148
Sports
    and Gibson Girl, 2
    1920s, 73–74
    1960s and 1970s, 174–75
    recent period, 219
Spousal abuse, 43, 172, 182
St. Denis, Ruth, 83
Stallone, Sylvester, 198
Stanton, Elizabeth Cady, 1, 4, 52, 64
Stanwyck, Barbara, 128
Steinbeck, John, 118
Stenographers. *See* Clerical workers
Stepford Wives (1978), 176
Steppenwolf, 165
Sterilization abuse. *See* Compulsory sterilization
Stern, Howard, 222
Stewardesses, 97
Stieglitz, Alfred, 86
Stiffed: The Betrayal of the American Man (Faludi),
    214
Stone, Lucy, 73–74
Stonewall riot, 180, 183
Strike! (Vorse), 109
Strikes, 58–61, 89, 113–114
Strip clubs, 195
Student Nonviolent Coordinating Committee
    (SNCC), 160
Suburban housewife, role of, 142–43
Suffrage, 64–68, 92
Summers, Donna, 191
Supremes, 159
Swanson, Gloria, 75, 98
Sweet Honey in the Rock, 173
Szold, Henrietta, 47

T

Taft-Hartley, Act, 138, 196
Tailhook Convention, 210
Take a Letter, Darling (1942) 123
Take Back the Night marches, 173
Tan, Amy, 184
Tarzan (fictional character, Burroughs),
    17–18
Taylor, Annie, 13
Taylor, Elizabeth, 146
Teachers, women as, 12, 15, 16, 129

Technology
  and housekeeping, turn of the twentieth century, 11
  in 1950s, 142–43
Teenagers, 102, 133, 157–58
Telephone operators, Bell System, 61
Television, female image in, 147–48, 176–77
Tell Me a Riddle (Olson), 109
Temple, Shirley, 121
Terminator films, 198
Textile industry, 59, 113
Their Eyes Were Watching God (Hurston), 84, 86
Third wave feminism, 195, 211, 214–18
Thomas, Clarence, 203–204, 206
Thomas, Marlo, 176
Title VII, Civil Rights Act (1964), 193
Title IX, Education Act (1972), 181, 219
Tootsie (1990), 198
Tranquilizers, 156
Travolta, John, 190
Triangle fire, 20, 60
Triangle Shirtwaist Company, 20, 60
True Confessions, 75
Truman, Harry, 138
Twiggy, 188

U

Undergarments, 2, 73, 120, 143–44, 203
Unemployment, women
  in 1930s, 110–111
  in 1960s, 169
  recent, 192, 208
  after World War II, 132
Union activities
  and Communist Party, 114–15
  and Mexican Americans, 114
  in 1900s, 58–62
  in 1920s, 89–90
  in 1930s, 109
  in 1960s, 169
  in 1970s and 1980s, 169, 196
  recent, 208
  and World War II, 133
  See also American Federation of Labor; Congress of Industrial Organizations; International Ladies Garment Workers Union
United Cannery, Agricultural, Packing, and Allied Workers of America (UCAPAWA), 114
United Farm Workers, 178
University of Chicago, 4
Unmarried Woman, An (1978), 176
"Unobtrusive mobilization" (Katzenstein), 209–210
Unwed mothers, 140
Urban Cowboy (1969), 176
Urban League, 45, 46, 103

V

Valentino, Rudolph, 75
Vamp, 98

Van Waters, Miriam, 91
Vargas, Alberto, 121
Vargas girls, 121
Vassar College, 4, 14
Verge, The, 56
Vertigo (1958), 147
V-girls, World War II, 133, 148
Victorian culture
  dress, 2
  rebellion against, 40
Victoria's Secret, 222
Video games, 198
Vietnam War, 163, 164, 170, 209
Virginian, The (Wister), 17
Vogue, 199
Vorse, Mary Heaton, 109

W

WACS (Women's Auxiliary Army Corps), 126
Wald, Lilliam, 45–46, 54
Walker, Alice, 86, 184
Walker, Maggie Lena, 13
Walker, Sarah Breedloe (Mrs. C. J.), 13–15
War Manpower Commission, 126, 129
WASPS (Women Air Force Service Pilots), 126, 129
Waters, Ethel, 125
WAVES (Women Accepted for Voluntary Emergency Service, 126
Wayne, John, 147
Webster v. Reproductive Health Services, 197, 205
"Welfare mothers," 212, 219
Wells, Ida B. (Barnett), 51
West, Mae, 122, 124, 201
Westerns, as films, 122
Wharton, Edith, 56
White, Pearl, 98
White House Conference on the Emergency Needs of Women, 108
Whitney, Gertrude Vanderbilt, 83
Wild One, The (1953), 147
Willard, Frances, 9, 41–42
Williams, Fannie Barrier, 36
Wills, Helen, 73
Wilson, Woodrow, 68
Wisconsin Women's Network, 205
Witches (feminism), 175
Wolff, Naomi, 214
Woman's Christian Temperance Union (WCTU), 9, 41, 68
Woman's Party, 92, 97
Women Against Pornography, 182–83
Women and Labor (Schreiner), 53
Women in the Modern World (Komarovsky), 153
Women of All Red Nations (WARN), 178
Women's Bureau, Department of Labor (federal), 91, 92, 102, 108, 112, 129, 132, 169
Women's clubs
  1890–1920, 41–43
  in 1920s, 91–93
  in 1950s, 153

Women's colleges, founding of, 3–4. *See also*
Education
Women's Committee for National Defense
(World War I), 67
Women's Equity Action League (WEAL), 169,
185
Women's Exchange movement, 51–52
Women's Health Action Network (WHAM),
215–16
Women's International League for Peace and
Freedom (WILPF), 93, 102
Women's Joint Congressional Committee, 91,
94
Women's moral superiority, feminism on, 182
Women's organizations
1890s and 1900s, 39–51, 58–62
1920s, 89–94
1930s, 102, 103, 108
1950s, 153–54
1960s and 1970s, 185
1980s and 1990s, 205, 208, 215–16
Women's Political Caucus, 169
Women's Reformatory, Bedford Hills, New
York, 44
Women's Reserve (Marine Corps), 126
Women's Reserve (U.S. Coast Guard), 126

Women's Strike for Peace, 143
Women's studies programs, 169
Women's Trade Union League (WTUL), 48,
62, 90, 92, 104, 108, 110, 114
Women's Two Roles: Home and Work (Myrdall
and Klein), 140
Wonder Woman (cartoon character), 127
Woodward, Ellen, 108
Working-class women
1900–1920, 20–21, 24–28
1920s, 81–82
1930s, 107–114
Works Progress Administration (WPA), 84,
105, 108, 110
Wylie, Philip, 140

Y

Yank, 129
"Yellow Wallpaper, The" (Gilman), 55
Young Americans for Freedom (YAF), 164
Young Women's Christian Association
(YWCA), 43, 49, 91, 154

Z

Ziegfeld Follies, 83
Zoot suits, 134